16th Joint ACL-ISO Workshop on Interoperable Semantic Annotation 2020

Marseille, France
11 – 16 May 2020

Editor:

Harry Bunt

ISBN: 978-1-7138-1262-3

LREC 2020 Workshop
Language Resources and Evaluation Conference
11–16 May 2020

**16th Joint ACL - ISO Workshop on
Interoperable Semantic Annotation**

PROCEEDINGS

Harry Bunt, Editor

Proceedings of the LREC 2020 Workshop
16th Joint ACL - ISO Workshop on
Interoperable Semantic Annotation

Edited by: Harry Bunt

For more information:
European Language Resources Association (ELRA)
9 rue des Cordelières
75013, Paris
France
http://www.elra.info
Email: lrec@elda.org

Introduction

Welcome to the proceedings of the 16th Joint ACL - ISO Workshop on Interoperable Semantic Annotation (ISA-16). These are the proceedings of a workshop that never happened. Planned to take place on May 12, 2020 in Marseille (France), as a side-event of the LREC 2020 conference, the spread of the COVID-19 virus made it impossible (and prohibited) to get together. The organisers of LREC 2020 decided to nonetheless go ahead with the publication of the conference proceedings as originally scheduled, while awaiting a decision on holding the conference later in the year or moving it to 2021 (like the Olympic games and the Euro 2020 football championship, and other major sports events). This way the efforts of the authors of accepted papers would not be lost, and their scientific contributions would be available to the rest of the world. The ISA-16 organisers decided to comply with this strategy, and so the papers that were accepted for presentation at the ISA-16 workshop are made available here as the workshop proceedings. The papers have been arranged in alphabetical order of the names of their first authors.

We thank the members of the ISA-16 program committee for reviewing the submitted papers timely in spite of uncertainty as to whether the workshop would actually happen, and we thank the authors of accepted papers for revising their contributions according to the original time schedule, taking the review comments into account, even though at that time it was clear that the workshop would not take place. Thank you!

The ISA-16 organisers,

Harry Bunt, Nancy Ide, Kiyong Lee, Volha Petukhova, James Pustejovsky, and Laurent Romary

Organizers:

Harry Bunt, Tilburg University (Netherlands)
Nancy Ide, Vassar College, Poughkeepsie, NY (USA)
Kiyong Lee, Korea University, Seoul (South Korea)
Volha Petukhova, Saarland University, Saarbrücken (Germany)
James Pustejovsky, Brandeis University, Waltham, MA (USA)
Laurent Romary, INRIA/Humboldt University, Berlin (Germany)

Program Committee:

Lasha Abzianidze, University of Groningen (Netherlands)
Jan Alexandersson, DFKI, Saarbrücken (Germany)
Ron Artstein, USC Institute for Creative Technologies, Playa Vista, CA (USA)
Johan Bos, University of Groningen (Netherlands)
Harry Bunt, Tilburg University (Netherlands)
Nicoletta Calzolari, ILC-CNR, Pisa
Jae-Woong Choe, Korea University, Seoul (South Korea)
Robin Cooper, University of Gothenburg (Sweden)
Ludivine Crible, University of Edinburgh (Scotland)
David DeVault, USC Institute for Creative Technologies, Playa Vista, CA (USA)
Simon Dobnik, University of Gothenburg (Sweden)
Jens Edlund, KTH, Stockholm University (Sweden)
Alex Fang, City University of Hong Kong
Robert Gaizauskas, University of Sheffield (UK)
Kallirroi Georgila, USC Institute for Creative Technologies, Playa Vista, CA (USA)
Jan Hajic, Charles University, Prague (Czech Republic)
Koiti Hasida, Tokyo University (Japan)
Nancy Ide, Vassar College, Poughkeepsie, NY (USA)
Elisabetta Jezek, Università degli Studi di Pavia (Italy)
Nikhil Krishnaswamy, Brandeis University, Waltham, MA (USA)
Kiyong Lee, Korea University, Seoul (South Korea)
Paul Mc Kevitt, University of Ulster, Londonderry (Northern Ireland)
Adam Meyers, New York University (USA)
Roser Morante, Free University of Amsterdam (Netherlands)
Philippe Muller, IRIT, Université Paul Sabatier, Toulouse (France)
Rainer Osswald, Heinrich-Heine University, Düsseldorf (Germany)
Patrizia Paggio, L-Università tà Malta, Msida (Malta)
Volha Petukhova, Saarland University, Saarbrücken (Germany)
Massimo Poesio, Queen Mary University, London (UK)
Eric Postma, Tilburg University (Netherlands)
Laurent Prévot, Aix-Marseille University (France)
James Pustejovsky, Brandeis University, Waltham, MA (USA)
Livio Robaldo, Université de Luxembourg
Laurent Romary, INRIA/Humboldt University, Berlin (Germany)
Ielka van der Sluis, University of Groningen (Netherlands)
Manfred Stede, Universität Potsdam (Germany)
Matthew Stone, Rutgers, the State University of New Jersey, Piscataway NJ (USA)
Thora Tenbrink, Bangor University (Wales)

Sara Tonelli, Fondazione Bruno Kessler, Trento (Italy)
Thorsten Trippel, University of Tübingen (Germany)
Carl Vogel, Trinity College, Dublin (Ireland)
Menno van Zaanen, North West University South Africa,Mahikeng (RSA)
Annie Zaanen, Stanford University, Palo Alto, CA (USA)
Heike Zinsmeister, Universität Hamburg (Germany)

Table of Contents

Proceedings of the 16th Joint ACL-ISO Workshop Interoperable Semantic Annotation (ISA-16), pages 1–12
Language Resources and Evaluation Conference (LREC 2020), Marseille, 11–16 May 2020

Annotation of Quantification: The Current State of ISO 24617-12

Harry Bunt

Department of Cognitive Science and Artificial Intelligence, Tilburg University

harry.bunt@uvt.nl

Abstract

This paper discusses the current state of developing an ISO standard annotation scheme for quantification phenomena in natural language, as part of the ISO Semantic Annotation Framework (ISO 24617). An approach that combines ideas from the theory of generalised quantifiers, from neo-Davidsonian event semantics, and from Discourse Representation Theory was proposed to the ISO organisation in 2019 as a starting point for developing such an annotation scheme. This scheme consists of (1) a conceptual 'metamodel' that visualises the types of entities, functions and relations that go into annotations of quantification; (2) an abstract syntax which defines 'annotation structures' as triples and other set-theoretic constructs; (3) an XML-based representation of annotation structures ('concrete syntax'); and (4) a compositional semantics of annotation structures. The latter three components together define the interpreted language QuantML. The focus in this paper is on the structuring of the semantic information needed to characterise quantification in natural language and the representation of these structures in QuantML.

Keywords: semantic annotation, quantification, ISO standards, QuantML

1. Introduction

The specification of an interoperable scheme for the semantic annotation of quantification phenomena in natural language has for some time been on the agenda for extending the ISO Semantic Annotation Framework. After preliminary studies, reported in Bunt (2017), Bunt et al. (2018), and Bunt (2019a), a concrete proposal for developing the specification of such a scheme, supported by a first 'working draft' (ISO/WD 24617-12), was adopted by the ISO organisation. This paper describes the current state of developing the proposed specification, elaborating the WD 24617-12 working draft. Although this work is still in a preliminary stage, the current state of the specification covers a fairly wide range of aspects and forms of quantification, including collective, cumulative, and group quantification, quantification over events, exhaustive quantification, negative-polarity quantification, quantified possessives, various forms of mass noun quantification, quantification involving parts of individuals, and quantification over complex domains including the use of quantifying modifiers with inverse linking. We refer to this annotation scheme under development by the name of its markup language, QuantML.

The interest in developing a semantic annotation scheme for quantification is twofold. First, there is the ubiquitous character of quantification in natural language. Quantification occurs when a predicate is applied to one or more sets of arguments. Since this happens in every clause when a verb is combined with its arguments (except perhaps in extremely simple sentences like *"John loves Mary"*, if proper names are regarded as referring expressions), quantification occurs in virtually every sentence. Quantification is moreover the most important source of structural ambiguity. Accurate question answering, information extraction, advice giving, negotiation, and other applications that rely on deep language understanding therefore struggle with the interpretation problems caused by quantification. Second, the ISO Semantic Annotation Framework (ISO 24617, 'SemAF') has parts for annotating temporal and spatial information, events, semantic roles, discourse relations, dia-

logue acts, and coreference relations, which together span a substantial range of semantic aspects of spoken and written language, but quantification forms a big gap in this range. Filling this gap would greatly enhance the coverage of SemAF.

Assuming that a semantic representation of a natural language (NL) expression is understood to be a formal expression that has a single well-defined interpretation corresponding to a possible meaning of the NL expression, a semantic *annotation* is somewhere in between a 'raw' NL expression and a semantic *representation*. A semantic annotation adds information to the annotated NL expression about its indented interpretation. In the simplest case, a semantic annotation identifies exactly one interpretation of the annotated NL expression, and thus corresponds to a single semantic representation, but in practice the situation is more complicated. First, semantic annotations are typically *constraints* on the possible interpretations, selecting a subset of its possible meanings rather than a single specific interpretation. Second, semantic representations do not necessarily carve out just one possible meaning. In fact, the pervasive ambiguity of quantifier scopes in NL expressions has prompted the definition of formalisms for underspecified semantic representations, thus blurring the distinction between semantic annotations and representations somewhat. Still, in practice the two are very different in two respects:

1. semantic annotations typically capture only certain aspects of natural language utterance meaning, such as properties of quantifications, or coreference relations, or spatiotemporal information;

2. semantic representations are typically designed as expressions in a formal logical language, while annotations are often designed to be a way of attaching certain labels to parts of NL expressions, such as semantic roles predicate-argument structures.

The various parts of the ISO Semantic Annotation Framework each deal with a certain type of semantic information, and thus with a certain type of constraints on semantic interpretation. Each of these parts defines an annotation scheme for the kind of information that it deals with, with the aim of specifying information that disambiguates an NL expression *in that respect*, such as which semantic role is played by an NP, or how is an anaphoric expression referentially related to which antecedent. Quantification is the most important source of structural ambiguity in natural language, and the annotation of the quantifications in an NL expression aims at disambiguating NL expressions in that respect. The main challenge in developing an annotation scheme for quantification is to identify a limited number of categories of information that is sufficient for characterising aspects, forms and uses of quantification that are found in natural language, and to define the combinations of these categories that form meaningful building blocks in annotations. Annotations should be constructed in accordance with the methodological principles laid out in ISO standard 24617-6 (Principles of semantic annotation), which means that the annotations should have an abstract and a concrete syntax, related through an encoding function (from abstract to concrete) and an inverse decoding function, and a semantics defined for the abstract syntax (and inherited by any concrete encoding).

Annotations should moreover be in stand-off format. The use of stand-off formats is motivated primarily by the consideration that the integrity of the primary data should always be respected, and has the methodological advantage that the pointers from elements in an annotation to elements in the primary data ('markables'), formalise the relation between annotation structures and linguistic elements, making explicit that the semantic annotation of an NL expression is not a stand-alone object, but is formally attached to NL elements.

This paper is organised as follows. Section 2 outlines the analytical framework for quantification annotation that is proposed in ISO WD 24617-12 (2019). Section 3 discusses the categories of semantic information identified in the QuantML annotation scheme for characterising aspects and forms of quantification. First, a number of traditional categories are considered such as scope and distributivity. Second, a number of less well-established categories are introduced, and some novel uses of traditional categories. Section 4 closes the main paper with some concluding remarks and directions for further work. The appendix contains a summary specification of the QuantML markup language and its underlying metamodel.

2. Analytical Framework

2.1. Quantification: GQT

Quantification is linguistically, logically, and computationally extremely complex, and has been studied for centuries by logicians, linguists, formal semanticists, and computational linguists (e.g. Aristotle, 4th century B.C., Frege, 1879; Montague, 1974; Barwise and Cooper, 1981; Westerståhl, 1985; Keenan and Stavi, 1986; Hobbs and Shieber, 1987; Partee, 1988; Cooper, 1983; Kamp and Reyle, 1993; Bos, 1995; Peters and Westerståhl, 2006, Szabolcsi, 2010; Ruys and Winter, 2011, Champollion, 2015; Coppock and Beaver, 2015). Mostowski (1957) and Lindström (1966) noted that the universal and the existential quantifier, as

used in predicate logic, can be viewed as expressing properties of sets of individual objects, involved in a predication: the universal quantifier expresses the property of containing all the elements of a given domain; the existential quantifier the property of containing at least one such element. This opened the way to generalise the notion of a quantifier to other properties of sets, such as the property of containing more than three elements, or of containing most of the elements of the quantification domain. The concepts in this broader class of quantifiers are called 'generalised quantifiers'.

The study of how generalised quantifiers are used and expressed in natural language has led to generalised quantifier theory (GQT, Barwise and Cooper, 1981). An important point in this theory is that there is a fundamental difference between quantification in natural language and quantification in logic in the following sense. Words like *"all"* and *"some"* in English, as well as their equivalents in other languages, may seem to be the counterparts of the universal ($\forall$ 'for all') and existential ($\exists$, 'for some' quantifiers of formal logic, and so-called 'cardinal quantifiers and 'proportional quantifiers' like *"three"*, and *"most"*, may seem to be the counterparts of certain generalised quantifiers, but they are not. In formal logic, if p is a formula that denotes a proposition then the expressions '$\forall x.p$' and '$\exists y.p$' are quantifications, saying that p is true of all individual objects and that p is true of at least one such object, respectively.

Such quantifications, which range over all individual objects in a universe of discourse, cannot be expressed in natural languages. Quantifying expressions in natural languages, instead, like *"all students"*, *"quelques gens"*, and *"mais que cinco melodias"*, include the indication of a restricted domain. This is reflected in the view that quantifiers in natural language are not determiners like *"all"* and *"some"*, but noun phrases (Barwise and Cooper, 1981).

The QuantML annotation scheme takes an approach which combines generalized quantifier theory with the neo-Davidsonian event-based approach.

2.2. Neo-Davidsonian event semantics

Abzianidze & Bos (2019) note that neo-Davidsonian event semantics is adopted in most if not all semantically annotated corpora. Davidson (1989) introduced events as individual objects into semantic representations, notably as an extra argument of predicates that correspond to verbs, as in 'read(e, x, y)'. In a variation of this approach, known as 'neo-Davidsonian' (Dowty, 1989; Parsons, 1990) the number of arguments of verb-related predicates is not increased, but instead one-place predicates are applied to existentially quantified event variables, and thematic roles, a.k.a. semantic roles, are used to represent the roles of the participants in events, as in 'read(e), agent(e,x), theme(e,y)'.

QuantML combines GQT with neo-Davidsonian event semantics. This has two advantages: it allows a treatment of adverbial temporal quantifiers such as *"twice"*, *"more than three times"*, *"daily"*, and *"twice an hour"*, and it is convenient since this approach is also taken in other parts of SemAF.

Using a neo-Davidsonian approach implies the use of an inventory of semantic roles. For reasons of intra-SemAF compatibility and in line with the recommendation by Abzianidze & Bos (2019) to use an existing role inventory, QuantML uses the set of roles defined in ISO 24617-4, which is based on the LRICIS and VerbNet inventories (see Bunt & Palmer, 2013; Bonial et al. 2011; Petukhova & Bunt, 2008).

2.3. Annotation theory

The QuantML scheme is designed according to the ISO principles of semantic annotation (ISO standard 24617-6, 'SemAF Principles', see also Bunt (2015) and Pustejovsky et al. (2017). This means that the QuantML markup language has a three-part definition consisting of (1) an abstract syntax that specifies the possible *annotation structures* at a conceptual level as set-theoretical constructs; (2) a semantics that specifies the meaning of the annotation structures defined by the abstract syntax; (3) a concrete syntax, that specifies a representation format for annotation structures (for example using XML). Defining the semantics at the level of the abstract syntax puts the focus of an annotation standard at the conceptual level, rather than at the level of representation formats. Annotators (human or automatic) work with concrete representations only, but they can rely on the existence of an underlying abstract syntax layer and its semantics for the interoperability of their annotations.

The abstract syntax is a detailed formalization of the meta-model of the annotation scheme. It specifies a store of basic concepts, called the 'conceptual inventory', and it decribes how the elements of the inventory can be used to build well-formed annotation structures in set-theoretical terms, like pairs, triples, and more complex nested structures. Two types of structure are distinguished: *entity structures* and *link structures*. An entity structure contains semantic information about a segment of primary data and is formally a pair ⟨m, s⟩ consisting of a markable, which refers to a segment of primary data, and certain semantic information. A link structure contains information about the way two or more entity structures are semantically related. The most important entity structures in QuantML are those that describe events and their participants, corresponding to the elements <event> and <entity> in XML representations; the most important link structures are those that link participants to events and those that specify quantifier scopes. See for example Figure 1.

The annotation structures defined by the abstract syntax can be represented (or 'encoded') in a variety of ways; XML is the most popular representation format, but other formats, such as attribute-value matrices or annotation graphs would be equally possible (Ide and Bunt, 2010).

The concrete syntax specifies a vocabulary and a class of syntactic structures, such as XML elements, which together define a class of well-formed representations, and an encoding function that assigns such a representation to every well-formed annotation structure.

The QuantML semantics has the form of an interpretation-by-translation into semantic representations; the recursive interpretation function I_Q 'translates' annotation structures to Discourse Representation Structures (DRSs) in a compositional way, compositional in the sense that the interpre-

tation of an annotation structure is obtained by combining the interpretations of its component entity structures and link structures. This particular form of the QuantML semantics is a choice of convenience rather than one of principle, inspired by the fact that DRSs have also been used as the semantic basis of several other (ISO) semantic annotation schemes. Other choices, such as the use of Minimal Recursion Semantics (Copestake et al., 2005) could work equally well, and although the compositionality of the semantics seems a desirable feature, not all existing proposals for interpreting quantifiers are compositional (e.g., Robaldo, 2011). The specification of the QuantML semantics most importantly shows exactly what QuantML annotations mean.

3. Information Categories

3.1. Overview

For the annotation of quantification in the QuantML scheme, so far the following information categories have been identified:

1. domain specificity
2. definiteness and determinacy
3. distributivity
4. individuation (count/mass)
5. cardinality and size
6. absolute and proportional involvement
7. exhaustivity
8. participant quantification scope
9. event quantification scope
10. modification scope
11. polarity and scope of negation
12. repetitiveness and frequency

Several of these categories are very well known and/or have been discussed for their use in QuantML in one of the previous publications on the development of QuantML, mentioned in Section1. The use of these categories will be very briefly summarised in the next subsection. The rest of this section describes novel QuantML uses of the categories listed above, in particular relating to possessives, negation, exhaustiveness, quantification over masses and parts of individuals, and participation in repetitive events.

3.2. Traditional categories

3.2.1. Domain, definiteness and determinacy

Full-fledged noun phrases consist of two parts: (1) one or more determiners of various kinds of (*"all"*, *"the"*, *"a"*, *"most"*, *"all five"*, *"two of his"*), and (2) a nominal head (bare noun or nominal complex). The latter part, called the *restrictor*, indicates a certain domain that is considered in the quantification. We use the term *'source domain'* to refer to the entities denoted by the restrictor. Quantifications are very often restricted to a contextually determined part of the source domain, the *'reference domain'*, also called 'context set' (Westerståhl, 1985; Partee et al., 1990). For example, the quantifier *"every student"* typically does not apply to literally every person who is a student, but only to the students in a particular class or school. The definiteness of an NP is often an indication that the reference domain of the quantification is a specific part of the source domain, rather than the entire source domain.

In English and in many other languages the determiner part of an NP is a prenominal sequence of determiners of different types. Grammars commonly distinguish different classes of determiners, with different possible sequencing and co-occurrence restrictions. In English grammar a distinction is made between predeterminers, central determiners, and postdeterminers (e.g. Quirk et al., 1972; Leech and Svartvik, 1975), having the following different functions:

- predeterminers express the quantitative involvement of the reference domain, and may, additionally, provide information about the distributivity of the quantification;

- central determiners determine the definiteness of the NP, and thus co-determine a reference domain;

- postdeterminers contain information about the cardinality of the reference domain.

This is illustrated by the NP *"All my nine grandchildren"* in (3.2.1.), where *"all"* is a predeterminer, *"my"* a central determiner, and *"nine"* a postdeterminer.

(1) All my nine grandchildren are boys.

While being definite is often an indication that some particular, determinate entity or collection of entities is considered, the relation between the semantic property of determinacy and the morphological category of definiteness is not straightforward (Coppock & Beaver, 2015; Peters & Westerståhl, 2013). The semantic difference between definite and indefinite expressions has been discussed in terms of familiarity, novelty, salience, uniqueness, and existence presuppositions. In QuantML the view is taken that definiteness is an indication of determinacy, interpreted as restricting a quantification to a reference domain that is somehow constrained through considerations of familiarity and salience, but that this can be overruled by contextual information. Conversely, an NP being indefinite does not necessarily mean that the quantification applies to the NP's entire source domain; contextual considerations often carve out a more restricted reference domain.

3.2.2. Relative scope

Studies of quantifier scope have focused almost exclusively on the relative scopes of quantifications over sets of participants, as in the classical example *"Everybody in this room speaks two languages"*. Relative scopes of this kind are not a property of one of the quantifications involved, but are a semantic relation between them. This is annotated in QuantML as follows:

```
(2) <entity xml:id="x1" target="#m1" involvement="all"
      definiteness="det" pred="person"/>
    <entity xml:id="x2" target="#m3" involvement="2"
      definiteness="indet" pred="language">
    <scoping arg1="#x1" arg2="#x2"
      scopeRel="wider"/>
```

(The reading with reverse scope order would be annotated with arg1="#x2" arg2="x1".) The relative scoping of participants and *events* is also a relevant issue. This is illustrated by the two possible readings of the sentence *"Everybody will die."* Besides the reading according to which everyone is mortal, there is also a reading which predicts an apocalyptic future event in which everyone will die. In the annotation in (3.2.2.) the relative scope of events and participants is marked up by means of the attribute @eventScope, which has been added to the XML element <srLink> as defined in ISO 24617-4.[1]

```
(3) <entity xml:id="x1" target="#m1" pred="person"/>
    <event xml:id="e1" target="#m2" pred="die"
      time-"fut"/>
    <srLink event="#e1" participant="#x1"
      semRole="theme" eventScope="wide"/>
```

Cumulative quantification, a case of branching quantification (Barwise, 1978, Hintikka, 1973; Scha, 1981), as occurring in (3.2.2.) (due to Reyle, 1993), is treated in QuantML as mutual outscoping of the quantifiers. That is, the reading where there is a set A of 3 breweries and a set B of 15 inns, such that the members of A supplied the members of B, and the members of B were supplied by the members of A, is annotated by the scope relation @scopeRel="dual".

(4) Three breweries supplied fifteen inns.

Group quantification is treated as a case of wide event scope in combination with collective distributivity; see Section 3.4. Other issues of scope concern the interaction between quantifiers and modifiers, and between quantifiers and negations; these are discussed below in the sections 3.5 and 3.6.

Scope underspecification is done in QuantML by simply omitting one or more <scoping> elements. The semantics of such a QuantML structure is an underspecified DRS (UDRS, Reyle 1993).

3.2.3. Distributivity

The distinction between distributive and collective quantification is well known, but other cases must be distinguished as well. Example (3.2.3.) may describe a situation where the boys involved did not necessarily do all the carrying either collectively or individually, but where they carried some heavy boxes collectively and some other, less heavy boxes individually. More importantly, the question whether a set of participants is involved in certain events collectively or individually is not always relevant. So in some contexts it is inappropriate to make the collective/distributive distinction and consider the quantification as ambiguous.

(5) The boys carried all the boxes upstairs

The quantifications in this sentence have 'unspecific' distributivity (Bunt, 1985); the sentence just says that all the boxes were somehow carried upstairs by the boys, and all

---

[1] The @scopeRel attribute in <scoping> elements, which is used to annotate the relative scopes of two participant sets, has possible values that are not applicable to the relative scoping of events and participants.

the boys somehow participated. This reading has also been called a 'cover reading' (Schwarzschild,1996), and can be seen as a cumulative reading with unspecific distributivity. (Ordinary cumulative readings have individual distributivity.) Cover readings are annotated in QuantML by both quantifiers having "unspecific" distributivity and "dual" relative scoping. Following Kamp & Reyle (1993), we use the notation X^* to designate the set consisting of the members of X and the subsets of X, and the predicate P^* to designate the characteristic function of the set X^*, where P is the characteristic function of X. Using moreover the notation R_0 to indicate the characteristic function of a reference domain that forms a subset of a source domain with characteristic function R, the 'unspecific' interpretation of (3.2.3.) can be represented in second-order predicate logic as follows:[2]

(6) $\forall x.[box_0(x) \rightarrow \exists y.\exists e.[boy_0{}^*(y) \wedge carry\text{-}up(e) \wedge agent(e,y) \wedge \exists z.[box_0{}^*(z) \wedge [x{=}z \vee x{\in}z] \wedge theme(e,z)]]] \wedge$
$\forall y.[boy_0(y) \rightarrow \exists u.\exists e.[box_0{}^*(u) \wedge carry\text{-}up(e) \wedge theme(e,u) \wedge \exists x.[boy_0{}^*(x) \wedge [y{=}x \vee y{\in}x] \wedge agent(e,x)]]]$

The distributivity of a quantification is not a property of the set of participants in a set of events, but a property of the way of participating. This is illustrated by example (3.2.3.), assuming that *"the men"* individually had a beer, and collectively carried the piano upstairs.

(7) The men had a beer before carrying the piano upstairs.

Distributivity should thus be marked up on the participation relation in the drinking and carrying events, as in the annotation fragment shown in (3.2.3.), where the XML element <srLink> from ISO 24617-4 has been enriched with the attribute '@distr':

(8)
```
<entity xml:id="x1" target="#m1"
    pred="man"/>
<event xml:id="e1" target="#m2" pred="drink"/>
<event xml:id="e2" target="#m3" pred="carry"/>
<srLink event="#e1" participant="#x1"
    semRole="agent" distr="individual"/>
<srLink event="#e2" participant="#x1"
    semRole="agent" distr="collective"/>
```

3.2.4. Size and cardinality

Cardinal determiners indicate the size of a set; in (3.2.4.), the central determiner "twenty-seven" indicates the cardinality of the reference domain, while the predeterminer "twenty-five" indicates the cardinality of the subset of the reference domain whose members were involved in vote-events.

(9) Twenty-five of the twenty-seven states voted in favour.

---

[2]Plural entities involved in quantifications can be viewed as mereological objects rather than as sets (Bunt1983; Champollion (2019); for the annotation as proposed in QuantML this makes little difference – see Bunt, 2019c).

At least the following quantitative aspects of a quantification must be taken into account: (1) the cardinality of the reference domain; (2) the number of elements in the reference domain involved in the predication; and (3) the size of sets, groups, or sums of individuals that are involved in a collective predication. See also Section 3.4 on group quantification.

3.3. Involvement and exhaustivity

The meaning of a cardinal determiner may depend on the speaker's intention, as expressed by the stress pattern of an utterance in which it is used. Used with focal stress, "two" may give rise to a partitive interpretation; for example, in (3.3.a) "two salesmen" means "two of the salesmen", different from (3.3.b) where the stress is on "salesmen".

(10) a. TWO salesmen came in.
     b. Two SALESmen came in.

The occurrence of a cardinal determiner in focus relates also to the much debated issue whether a determiner (or a numeral) like "two" should be interpreted as "exactly two", as "two or more", or as "at most two". Consider the following examples:

(11) a. Two dogs are growling.
     b. Do you have two AA batteries?
     c. How many children does Mary have?
        Mary has two children.
     d. Mary has at most two children.

The standard GQT interpretation of quantifiers of the form *"two N"* is the property of being a set that contains two Ns. So for example, in DRT (Kamp and Reyle, 1993) sentence (3.3.a) is interpreted as claiming the existence of a set X containing two growling dogs. Now suppose there are in fact three growling dogs - in that case it is also true that there are two growling dogs. So *"two"* in (3.3.a) is in fact interpreted as 'two or more'. This seems reasonable for sentence (3.3.a). For sentence (3.3.b), uttered in a context where the speaker is examining a remote control with two apparently flat batteries, this is the only reasonable interpretation. But in (3.3.c) the answer to the question licences the inference that Mary does not have more than two children or less than two children, so in this case *"two"* means 'exactly two'.

It is widely assumed (e.g. Partee, 1988; Kamp and Reyle, 1993; Krifka, 1999) that the numeral *"two"* indicates that the cardinality of the set (or individual sum) denoted by the NP that it modifies is exactly 2, but that the generalized quantifier *"two N"* is interpreted in some contexts as "at least two N' and in others as "exactly two N', due to context-specific (Gricean) pragmatic inferences - see Kadmon (2001). Quantifier readings of the type "exactly two N" are called 'exhaustive', and can be thought of as generated by a covert operator, an 'exhaustivizer', that could be lexicalized as *"only"* (see Szabolcsi, 2010). In (3.3.), replacing *"two"* by *"only two"* in case a and case c enforces or reinforces the 'exactly two' reading, whereas in case b the replacement would be distinctly odd. Similar issues arise when *"two"* forms part of a monotone-decreasing

Markables: m1 = "Each machine", m2 = "machine", m3 = "assembles", m4 = "more than fifty parts", m5 = "parts"

QuantML annotation representation:
```
<entity xml:id="x1" target="#m1" domain="#x2" involvement="all" definiteness="det"/>
<sourceDomain xml:id="x2" target="#m2" pred="machine" indiv="count"/>
<event xml:id="e1" target="#m3" pred="assemble"/>
<entity xml:id="x3" target="#m4" domain="#x2" involvement=">50" definiteness="indet"/>
<sourceDomain xml:id="x4" target="#m5" pred="part" indiv="count"/>
<participation event="#e1" participant="#x1" semRole="agent" distr="individual" eventScope="narrow"/>
<participation event="#e1" participant="#x3" semRole="agent" distr="collective" eventScope="wide"/>
<scoping arg1="#x1" arg2="#x3" scopeRel="wider"/>
```

Figure 1: Annotation of group quantification

quantifier, as in (3.3.d), which is inherently exhaustive. The exhaustiveness of a quantifier relates to focus placement, as illustrated by (3.3.a).

Exhaustive linking occurs when the set of individuals involved in a quantified predication contains all the participants of which the predication is said to hold, as in *"(Only) Two people attended the wedding"* and in *"(Only) Two colleagues did not attend the wedding"*.

(12) (Only) TWO dogs barked.
    Markables: m1=Two dogs, m2=dogs, m3=barked

    QuantML annotation:
```
<entity xml:id="x1" target="#m1" domain="#x2"
    involvement="2" exhaustiveness="exhaustive"
    definiteness="indet"/>
<sourceDomain xml:id="x2" target="#m2"
    individuation="count" pred="dog"/>
<event xml:id="e1" target="#m3" pred="bark"/>
<participation event="#e1" participant="#x1"
    semRole="agent" distr="individual"
    eventScope="narrow"/>
```

3.4. Group quantification

Quantifications with wide event scope and collective distributivity allow readings with so-called 'group quantification', as illustrated by the quantification over *"parts"* in example (3.4.).

(13) Each of these machines assembles more than fifty parts.

Upon the 'group' reading, in every assembly-event where one of the machines under considerations is the agent, a collection of more than 50 parts is involved in the theme role. The annotation of this sentence is shown in figure 1.

3.5. Individuation

Studies of quantification in natural language have often been restricted to cases where the NP head is a count noun. Quantification by means of a mass NP is in many respects similar, but there are some interesting differences. Compare the two sentences in (3.5.):

(14) a. The boys polished all the knives in the drawer.

    b. The boys drank all the milk in the fridge.

In (3.5.a) a predicate is applied to a set of knives, and likewise in (3.5.b) a predicate is applied to a set of quantities of milk. A difference is that (3.5.a) can be analysed as: *Every knife in the drawer was the theme in a polish-event with one of the boys as the agent*, but it is not clear that the analogous analysis *Every quantity of milk in the fridge was the theme in a drink-event with one of the boys as the agent* would make sense, since the set of quantities of milk in the fridge may include bottles of milk, pints of milk and, other quantities that were not as such the object of a drink-event. A universal mass noun quantification of the form *"all the M"* does not necessarily refer to *all* the quantities of M. A detailed analysis of mass noun quantification can be found in Bunt (1985), where elements from lattice theory and set theory are formally integrated. Quantities are analysed as having a part-whole structure (just like sets), defining a sum operation Σ such that the sum of two quantities of M forms another quantity of M. One interpretation of expressions of the form *"all the M"* is as referring to a set X of quantities of M that together make up the reference domain M_0, in the sense that their sum equals the sum of all quantities in the reference domain: $\Sigma(X) = \Sigma(M_0)$.

Since mass nouns do not individuate their reference (Quine, 1960), quantification by mass NPs would seem not to allow individual distribution. Yet there is a distinction similar to the individual/collective distinction of count NP quantifiers, as (3.5.) illustrates.

(15) a. All the water in these lakes is polluted.

    b. The sand in the truck weighs twelve tons.

    c. The boys carried all the sand to the back yard.

In (3.5.a) the predicate of being polluted applies to any sample of *"the water in the lake"*; this distribution is called *homogeneous*. In (3.5.b) the predicate of weighing 12 tons applies to the quantities of sand taken together, so this is a form of collective quantification. In (3.5.c) the boys did not carry every quantity of sand, but certain quantities that together make up "all the sand"; in this case the distribution is called *unspecific*.

These examples illustrate three different ways in which the quantification domain of a mass NP can be completely involved in a predication, corresponding to three different senses of expressions of the form *"all M"* (or *"all the M"*) in English, and similarly in other languages. Complete involvement with homogeneous distribution, as in (3.5.a), where *"all the water"* quantifies over the set of all contextually distinguished quantities of water, is annotated with the @involvement attribute having the value "all". In cases like (3.5.c), where *"all the sand"* refers to a subset of quantities of sand that together make up all the (contextually distinguished) sand - the @involvement attribute has the value "total". Finally, on the collective reading of (3.5.b), where *"(all) the sand"* refers to the quantity of sand formed by all contextually relevant quantities of sand together, the involvement will be annotated as "whole". This is summarized in Table 1.

Although count nouns do individuate their reference in terms of individuals, there is a form of quantification with count NPs that resembles the 'total, unspecific' quantification with mass NPs (Bunt, 2017). Consider the example *"Mario ate three pizzas for dinner"*. The standard interpretation would go something like this: There is a set of three pizzas that were the object in an eat-event at dinner time with Mario as the agent. But now consider: *"Mario ate five pizzas last week"*. A plausible interpretation could now be: Last week Mario ate in total 5 pizzas in some eat-events (for example, 2.75 pizza in one event and 2.25 pizza in another). This interpretation requires the consideration of pizza parts as the participants in eat-events, and a notion of summation of parts (in this example adding up to 5 pizzas). Quantifications of this kind are annotated in QuantML by the @individuation attribute in <sourceDomain> elements having the value "count/parts".

3.6. Modification scope

Relative scope is an issue not only between two participant quantifications, or between a participant quantification and an event quantification, but also when the head noun of a quantifying NP is modified by a relative clause, a prepositional phrase, or a possessive phrase that contains quantifiers. In that case a quantifier in the modifier may outscope the quantification over the head noun. The following examples illustrate this phenomenon, which is known in the linguistic literature as 'inverse linking' (May, 1977; May and Bale, 2007; Szabolcsi, 2010; Ruys and Winter, 2011; Barker, 2014).

(16) a. Two students from every college participated.
      b. The children's toys were stolen.

The relative scoping of the two quantifiers is in these case annotated as a property of the modifying relation, expressed by the value "inverse" of the attribute @linking in a <ppMod> or a <possRestr> element, as shown in Fig. 2.

Possessive expressions introduce a relation that is not made explicit, or that is expressed using a rather vague preposition like *"of"* in English and *"de"* in Romance languages. Typical examples are shown in (3.6.). All these (and other) forms have in common that they express some sort of possession relation between a (set of) possessor(s) and a set of possessions. Possessive expressions involve quantification over possessions (and possibly also over possessors). A case like (3.6.a1) can be analysed schematically as in (3.6.b), introducing a generic 'Poss' relation as proposed by Peters and Westerståhl (2013).

(17) a. 1. Tom's house
         2. John and Mary's two children
         3. two of my books
         4. the headmaster's children's toys
         5. the children of the headmaster
         6. every student's library card

      b. house(x) $\wedge$ tom(y) $\wedge$ Poss(x,y)

3.7. Polarity and scope of negation

The QuantML scheme does not offer a general treatment of the annotation of polarity and modality, but it provides devices for dealing with the relative scopes of quantifications and negations. The example sentence in (3.7.) illustrates the possible scopes of a negation at clause level, the negation scoping either over the entire clause, over the clause minus *"the unions"*, or just over the determiner in *"the unions"*. The first two readings can be distinguished in annotations by means of a @polarity attribute in <participation> elements with the value "neg-wide" for wide-scope negation and "neg-narrow" for the second reading, while the third reading is distinguished by the value of the @involvement attribute in the corresponding <entity> element indicating that less than all of the individuals in the reference domain are involved.

(18) a. The unions do not accept the proposal.

      b. It is not the case that all the unions accept the proposal [some of them don't]
         <participant event="#e1" participant="#x1" semRole="agent" distr="individual" polarity="neg-wide"/>

      c. All the unions do not accept the proposal [none of them does]
         <participant event="#e1" participant="#x1" semRole="agent" distr="individual" polarity="neg-narrow"/>

      d. Not all the unions accept the proposal [though most of them do]
         <entity xml:id="x1" target="#m1" pred="union" involvement="not-all"/>

Note that this way of annotating negation scope makes it possible to handle cases of double or triple negation, as in *"Not all the unions do not accept the proposal"*.

3.8. Repetitiveness

The annotation of repeated participation in recurring events has been treated in ISO 24617-1 as a quantification over temporal objects, but in spite of the suggestion that comes from the word "times" in the English language, expressions like *"once"*, *"twice"* and *"three times"* do not really quantify over time, but rather over sets of eventualities (Lewis, 1975). The QuantML scheme does not provide a complete proposal for dealing with adverbial temporal or spatial quantification, but repetitiveness can be covered in a natural way by using the concepts available in QuantML. Participation in a k-times repetitive event is annotated by means of a <participation> element with @repetitiveness

distribution	involvement	interpretation	example
homogeneous	all	For all quantities of M	(3.5.a)
unspecific	total	For the elements in a set of quantities of M	
		that together make up the whole of M	(3.5.c)
collective	whole	For M as a whole	(3.5.b)

Table 1: Involvement and distributivity in mass NP quantification.

Markables in sentence (3.6.a):
m1="Two students from every university", m2="students", m3="students from every university", m4="from every university", m5="every university", m6="university", m7="participated"

QuantML annotation:
```
<entity xml:id="x1" target="#m1" domain="#x2" involvement="2" definiteness="indef"/>
<refDomain xml:id="x2" target="#m3" source="#x3" restrs="#r1"/>
<sourceDomain xml:id="x3" target="#m2" individuation="count" pred="student"/>
<ppMod xml:id="r1" target="#m4" pRel="from" pEntity="#x4" distr="individual" linking="inverse"/>
<entity xml:id="x4" target="#m5" domain="#x5" involvement="all" definiteness="det"/>
<sourceDomain xml:id="x5" target="#m6" individuation="count" pred="university"/>
<event xml:id="e1" target="#m7" pred="participate"/>
<participation event="#e1" participant="#x1"semRole="agent" distr="unspecific" eventScope="narrow"/>
```

Figure 2: QuantML annotation of modification scope

= "k", the semantics of which is given by (3.8.) for individual, non-exhaustive participation in the Agent role with narrow event scope and positive polarity.[3] (Note that k can be any numerical predicate that identifies a range of natural numbers, such as 'only once', 'more than three times' or 'two or three times'.)

(19) I_Q(Agent, individual, narrow, non-exhaustive, k, positive) =
$[X \mid x \in X \rightarrow [E \mid k(E), e \in E \rightarrow agent(e,x)]]$

This leads for example to the semantic interpretation (3.8.b) for the sentence (3.8.a), where 'child$_0$" designates the predicate 'child' restricted to the reference domain formed by the contextually distinguished children:

(20) a. Two of the children called twice.

b. $[X \mid |X|{=}2, x \in X \rightarrow [E \mid |E|{=}2, child_0(x),$
$e \in E \rightarrow [call(e), agent(e,x)]]$

4. Conclusions

Although the development of QuantML as an ISO standard is still in a preliminary stage, the scheme as developed so far supports the annotation of quite a variety of forms and aspects of quantification in a way that is interoperable (a) in the sense that its XML-based representation format is just one possible encoding of the underlying abstract annotation structures with their formal semantics, and (b) in the sense of sharing a view on sentence meaning rooted in Neo-Davidsonian event semantics, and DRT with other parts of ISO SemAF.

Current limitations of QuantML have to do with the limitations of the events-and-participants view and with lack of agreement on the analysis of certain forms of quantification. The events-and participants approach seems to be stretched to its limits for verbs that take abstract concepts like thoughts, beliefs, desires, etc. as their arguments, as in *"Bob wants to catch a fish"*.

Forms of quantification that have so far escaped a generally agreed analysis include generics and habituals, whose theoretical status has not been fully resolved; see e.g. Kamp and Reyle (1993), Section 3.7.4. Krifka et al. (1995) analyse generics in terms of a special default quantifier; others introduce a notion of 'normal' or 'prototypical' into the interpretation framework (cf. Eckhardt, 2000; van Rooij and Schulz, 2020).

Another issue for further work concerns the overlaps between QuantML and schemes for annotating other phenomena, such as events and coreference. The recently introduced notion of an annotation scheme plug-in with its interface (Bunt, 2019b) may provide a mechanism for dealing with such overlaps.

Most importantly, the QuantML annotation scheme needs to be validated in manual and automatic annotation. For manual annotation, the scheme reflects the fact that quantification in natural language is an extremely complex matter. To do justice to this complexity, the annotation scheme is inevitably quite complex itself, and impossible for use by untrained annotators, except perhaps if annotators are supported by an interactive annotation tool that for example asks questions like "Did the men act together or each one by himself?", to distinguish between collective and distributive readings, and suggests appropriate default values of certain attributes. An extensive user manual and a repository of annotated examples would also seem to be indispensable for training annotators, and such material could be useful as well as training material for automatic annotation.

---

[3]Alternatively, repetitiveness could be annotated in <event> elements, but that would make the formulation of the semantics of annotation structures slightly more complex.

Abzianidze, L. and J. Bos (2019). Thirty musts for meaning banking. In *Proceedings of ACL 2019 First International Workshop on Designing Meaning Representations*, pp. 15–27.

Barker, C. (2014). Scope. In S. Lappin and C. Fox (Eds.), *The Handbook of Contemporary Semantic Theory*, pp. 40–76. New York: John Wiley.

Barwise, J. (1978). On Branching Quantifiers in English. *Journal of Philosophical Logic 8*, 47–80.

Barwise, J. and R. Cooper (1981). Generalized Quantifiers and Natural Language. *Linguistics and Philosophy 4*, 159–219.

Bonial, C., W. Corvey, M. Palmer, V. Petukhova, and H. Bunt (2011). A hierarchical unification of LIRICS and VerbNet semantic roles. In *Proceedings IEEE-ICSC 2011 Workshop on Semantic Annotation for Computational Linguistic Resources*, Stanford, CA.

Bos, J. (1995). Predicate logic unplugged. In *Proceedings 10th Amsterdam Colloquium*, Amsterdam, pp. 133–142. ILLC.

Bunt, H. (1985). *Mass Terms and Model-Theoretic Semantics*. Cambridge University Press.

Bunt, H. (2015). On the principles of semantic annotation. In *Proceedings 11th Joint ACL-ISO Workshop on Interoperable Semantic Annotation (ISA-11)*, London, pp. 1–13.

Bunt, H. (2017). Towards interoperable annotation of quantification. In *Proceedings ISA-13, Thirteenth International Workshop on Interoperable Semantic Annotation*, Montpellier, pp. 84–94.

Bunt, H. (2018). *Semantic Annotation of Quantification in Natural Language*. *TiCC Technical Report* 2018-15. Tilburg Center for Cognition and Communication, Tilburg University.

Bunt, H. (2019a). An annotation scheme for quantification. In *Proceedings 14th International Conference on Computational Semantics (IWCS 2019)*, Gothenburg, Sweden, pp. 31–42.

Bunt, H. (2019b). Plug-ins for content annotation of dialogue acts. In *Proceedings 15th Joint ISO-ACL Workshop on Interoperable Semantic Annotation (ISA-15)*, Gothenburg, Sweden, pp. 34–45.

Bunt, H. (2019c). *Semantic Annotation of Quantification in Natural Language, Ed. 2. TiCC Technical Report* 2019-12. Tilburg Center for Cognition and Communication, Tilburg University.

Bunt, H. and M. Palmer (2013). Conceptual and representational choices in defining an ISO standard for semantic role annotation. In *Proceedings of the 9th Joint ISO - ACL Workshop on Interoperable Semantic Annottiion (ISA-9)*, Potsdam, pp. 41–50.

Bunt, H. and J. Pustejovsky (2010). Annotating temporal and event quantification. In *Proceedings ISA-5, Fifth International Workshop on Interoperable Semantic Annotation*, pp. 15–22. City University of Hong Kong.

Bunt, H., J. Pustejovsky, and K. Lee (2018). Towards an ISO Standard for the Annotation of Quantification. In *Proceedings 11th International Conference on Language Resources and Evaluation (LREC 2018)*, Myazaki, Japan. ELRA.

Champollion, L. (2015). The interaction of compositional semantics and event semantics. *Linguistics and Philosophy 38 (1)*, 31–66.

Champollion, L. (2019). Distributivity in Formal Semantics. *Annual Review of Linguistics 5*, 289–308.

Cooper, R. (1983). *Quantification and syntactic theory*. Dordrecht: Reidel.

Copestake, A., D. Flickinger, C. Pollard, and I. Sag (2005). Minimal Recursion Semantics: An Introduction. *Research on Language and Computation 3*, 281–332.

Coppock, E. and D. Beaver (2015). Definiteness and determinacy. *Linguistics and Philosophy 38*, 377–435.

Davidson, D. (1967). The Logical Form of Action Sentences. In N. Resher (Ed.), *The Logic of Decision and Action*, pp. 81–95. Pittsburgh: The University of Pittsburgh Press.

Dowty, D. (1989). On the Semantic Content of the Notion of 'Thematic Role'. In G. Chierchia, B. Partee, and R. Turner (Eds.), *Properties, Types and Meaning*, Volume 2. Dordrecht/Boston/London: Kluwer Academic Publishers.

Eckhardt, R. (2000). Normal objects, normal worlds, and the meaning of generic sentences. *Journal of Semantics 16*, 237–278.

Frege, G. (1897). *Begriffsschrift, eine der arithmetischen nachgebildete Formelsprache des reinen Denkens*. Halle: Nebert.

Hintikka, J. (1973). Quantifiers vs. quantification theory. *Dialectica 27*, 329–358.

Hobbs, J. and S. Shieber (1987). An algorithm for generating quantifier scopings. *Computational Linguistics 13*(1-2), 47–63.

Ide, N. and H. Bunt (2010). Anatomy of annotation schemes: Mapping to GrAF. In *Proceedings 4th Linguistic Annotation Workshop (LAW IV)*, Uppsala.

ISO (2012). *ISO 24617-1: 2012, Language Resource Management - Semantic Annotation Framework (SemAF) - Part 1: Time and events*. Geneva: International Organisation for Standardisation ISO.

ISO (2014a). *ISO 24617-4: 2014, Language Resource Management - Semantic Annotation Framework (SemAF) - Part 4: Semantic roles*. Geneva: International Organisation for Standardisation ISO.

ISO (2014b). *ISO 24617-7: 2014, Language Resource Management - Semantic Annotation Framework (SemAF) - Part 7: Spatial information*. Geneva: International Organisation for Standardisation ISO.

ISO (2015). *ISO 24617-6:2015, Language Resource Management - Semantic Annotation Framework (SemAF) - Part 6: Principles of semantic annotation*. Geneva: International Organisation for Standardisation ISO.

ISO (2016). *ISO 24617-8:2016, Language Resource Management - Semantic Annotation Framework (SemAF) - Part 8: Semantic relations in discourse, Core annotation scheme (DR-Core)*. Geneva: International Organisation for Standardisation ISO.

ISO (2019). *ISO/WD 24617-12:2019, Language Resource Management: Semantic Annotation Framework (SemAF) - Part 12: Quantification*. Geneva.: International Standard. International Organisation for Standardisation ISO.

Kadmon, N. (2001). *Formal Pragmatics*. Oxford: Blackwell.

Kamp, H. and U. Reyle (1993). *From Discourse to Logic*. Dordrecht: Kluwer Academic Publishers.

Keenan, E. and J. Stavi (1986). A semantic characterization of natural language determiners. *Linguistics and Philosophy 9*, 253–326.

Krifka, M. (1999). At least some determiners aren't determiners. In K. Turner (Ed.), *The Semantics/Pragmatics Interface From Different Points of View*, pp. 257–291. Amsterdam: Elsevier.

Krifka, M., F. Pelletier, G. Carlson, A. ter Meulen, G. Chierchia, and G. Link (1995). Genericity: An introduction. In G. Carlson and F. Pelletier (Eds.), *The generic book*, pp. 1–124. Chicago: University of Chicago Press.

Leech, G. and J. Svartvik (1975). *A communicative grammar of English*. London: Longman.

Lewis, D. (1975). Adverbs of quantification. In E. Keenan (Ed.), *Formal Semantics of Natural Language*, pp. 3–15. Cambridge: Cambridge University Press.

Lindström, P. (1966). First order predicate logic with generalized quantifiers. *Theoria 32*, 186–195.

May, R. (1977). *The Grammar of Quantification*. Ph.D. Dissertation, MIT.

May, R. and A. Bale (2005). Inverse linking. In M. Everaert and H. van Riemsdijk (Eds.), *The Blackwell Companion to syntax, Vol. 2*, pp. 639–667. Oxford: Blackwell.

Montague, R. (1971). The proper treatment of quantification in ordinary language. In R.Thomason (Ed.), *Formal Philosophy*. New Haven: Yale University Press.

Mostowski, A. (1957). On a generalization of quantifiers. *Fundamentae Mathematicae 44*, 12–36.

Parsons, T. (1990). *Events in the Semantics of English: A Study in Subatomic Semantics*. Cambridge, MA: MIT Press.

Partee, B. (1988). Many quantifiers. In *ESCOL 89: Proceedings of the Eastern States Conference on Linguistics, Reprinted in Compositionality in Formal Semantics: Selected Papers by Barbara Partee*, Oxford, pp. 241–158. Blackwell 2004.

Partee, B., A. ter Meulen, and R. Wall (1990). *Mathematical Models in Linguistics*. Berlin: Springer.

Peters, S. and D. Westerståhl (2006). *Quantifiers in Language and Logic*. New York: Oxford University Press.

Peters, S. and D. Westerståhl (2013). The semantics of possessives. *Language 89(4)*, 713–759.

Petukhova, V. and H. Bunt (2008). LIRICS semantic role annotation: design and evaluation of a set of data categories. In *Proceedings of the Sixth International Conference on Language Resources and Evaluation (LREC 2008)*, Marrakech, Morocco. ELRA, Paris.

Pustejovsky, J., H. Bunt, and K. Lee (2010). ISO-TimeML. In *Proceedings of the 7th International Conference on Language Resources and Evaluation (LREC 2010)*, Malta. ELDA, Paris.

Pustejovsky, J., H. Bunt, and A. Zaenen (2017). Designing annotation schemes: From theory to model. In N. Ide and J. Pustejovsky (Eds.), *Handbook of Linguistic Annotation*, pp. 21–72. Berlin: Springer.

Quine, W. (1960). *Word and Object*. Cambridge, Mass.: MIT Press.

Quirk, R., A. Greenbaum, G. Leech, and J. Svartvik (1972). *A Grammar of Contemporary English*. London: Longman.

Reyle, U. (1993). Dealing with ambiguities by underspecification: Construction, representation, and deduction. *Journal of Semantics*, 123–179.

Robaldo, L. (2011). Distributivity, collectivity, and cumulativity in terms of (in)dependence and maximality. *Journal of Logic, Language and Information 23(1)*, 233–271.

Rooij, R. v. and K. Schulz (2020). Generics and typicality: a bounded rationality approach. *Linguistics and Philosophy 43(1)*, 83–117.

Ruys, E. and Y. Winter (2011). Quantifier Scope in Formal Linguistics. In D. Gabbay and F. Guenthner (Eds.), *Handbook of Philosophical Logic*, pp. 195–225. Dordrecht: Foris.

Scha, R. (1981). Collective, distributive and cumulative quantification. In J. Groenendijk and M. Stokhof (Eds.), *Formal Methods in the Study of Language*, pp. 483–512. Amsterdam: Mathematisch Centrum.

Schwarzschild, R. (1996). *Pluralities*. Dordrecht: Kluwer Academic Publishers.

Szabolcsi, A. (2010). *Quantification*. Cambridge (UK): Cambridge University Press.

Westerståhl, D. (1985). Determiners and context sets. In J. van Benthem and A. ter Meulen (Eds.), *Generalized Quantifiers in Natural Language*, pp. 45–71. Dordrecht: Foris.

Appendix:
Outline of QuantML specification

Metamodel

The metamodel underlying QuantML annotations shows the concepts that make up annotation structures corresponding to the information categories discussed in Section 3, with their grouping into entity structures and link structures – see Figure 3.

Abstract syntax

The structures defined by the abstract syntax are n-tuples of elements that are either basic concepts, taken from a store called the 'conceptual inventory', or, recursively, of such n-tuples. Two types of structure are distinguished: entity structures and link structures. An entity structure contains semantic information about a segment of primary data and is formally a pair ⟨m, s⟩ consisting of a markable, which refers to a segment of primary data, and certain semantic information. A link structure contains information about the way two or more segments of primary data are

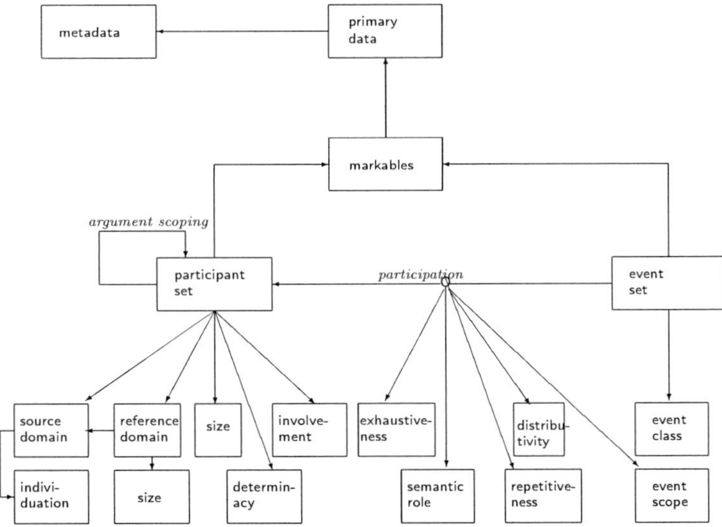

Figure 3: QuantML Metamodel.

semantically related.

QuantML conceptual inventory:

- unary predicates that characterize source domains (such as 'book', 'student', and 'water) or event domains (such as 'lift', 'carry', 'drink'), or that correspond to adjectives or to prepositions;
- binary predicates that correspond to semantic roles, notably the roles as defined in ISO 24617-4 (Semantic roles);
- numerical predicates for specifying reference domain involvement, reference domain size, size of certain parts of a reference domain, or number of repetitions or frequency of recurrence in event structures;
- predicates for specifying proportional reference domain involvement, such as 'all', 'some', 'most';
- parameters for specifying definiteness: 'determinate' and 'indeterminate'; domain individuation: 'count', 'mass', 'count/parts'; and distributivity: 'collective', 'individual', 'homogeneous', 'single' (used for singular proper names and definite descriptions), 'unspecific';
- basic units of measurement, such as 'meter', 'kilogram', 'litre', and the operators 'division' and 'multiplication' for forming complex units;
- the polarity values 'positive' and 'negative';
- the values 'exhaustive' and 'non-exhaustive';
- parameters for specifying event scope: 'wide' and 'narrow' (default value), and for specifying whether scope inversion occurs: 'inverse' or 'linear' (default value).
- ordering relations for specifying the relative scopes of quantifiers over sets of participants: 'wider', 'dual', and 'unscoped'.

QuantML has three kinds of entity structures: (1) for events; (2) for participants; (3) for restrictions on sets of participants. A quantified set of participants is characterized by the following properties:

- the source domain, from which the participants are drawn, and its individuation;

- the reference domain, typically a subset of the source domain;
- the quantitative (absolute or proportional) involvement of the reference domain;
- the size of the reference domain, or of groups, subsets, or parts of the reference domain involved in the quantified predication.

The entity structure $\langle m, s \rangle$ for a set of participants thus contains a triple $s = \langle\langle D, v \rangle, q, d \rangle$ with D = characteristic domain predicate, v = individuation, q = reference domain involvement, and d = determinacy, with possibly an additional size specification. The domain component is more complex when the restrictor of an NP contains head noun modifiers and/or multiple, conjoined heads (see Bunt 2018 for details). Entity structures for sets of events are very simple; they contain just a predicate that characterizes a domain of events.

Modifier structures come in five varieties, depending on whether the head noun of an NP is modified by an adjective, noun, PP, relative clause, or possessive restriction. These are not spelled out in Fig. 3.

Two kinds of link structure are defined: participation structures, which link participants to events, and scope link structures. Participation structures are a 7- or 8-tuple, specifying (1) a set of events; (2) a set of participants; (3) a semantic role; (4) a distributivity; (5) the exhaustiveness of the participation; (6) the relative scope of the event quantification; (7) the polarity, which is "positive" by default; and possibly (8) a repetitiveness. Scope link structures specify the relative scope of two participant entity structures.

Annotation structures for quantification are associated mostly with clauses and their constituent NPs and verbs. The annotation structure for a clause is a quadruple consisting of an event structure, a set of participant structures, a set of participation link structures, and a set of scope link structures. In a complete clause annotation structure all participant structures are linked to the verb's event structure, and the relative scopes of all participant entity structures are specified.

Concrete syntax

A concrete syntax is specified here in the form of an XML representation of annotation structures. For each type of entity structure, defined by the abstract syntax, a corresponding XML element is defined; each of these elements has an attribute @xml:id whose value is a unique identifier (unique within the annotation structure), and an attribute @target, whose value anchors the annotation in the primary data, having a markable as value (or a sequence of markables). In addition, these elements have the following attributes:

<**entity**>: @domain, @involvement, @definiteness and @size (optional);
<**event**>: @pred (event class);
<**refDomain**>: @source (with multiple values in the case of a conjunctive head) and @restrictions;
<**sourceDomain**>: @pred, @individuation;
<**adjMod**>: @pred, @distr, and @restrictions (optional);
<**nnMod**>: @pred, @distr, and @restrictions (optional);
<**ppMod**>: @pRel, @pEntity, @distr, @linking;
<**relClause**>: @semRole, @clause, @distr, @linking;
<**amount**>: @num, @unit;
<**complexUnit**>: @unit1, @operation, @unit2.

For each of the two types of link structure defined by the abstract syntax, an XML element is defined:

<**participation**> with attributes @event, @participant, @semRole, @distr, @eventScope, @exhaustiveness, [optionally: @repetitiveness]; and @polarity;

<**scoping**> with the attributes @arg1, @arg2, @scopeRel.

Semantics

The QuantML semantics specifies a recursive interpretation function I_Q that translates annotation structures into DRSs in a compositional way: the interpretation of an annotation structure is obtained by combining the interpretations of its component entity structures and participation link structures, in a way that is determined by scope link structures (if any). For a full specification of the QuantML semantics see Bunt (2019c). Here we outline the overall approach and present some interesting parts of the definition of I_Q.

The QuantML interpretation function translates every participant entity structure, event entity structure, and participation link structure into a DRS and combines these. Consider the example in (4.). The entity structures for *"More than two thousand students"*, and *"protested"* are translated into the DRSs shown in (4.)b and c. For the participant entity structure this is achieved by applying an instance of clause (4.a) in the I_Q definition, which interprets entity structures with source domain D, individuation v, involvement q, and definiteness *indef*. The interpretation q' of domain involvement specification q is defined in (4.b-c), and that of the domain specification in (4.d-e).

(21) a. $I_Q(\langle m1, \langle\langle\langle m2, D\rangle, v\rangle, q, \mathit{indef}\rangle\rangle) = [\,X \mid q'(X), [x \in X \to D'(x)]]$

b. $q' = I_Q(q) \circ F_Q(v)$

c. $F_Q(v)$: $F_Q(count) = \lambda X.|X|$; $F_Q(mass) = F_Q(count/parts) = \lambda X.|\Sigma X|$

d. $D' = I_Q(\langle D, v\rangle)$

e. $I_Q(\langle D, v\rangle)$: $I_Q(\langle D, count\rangle) = I_Q(\langle D, mass\rangle) = I_Q(D)$; $I_Q(\langle D, count/parts\rangle) = I_Q(D)^+$

(22) a. More than two thousand students protested.

b. $I_Q(\langle m1, \langle\langle\langle m2, student\rangle, count\rangle, \lambda z.|z| > 2000, \mathit{indet}\rangle\rangle) = [\,X \mid |X|{=}2000, [x \in X \to student(x)]]$

c. $I_Q(\langle m3, \langle protest\rangle\rangle) = [\,E \mid [\,e \in E \to protest(e)]]$

The DRS in (4.b) says that there exists a set with the property of containing two thousand students, reflecting the GQT approach to NP interpretation. The DRS in (4.c) together with (4.) illustrates the adoption of neo-Davidsonian event semantics.

The participation link structure has in this example the form $\langle \epsilon_E, \{\epsilon_{P1}\}, R, d, \xi, \sigma, p\rangle$, where ϵ_E and ϵ_{P1} are the participant and event entity structures that are linked in the Agent role (R = Agent), with d = collective, ξ = non-exhaustive, σ (event scope) = narrow, and p (polarity) = positive. The semantic interpretation of such a structure is defined as follows, where '$\cup$' designates the familiar merge operation for DRSs:

(23) $I_Q\langle \epsilon_E, \{\epsilon_{P1}\}, R, d, \sigma\rangle = I_Q\langle \epsilon_{P1}\rangle \cup (I_Q\langle \epsilon_E\rangle \cup I_Q(R, d, \xi, \sigma, p)$

A triple like $\langle\, R, d, \sigma\rangle$ is interpreted as shown in (4.):

(24) a. $I_Q(R, individual, narrow) = [\,X \mid x \in X \to [\,E \mid e \in E \to agent(e, x)\,]$

b. $I_Q(R, individual, wide) = [\,E \mid e \in E \to [\,X \mid x \in X \to agent(e, x)\,]$

c. $I_Q(R, collective, \sigma) = [\,X, E \mid x \in X \to [\,e \mid e \in E, R(e, X)\,]$

Applying rule (4.) to the right-hand sides of (4.) and (4.c), with the values for R, d and σ substituted, gives the desired result shown in (4.):.

(25) $[X \mid |X| > 2000, [x \in X \to student(x)], [E \mid e \in E \to [\,protest(e), agent(e,X)]]]$

Hindi TimeBank: An ISO-TimeML Annotated Reference Corpus

Pranav Goel, Suhan Prabhu, Alok Debnath, Priyank Modi & Manish Shrivastava
Language Technologies Research Center
International Institute of Information Technology
Hyderabad, India
{pranav.goel, suhan.prabhuk, alok.debnath, priyank.modi}@research.iiit.ac.in
m.shrivastava@iiit.ac.in

Abstract

ISO-TimeML is an international standard for multilingual event annotation, detection, categorization and linking. In this paper, we present the Hindi TimeBank, an ISO-TimeML annotated reference corpus for the detection and classification of events, states and time expressions, and the links between them. Based on contemporary developments in Hindi event recognition, we propose language-independent and language-specific deviations from the ISO-TimeML guidelines, but preserve the schema. These deviations include the inclusion of annotator confidence, and an independent mechanism of identifying and annotating states (such as copulars and existentials) With this paper, we present an open-source corpus, the Hindi TimeBank. The Hindi TimeBank is a 1,000 article dataset, with over 25,000 events, 3,500 states and 2,000 time expressions. We analyze the dataset in detail and provide a class-wise distribution of events, states and time expressions. Our guidelines and dataset are backed by high average inter-annotator agreement scores.
Keywords: Annotation Corpora, Hindi, Temporal Information Extraction

1. Introduction

Temporal information retrieval is a rapidly growing branch of natural language processing and information extraction, due to numerous applications such as question answering and summarization systems. The detection of events, states, temporal expressions and their relations provides a rich source of temporal information, and acts as the representation of real world information in text. This has two-fold implications, first, that the representation mechanism depends on the syntactic and semantic properties of the language, and second, that in order to create systems that use this information, large amounts of annotated data are a prerequisite.

An attempt towards solving the issue of disparate representations was made by ISO-TimeML (Pustejovsky et al., 2010), by developing an international standard based on the earlier, highly popular event annotation framework known as TimeML (Pustejovsky et al., 2003a). ISO-TimeML is an inter-operable semantic framework for linguistic annotation of temporal expressions such as events (e.g. occurrences and happenings) and time expressions (e.g. mentions of days, dates and times). The international standard had been created such that the annotation framework could be applied across languages extensively. The issue of training data for large systems was solved by creating large annotated corpora based on the prevalent annotation mechanism, known as TimeBanks. After the English TimeBank (Pustejovsky et al., 2003b), TimeBanks have been developed for various languages, elaborated upon in section 2..

Recently, Hindi has been added to the list of languages with literature working towards the annotation of events and temporal expressions. Temporal expression identification in Hindi and their basic classification has been done as a part of the FIRE 2011 corpus[1], but a more focused approach has also been adopted (Ramrakhiyani and Majumder, 2013; Ramrakhiyani and Majumder, 2015). For

event detection and recognition, the framework and basic guidelines for a binary recognition of event nugget has been established by Goud et al. (2019), which also differentiates between events and states and makes a case for the complexity of recognition of events in a semantico-syntactic grammatical framework of Hindi. We continue to follow this distinction, as mentioned in section 3..

Event analysis as a temporal phenomena is a question not only in NLP but also in linguistic philosophy, which is deeply rooted in the manner languages express events. ISO-TimeML event schema is an improvement over the TimeML event analysis framework to make it more general for all languages. TimeML's definition of an event seems to be derived from the Davidson's notion of eventualities (Davidson, 1967), which provided a definition of events as *"spatio-temporal phenomena with functionally integrated participants"*. Therefore, extensionally, TimeML events (Pustejovsky et al., 2007) are based on a neo-Davidsonian analysis of eventualities, and are detected based entirely on properties.

In this paper, we extend both the idea and the initial seed dataset from binary event classification in Hindi (Goud et al., 2019) and include the annotation of states (which was deliberately eliminated earlier), the classification of both events and states, as well as inclusion of time expressions in an augmented dataset of 1,000 Hindi articles. We provide a comprehensive set of guidelines for the identification and differentiation of events from states. The classification scheme for events and states in Hindi has been augmented from TimeML for consistency. Further, changes have been implemented in later stages of the annotation cycle. These are both language specific changes and changes to the ISO-TimeML schema that can be applied to other languages as well. Lastly, the robustness of the annotation guidelines is evaluated by inter-annotator scores, as well as other statistics about the dataset.

To summarize, this paper contributes a corpus of 1,000 articles with 25,829 events and 3,516 states for the purpose

---

[1]http://fire.irsi.res.in/

of temporal information retrieval in Hindi, the Hindi Time-Bank. This resource has been annotated on a modified ISO-TimeML schema and guidelines, which have been elucidated below. We provide a comprehensive analysis of the data, the schema, the guidelines and the annotation mechanism, which can be used for event and temporal expression annotation of multiple other languages.

2. Related Work

TimeBanks have been introduced for multiple languages after English. These TimeBanks were developed after fundamental additions and modifications to ISO-TimeML guidelines for language specific syntactic properties.

In the French TimeBank(Bittar et al., 2011), the authors propose that those verbs be tagged as modal since modality is expressed by fully inflected verbs. Furthermore, the authors also provide a way of capturing the difference between support verb constructions with a neutral aspectual value (mener une attaque (carry out an attack)) and those with an inchoative aspectual value.

The Italian TimeBank(Caselli et al., 2011) focuses on the EVENT and TIMEX3 tag and modifies their properties to suit Italian. The main difference with regards to the EVENT tag is in the tag attribute list and attribute values. The TIMEX tag used in the Ita-TimeBank is as much as possible compliant with the TIDES TIMEX2[2] annotation.

In the Romanian (Forascu and Tufiș, 2012) and Spanish (Saurı and Badia, 2012) TimeBanks, the authors opted to indicated whether an EVENT is a state (with the 'class' attribute having the value 'STATE'), instead of using the attribute 'type' to indicate if the EVENT is a state, a process or a transition.

The Portuguese TimeBank (Costa and Branco, 2012) uses the same guidelines as the English TimeBank, and use a combination of the Portuguese OpenWordNet and temopral-aware systems.

Finally, in the Persian TimeBank (Yaghoobzadeh et al., 2012), gerund phrases, known as *"esm-e masdar"*, must always be annotated as events, even when they represent generic events. Furthermore, the authors also consider objective deverbal adjectives in PersTimeML. Syntactically, Persian TimeBank differs from ISO-TimeML in the way that all the tokens part of an event are marked under the same event ID irrespective of whether they are consecutive or not.

3. Annotation Guidelines

In this section, we shall cover the basic guidelines for the annotation of events and states, their classification mechanism and the annotation and classification of TIMEX3 time expressions. We present the modified definitions and then use the relevant syntactic cues which will be used in order to determine, annotate and classify both events and states.

3.1. Events and States

TimeML defined *events* as situations that occur, hold or take place, or as states or circumstances in which something

obtains or holds true (Saurí et al., 2006). In annotation of Hindi events by this definition, annotators portrayed low confidence, given that event normalization, subordinating verbs and "generics" were not to be marked.

Therefore, states have been defined with respect to these distinctions in order to be easier to annotate. A state may be defined as *a verbal predicate which provides a spatio-temporal description participating entities, including a description of properties, location or existence.* Such a definition accounts for verbal modifiers and copular constructions. Note that subjunctives are not considered states under this definition and neither are they considered events, due to the fact that the participating entities do not undergo any change (Goud et al., 2019). Therefore, subjunctive phrases are not annotated as either events or states.

Furthermore, given an extensional understanding of events based on the change in the properties of entities, certain reporting verbs with sentential predicates are not considered events if they do not contain a participating entity. Hindi allows subject ellipsis constructions, therefore those verbs do not contain any entities, and are therefore not annotated. For example:

1.
kahā	*jātā*	*hai*	*tūphāna*	*gabhīra*	*hai*
say	go	is	storm	serious	is

It is said that the storm is serious.

Due to the lack of expletive subjects, the verb "*kahA*" can not be attributed to any entity.

3.2. Time Expressions

Time expressions are defined as a span of text which denote a specific time, the duration of an event or state, or a point in time relative to an event or time expression (Group and others, 2009). Annotation and evaluation of temporal annotations is a fundamental concept in information retrieval based on events, as events are anchored on time expressions and therefore it is ubiquitous in semantic evaluation literature (Verhagen et al., 2010).

A time expression consists of a t_id which is a unique ID given to each time expression which is useful when they act as anchors to TLINKs (explained in Section 3.5.), a class which can be a DATE, TIME, DURATION and SET, the tokens in the span of the time expression and the AnnConf (annotator confidence parameter).

The classes of time expressions in Hindi are described as follows:

- TIME: The TIME category is used to annotate times of the day, which may be specific such as *pAnch baje* (5 o'clock) or a general period such as *subah* (morning). Note that the case markers or *karakas* associated with the time expression are also considered as a part of the time expression when it provides durativity information. For example:

  2.
āja	**pāca**	**baje**	*vaha*	*āegā*
Today	five	o'clock	he/she	come

  He/She will come at 5 o'clock today.

- DATE: The DATE category is used to annotate calendar days and dates, weekdays and other temporal expressions which consist of multiple days or dates, such

[2]https://www.ldc.upenn.edu/sites/www.ldc.upenn.edu/files/english-timex2-guidelines-v0.1.pdf

as weeks, months or years. Note that spans of time with specified start and end dates are not considered in this category. For example:

3. **do** **mahīne** *bāda* *vaha* *āegā*
   Two months after he/she come
   He/She will come after two months.

- DURATION: The DURATION category is applicable to spans of text which refer to a range of time with start and end times specified in the text.

4. **cāra** **mahīno** *se* *gāyaba* *hai*
   four months from missing is
   He/she has been missing for four months.

- SET: The SET class of time expressions is used to define the periodicity of an action or refer to an event a definite time in the past or future relative to the current time. The inclusion of *karaka* is important because it denotes the durativity or recursion of the event. For example:

5. **hara** **cāra** **sāla** *olapiksa* *hote* *hai*
   every four years Olympics happen is
   The Olympics take place every four years.

In using a syntactico-semantic approach to annotate time expressions in Hindi, we need to account for nested time expressions. We do so using a dependency perspective of the time expression itself, by considering the relations between annotations. For example:

6. **bīte** **sāla** **apraila** *se* **jūna** *taka* -
   Past year April from June till -
   This past year from April to June -

has the standoff annotation:

```
<TIMEX id="t1" class="DURATION"
tokens="1,2", AnnConf="High"/>
<TIMEX id="t2" class="DATE" tokens="3",
AnnConf="High"/>
<TIMEX id="t3" class="DATE" tokens="5",
AnnConf="High"/>
```

3.3. State Categories

TimeML has an event category for STATE and I-STATE. However, as mentioned in Section 4., we do not consider states or intentional states to be events and therefore present the following schema for categorizing states on more syntactic rather than semantic grounds. The category of states introduced in the schema are declarative (DECL) and descriptive (DESC) states.

- DECL: A verb is marked as a declarative state if it provides information about the properties or attributes of a participating entity. They are uniquely identified by copular constructions. For example:

7. *yaha* *gāī* *lāla* *raga* *kī* **hai**
   this car red colour (gen.) is
   This car is red in colour.

- DESC: A verbal modifier or participle is marked as a descriptive state when it can be rephrased as a copular, and as a modifier provides information about the entity or event it is describing. For example:

8. **khelatā** **huā** *baccā* *pahāī* *karegā*
   playing doing child study will do
   The child who is now playing will study.

3.4. Event Categories

The event categories are mostly the same as the TimeML event categories (Pustejovsky et al., 2003a). Therefore, the annotated event categories are:

- REP: Reporting events, marked by REP are those events in which an event or state is explained, talked about, spoken, written about or reported. For example:

9. *maine* **kahā** *mujhe* *bhūka* *lagī* *hai*
   I said I hunger feel is

   I said that I feel hungry.

- ASP: Aspectual events, marked as ASP are the events which denote the beginning, ending, continuation or any other aspectual state of another event. For example:

10. *maine* *khānā* **śurū** **kara** **diyā**
    I eating start do did

    I started eating.

- PER: Perception events are those events which involve the direct sensing of an event or entity, such as sight, sound or taste. Perception events require an experiencer. For example:

11. *maine* *use* **dekhā** **thā**
    I him see had

    I had seen him.

- IAC: I_Action events, marked as IAC are the events which explicitly introduce another event as an argument, but not as the aspectual state of that event. In Hindi, there are two syntactic types of IAC events. Either the I_Action occurs as the main verb of the sentence, subordinating the other verb in the sentence, or as the subordinating verb itself. In either case, the I_Action is incomplete without another event or state. For example:

12. *me* **padhakara** *so* *jāūgā*
    I read after sleep will go

    I will go to sleep after reading.

- OCC: All other events, which are not categorized above are categorized as occurrences, marked as OCC. All nominal events are inherently occurrences. For example:

13. *yuddha* *me* *sainika* **ghāyala** **hue**
    war in soldiers hurt got

    Soldiers were hurt in the war.

3.5. Linking Events and TIMEX3 Annotations

TimeML introduces three links, known as `TLINK`, `SLINK` and `ALINK`, which are described below (Saurí et al., 2006).

- `TLINK`: A temporal link or `TLINK` is a relationship between two events or states (represented by their instance IDs), or of an event or state with a time. It is categorized into `BEFORE`, `BEFORE-OVERLAP` and `OVERLAP` (O'Gorman et al., 2016).

14.
yuddha	*me*	*sainika*	**ghāyala**	**hue**
war	in	soldiers	hurt	got

Soldiers were hurt in the war.

```
<TLINK f_id='e1', s_id='e2',
class='OVERLAP' AnnConf='High'/>
```

- `SLINK`: A subordination link or `SLINK` is used to annotate the relations between two events, specifically reporting and other events. We also consider certain intensional events with other events given that the latter event expects or determines the former event. Conditional constructions are annotated as `SLINK` as well.

15.
rāma	**kahatā**	**hai**	*kī*
ram	says	is	that
yuddha	**gabhīra**	**hai**	
war	serious	is	

Ram says that the war is serious.

had the annotation :
```
<SLINK f_id='e1', s_id='e2'
AnnConf='High'/>
```

- `ALINK`: An aspectual link or `ALINK` shows the relation between an aspectual event and its argument event or state. The `ALINK` tag had 4 classes viz. `INITIATION`, `TERMINATION`, `CONTINUATION` and `CONCLUSION` inspired by Pustejovsky et al. (2003a).

16.
rāma	*ne*	*khānā*	**śurū**	**kara**
ram	(Erg.)	eat	start	did

Ram started eating.

had the annotation :
```
<ALINK f_id='e1', s_id='e2',
class='INITIATION' AnnConf='High'/>
```

4. Modifications to ISO-TimeML

In this section, we review some of the basic modifications to the ISO-TimeML event annotation schema and guidelines that have been used to annotate the Hindi TimeBank. The modifications are twofold, one which are language independent or cross lingual, and can be applied for creating new TimeBanks in other languages as well as extending the Hindi TimeBank, and the second which are particular to Hindi due to the semantico-syntactic nature of its grammar.

4.1. Language Independent Modifications

Pustejovsky et al. (2008) introduces the `<CONFIDENCE>` tag in order to provide the notion of a confidence metric to each attribute of each tag. The confidence tag used was in the range of 0 to 1 and was used to determine the annotator's confidence in every attribute annotation. However, this notion was found to be too granular. Given the attributes we annotate in the Hindi TimeBank, considering annotator confidence as an attribute rather than a standoff tag seemed more appropriate.

In our system, the annotator confidence metric is a ternary annotation parameter with values `HIGH`, `MEDIUM` and `LOW`, and is meant to signify how confident an annotator is about an annotation. Thus, we found that the annotator confidence metric is a very useful parameter in determining the clarity of definitions to annotators specifically in event and time expression classification.

The annotator confidence parameter helps in justifying the changes over iterations of guideline development, and also serve to point of ambiguous constructions which rely heavily on context, and/or represented a facet of the grammar that can not be captured by the current guidelines, and may pose a problem for further processes done using this data. One significant point based on which annotator confidence proved pertinent is the removal of subjunctives from event representation.

4.2. Language Specific Modifications

There are a number of modifications made to the ISO-TimeML guidelines which needed to be made due to the discourse structure and the grammatical framework associated with the identification and classification of events in Hindi. These changes include the identification of states, modifying the classification of events due to state categorization and a entity-centric event descriptions.

Identification of States TimeML presents events "as a cover term for situations that happen, occur, hold, or take place as well as those predicates describing states or circumstances in which something obtains or holds true" (Pustejovsky et al., 2003a). However, Goud et al. (2019) mentions the difficulties in direct annotation of events and states from a linguistic philosophy perspective as well as from an annotation guidelines standpoint.

As mentioned in Section 1., TimeML's definition of events seems similar to the syntactically motivated new-Davidsonian definition of an event. However, our analysis of events and states is based on Bach's definition of events, states and processes (Bach, 1986), which is similar to Panini's event semantic representation. We present the need for a separate notion of state by showing the following example from Goud et al. (2019):

17.
ijarāila	*me*	*gaisa*	*māska*	*kī*	**kamī**
Israel	in	gas	mask	of	shortage
se	*unhe*	*takalīpha*	*honī*	*lagī*	
reason	they	hardship	happen	began	

Due to a shortage of gas masks in Israel, they began to suffer.

18.

ijarāila	*me*	*gaisa*	*māska*	*kī*	***kamī***
Israel	in	gas	mask	of	shortage
hone	*se*	*unhe*	*takalīpha*	*honī*	*lagī*
to-be	reason	they	hardship	happen	began

Due to a shortage of gas masks in Israel, they began to suffer.

While these sentences are semantically equivalent, the syntactic representation of the subordinate verb clause is very different, as the presence of the verbal auxiliary *hone* explicitly marks a notion of a telic and adurative situation. According to TimeML, generics and verbal clauses with generic arguments are not to be annotated as events. However, the auxiliary *hone* is used with generics to construct semantically equivalent sentences. Therefore, according to TimeML annotation guidelines, annotators would not mark *kamI* as an event, but would mark *kamI hone*, even though they have been used in the same way in the sentence.

In order to resolve this discrepancy, we turn to the Paninian grammatical framework. The presence of auxiliaries in the verbal predicate are used to denote emphasis, tense and aspect information (Palmer et al., 2009). From the perspective of event and state representation, the auxiliaries are representative of the telic and durative properties of the predicate, which makes both their representation as well as participation of entities different depending on the type of verbal auxiliary used. Therefore:

- Verbal auxiliaries provide syntactic as well as semantic information about the verbal predicate, which is crucial.

- A verbal predicate may therefore be considered either a state or an event if compared to Bach's notion of eventualities

Since Bach's definition helps in the identification and classification of generics, habitual verbal predicates as well as other semantically equivalent but syntactically distinct forms, we adopt its definition for identifying states as a unique concept. Therefore, for the example above, we uniformly mark both *kamI* and *kamI hone* as descriptive states which have been described in the annotation guidelines (Section 3.3.).

We found that on introducing and defining states, annotator confidence regarding verbal modifiers as well as clauses with ambiguous constructions rose significantly, as it made the guidelines more naturally aligned to the annotator's understanding of the language. This solidified the inclusion of states into the Hindi TimeBank.

Modification in Classification Mechanism Given that both states and events are being annotated as independent concepts, the classification prescribed by TimeML (Pustejovsky et al., 2003a) can not be used directly. Instead, the STATE and I-STATE event categories have been removed. We have seen that our analysis of states are different from the TimeML representation of states. TimeML defines I-STATE as states that refer to alternate or possible worlds. Hindi only presents these constructions as subjunctives, which explicitly do not include a participant. Therefore, by definition, I-STATE are not annotated as states, but are identified as OCC events.

We introduce a classification schema for states, which are DESC and DECL, the description of which are given in Section 3. For example:

19.

khelatā	**huā**	*baccā*	**bhāga**	**rahā**	**hai**
play	doing	child	run	-ing	is

The child who is running, is playing.

has the standoff annotations:

```
<STATE id="s1" class="DESC" tokens="1,2"
annconf="HIGH" />
<EVENT id="e1" class="OCC" tokens="4,5,6"
annconf="HIGH" />
```

using the ISO-TimeML XML schema. The phrase "*KelawA huA baccA*" translates to "the child who is playing", but the verb form used is a verbal modifier and not a participle, and therefore it does not change the state of the participating entity, rather describes it.

Modifications to TIMEX3 TIMEX3 in Hindi has been studied (Ramrakhiyani and Majumder, 2013; Ramrakhiyani and Majumder, 2015) in order to analyze, identify and classify time expressions in Hindi. The procedure for annotating and extracting time expressions manually has been detailed in section 3.. We deviate in the annotation of fragmented time expressions by taking only those tokens which give us a local time expression and grouping them under a single TIMEX id. Relative time expressions such as *cāra sāla* (four years) can only be annotated as a TIMEX only if the duration can be estimated. We also account for dependency and semantic role information when annotating time expressions, which is not considered in TIMEX3.

5. Annotation Pipeline

Goud et al. (2019) proposed an event tagged dataset comprising of 810 news articles, which were primarily from the financial and crime domain, annotated only by the presence of events. We discarded all the articles which had less than 100 tokens, since these files did not contribute to the information base.

We chose a group of 8 annotators for the task of annotation as well as evaluation of the bootstrapped dataset. The annotators are native Hindi speakers, educated in both English and Hindi. All annotations were carried out using the BRAT Annotation Framework (Stenetorp et al., 2012). Figure 1 shows the annotation procedure in detail. There are multiple rounds of annotation in each stage of the pipeline.

5.1. Event and State Identification

Since Goud et al. (2019) only had events identified, the first task at hand was to annotate the states in these articles.The files were annotated by 8 annotators in batches of 100 articles, over 2 rounds of annotation.

Since all the articles from Goud et al. (2019) were from the financial crime domain, this dataset was not balanced well in terms of the types of syntactic and semantic environments in which events and states can occur in Hindi.

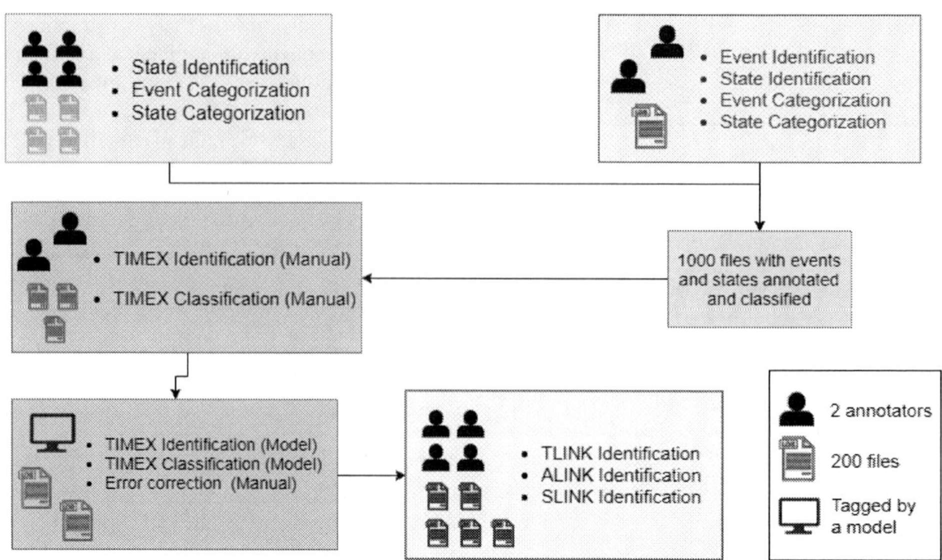

Figure 1: Annotation Steps for Hindi TimeBank. The legend for each icon used in the diagram is provided in the bottom right.

Thus, 200 articles were added to the seed dataset, out of which 150 were news articles and the remaining 50 were short fiction stories. We collected these news articles from Navbharat Times[3], a national Hindi daily newspaper with over 2 million copies circulated nationwide. The distribution of these scraped articles can be found in Table 2. The short stories are by Premchand, who is a renowned Hindi author[4]. The addition of these articles will allow the models trained on the Hindi TimeBank to be more reliable in detecting events, states, and temporal expressions in Hindi text.

For these 200 articles, they were first tokenized using a freely available tokenizer (Reddy and Sharoff, 2011)[5] and then the identification of both events and states were done by 4 annotators in batches of 50 articles over 4 rounds. Large inter-annotator disparity was found between annotators for reporting verbs with no participating entity, due to which those constructions were removed from the purview of event and state annotation.

5.2. Event and State Categorization

The above mentioned 200 articles were annotated for event and state categories by 4 annotators in batches of 50 articles over 4 rounds. The classification guidelines are based on easily identifiable syntactic differences, which made the manual annotation of events and state categories a high-confidence task among annotators. Once these 200 articles were annotated, the dataset of Goud et al. (2019) was annotated for the same by 8 annotators in batches of 100 articles over 3 rounds of annotation.

[3]https://navbharattimes.indiatimes.com/
[4]https://hindisamay.com/premchand%
20samagra/Indexpremchand.htm
[5]https://bitbucket.org/sivareddyg/
hindi-part-of-speech-tagger/src/master/

Features	Description
WI	Word Identity
POS	Part-of-Speech
BT	Bi-gram and tri-gram features
BOS	Beginning Of Sentence
ISTIMEX	Current Word is part of a TIMEX tag

Table 1: CRF Features

This resulted in a corpus of 1000 articles with event and state phrase boundaries identified and classified.

5.3. TIMEX Annotation and Classification

Automated Identification: For the first sub-task, our CRF model was trained on the set of 600 articles tagged manually and tested on the remaining 400 articles, in which, time expressions were identified. This CRF used the first 4 features of Table 1 and had a precision of 0.79 in this sub-task. The resultant labeling was evaluated manually by 4 annotators, and the relevant changes to the dataset were made.

Automated Categorisation: For the second sub-task, which was the categorization of the annotated time expressions, our CRF was trained on the set of 600 articles tagged manually and tested on the remaining 400 articles. For this CRF, the ISTIMEX feature of Table 1 was used in addition to the rest of the features. Our CRF had a precision of 0.84 in this sub-task. The labeled data was then corrected manually by 4 annotators in 2 rounds of annotation.

Finally, the resultant dataset was manually annotated with temporal links (TLINK), aspectual links (ALINK) and and subordination links (SLINK). This phase of annotation required 8 annotators with 4 rounds of annotations in batches of 125 articles each.

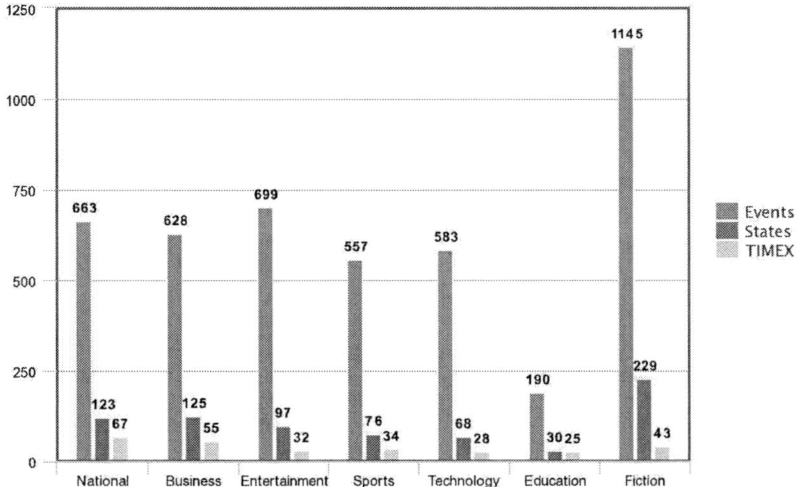

Figure 2: Domain Wise Distribution for Event, State and TIMEX tags

Domain	Number of Articles
Financial (Goud et al., 2019)	800
Fiction	50
National (News)	30
Business Analysis (News)	30
Entertainment (News)	30
Sports (News)	25
Technology & Development	25
Education (News)	10
Total	**1000**

Table 2: Distribution of Articles by Domain

	Category	Total
Event	OCC	22,606
	REP	1,599
	IAC	783
	ASP	421
	PER	420
	Total	**25,829**
State	DESC	1,865
	DECL	1,651
	Total	**3,516**

Table 4: Event and State Categories and Distribution

Feature	Total
Number of Tokens	292,517
Number of Events	25,829
Number of States	3,516
Number of TIMEX	2,396
Number of TLINK	7,289
Number of SLINK	4,741
Number of ALINK	433

Table 3: Count of Event, States, TIMEX and all types of links

6. Corpus Statistics

In this section we present some basic statistics of the Hindi TimeBank, such as the number of events, states, categories and links. As mentioned in the Section 5., we annotate 1000 articles from multiple domains. Table 3 shows the total number of events, states, TIMEX and all of the links in the corpus. In the following subsections, we present the ratio of classes of events, states, time expressions and links. We also present the statistics on annotator confidence and the inter-annotator agreement scores.

6.1. Event and State Statistics

In this section we provide insight into the distribution of the event and state categories. Table 4 provides the details of the distribution of events in the dataset. We see that the occurrence type (OCC) is the most popular, accounting for 87.52% of the total number of events. The aspectual type (ASP) accounts for 1.62%, the intensional action (IAC) for 3.03%, the perception events (PER) for 1.62%, and the reporting (REP) event 6.19% of the total events.

The occurrence type is the most popular type of event due to limited syntactic and semantic constraints on its classification and the fact that an event was annotated as an occurrence if did not belong to any other category.

We provide a similar analysis of states, with 53.04% of the states being descriptive (DESC) and 46.96% being declarative (DECL) in nature.

In Figure 2, we show the domain wise distribution of Event, State and TIMEX tags. We observe that the number of events are significantly higher than the number of states and time expressions across all domains. For Goud et al. (2019), the number of events, states and time expressions are $21,364, 2,768$, and $2,112$. These numbers are not represented in Figure 2 as they account for 800 articles (80%) of the dataset.

TIMEX Category	Total
DATE	1,390
DUR	545
TIME	433
SET	28
Total	**2,396**

Table 5: Time Expressions Categories and Distribution

Annotation	Fleiss' Kappa Score
Detection of Events	0.84
Detection of States	0.81
Event Categories	0.77
State Categories	0.86
TIMEX Detection	0.88
TIMEX Categories	0.86

Table 6: Inter Annotator Agreement for Various Annotation Phases

Category	High	Medium	Low
Event Categories	92.24%	5.86%	1.90%
State Categories	91.07%	5.52%	3.41%
TIMEX Categories	95.69%	4.31%	0.00%
TLINK	90.86%	4.25%	4.89%
ALINK	93.35%	4.60%	2.05%
SLINK	89.77%	5.71%	4.52%

Table 7: Category-wise Breakdown of Annotator Confidence Scores

6.2. Time Expression Statistics

In this section, we look into the time expressions in the Hindi TimeBank. We see in Table 5 that a majority of the time expressions belong to the $DATE$ class.

6.3. Annotator Confidence and Inter-Annotator Agreement Scores

In this section, we calculate the inter-annotator agreement scores for the event and state detection. This is done by Fleiss' Kappa metric (Fleiss and Cohen, 1973) as:

$$\kappa = \frac{\bar{P} - \bar{P}_e}{1 - \bar{P}_e} \tag{1}$$

where $P - P_e$ is the actual degree of agreement achieved and $1 - P_e$ is the degree of agreement above chance. Given N tokens to be annotated and n annotators, with k categories to annotate the data. We first calculate the proportion of annotations in the jth domain as:

$$p_j = \frac{1}{Nn} \sum_{i=1}^{N} n_{ij} \ , \quad 1 = \sum_{j=1}^{k} p_j \tag{2}$$

We then calculate P_i, the degree of agreement with the ith annotator as:

$$P_i = \frac{1}{n(n-1)} \sum_{j=1}^{k} n_{ij}(n_{ij} - 1) \tag{3}$$

$$= \frac{1}{n(n-1)} \left[\left(\sum_{j=1}^{k} n_{ij}^2 \right) - n \right] \tag{4}$$

Finally we calculate $\bar{P}$ and $\bar{P}_e$ as:

$$\bar{P} = \frac{1}{N} \sum_{i=1}^{N} P_i \tag{5}$$

$$\bar{P}_e = \sum_{j=1}^{k} p_j^2 \tag{6}$$

We also provide the domain wise breakdown of annotator confidence in the final corpus in Table 7. We do not remove annotations which are marked as MEDIUM or LOW by the annotators. Annotator confidence variations are seen most for events which have some ambiguity of being considered states. Lower confidence is associated with those verbal predicates which have only tense auxiliaries but either belong to a fragmented event or are in light verb constructions. State annotations show low confidence for descriptive states which are emphasized. TIMEX classification has no low confidence scores. Classification causes some low and medium confidence scores among TLINKS and ALINKs. In the case of SLINKs, subordination of OCC-OCC links are most ambiguous and result in low confidence among the annotators.

In the future, we hope this effort can help in the development of TimeBanks for other languages. The current corpus can also be enriched with the annotation of relations between the events and states based on causality and correlation. In it current form, the corpus can be used for generating a minimal knowledge graph which may also be enriched by entity and event linking.

7. Conclusion

In this paper, we present the Hindi TimeBank, a large event, state and time expression annotated corpus. We describe the annotation mechanism and modifications we made to the ISO-TimeML guidelines in order to annotate the data. We provide extensive analysis of the annotation methodology, so that the process of creating TimeBanks for other languages can be a structured effort, especially for languages with similar syntactic and semantic constraints as Hindi. We also present a detailed analysis of the corpus itself, including the distribution of events and states, their categories and the links between them, as well as the distribution of extents and types of time expressions.

The Hindi TimeBank has been created such that it can be used to further event annotation and detection research in Hindi, and the modifications to ISO-TimeML can be used to annotate TimeBanks for other Indo-Aryan languages. The current corpus can also be enriched with the annotation of relations between the events and states based on causality and correlation. A better annotation by nuanced clustering of dates as a duration, and the analysis of TIMEX types such as duration and set is also a direction for further exploration. In its current form, the corpus can be used for generating a minimal knowledge graph, which may also be enriched by entity and event linking. The corpus can also act as a gold standard dataset for machine learning applications for Hindi.

To get access to the dataset, please e-mail the authors [6].

8. Bibliographical References

Bach, E. (1986). The algebra of events. *Linguistics and philosophy*, 9(1):5–16.

Bittar, A., Amsili, P., Denis, P., and Danlos, L. (2011). French timebank: an iso-timeml annotated reference corpus. In *Proceedings of the 49th Annual Meeting of the Association for Computational Linguistics: Human Language Technologies: short papers-Volume 2*, pages 130–134. Association for Computational Linguistics.

Caselli, T., Bartalesi Lenzi, V., Sprugnoli, R., Pianta, E., and Prodanof, I. (2011). Annotating events, temporal expressions and relations in Italian: the it-timeml experience for the ita-TimeBank. In *Proceedings of the 5th Linguistic Annotation Workshop*, pages 143–151, Portland, Oregon, USA, June. Association for Computational Linguistics.

Costa, F. and Branco, A. (2012). Timebankpt: A timeml annotated corpus of portuguese. In *LREC*, pages 3727–3734.

Davidson, D. (1967). The logical form of action sentences.

Fleiss, J. L. and Cohen, J. (1973). The equivalence of weighted kappa and the intraclass correlation coefficient as measures of reliability. *Educational and psychological measurement*, 33(3):613–619.

Forascu, C. and Tufiș, D. (2012). Romanian timebank: An annotated parallel corpus for temporal information. In Nicoletta Calzolari (Conference Chair), et al., editors, *Proceedings of the Eight International Conference on Language Resources and Evaluation (LREC'12)*, Istanbul, Turkey, may. European Language Resources Association (ELRA).

Goud, J. S., Goel, P., Debnath, A., Prabhu, S., and Shrivastava, M. (2019). A semantico-syntactic approach to event-mention detection and extraction in hindi. In *Workshop on Interoperable Semantic Annotation (ISA-15)*, page 63.

Group, T. W. et al. (2009). Guidelines for temporal expression annotation for english for tempeval 2010.

O'Gorman, T., Wright-Bettner, K., and Palmer, M. (2016). Richer event description: Integrating event coreference with temporal, causal and bridging annotation. In *Proceedings of the 2nd Workshop on Computing News Storylines (CNS 2016)*, pages 47–56.

Palmer, M., Bhatt, R., Narasimhan, B., Rambow, O., Sharma, D. M., and Xia, F. (2009). Hindi syntax: Annotating dependency, lexical predicate-argument structure, and phrase structure. In *The 7th International Conference on Natural Language Processing*, pages 14–17.

Pustejovsky, J., Castano, J. M., Ingria, R., Sauri, R., Gaizauskas, R. J., Setzer, A., Katz, G., and Radev, D. R. (2003a). Timeml: Robust specification of event and temporal expressions in text. *New directions in question answering*, 3:28–34.

Pustejovsky, J., Hanks, P., Sauri, R., See, A., Gaizauskas, R., Setzer, A., Radev, D., Sundheim, B., Day, D., Ferro, L., et al. (2003b). The timebank corpus. In *Corpus linguistics*, volume 2003, page 40. Lancaster, UK.

Pustejovsky, J., Littman, J., and Saurí, R. (2007). Arguments in timeml: events and entities. In *Annotating, Extracting and Reasoning about Time and Events*, pages 107–126. Springer.

Pustejovsky, J., Lee, K., Harry, H. B., Boguraev, B., and Ide, N. (2008). Language resource management—semantic annotation framework (semaf)—part 1: Time and events. *International Organization*.

Pustejovsky, J., Lee, K., Bunt, H., and Romary, L. (2010). Iso-timeml: An international standard for semantic annotation. In *LREC*, volume 10, pages 394–397.

Ramrakhiyani, N. and Majumder, P. (2013). Temporal expression recognition in hindi. In *Mining Intelligence and Knowledge Exploration*, pages 740–750. Springer.

Ramrakhiyani, N. and Majumder, P. (2015). Approaches to temporal expression recognition in hindi. *ACM Transactions on Asian and Low-Resource Language Information Processing (TALLIP)*, 14(1):2.

Reddy, S. and Sharoff, S. (2011). Cross language pos taggers (and other tools) for indian languages: An experiment with kannada using telugu resources. In *Proceedings of the Fifth International Workshop On Cross Lingual Information Access*, pages 11–19, Chiang Mai, Thailand, November. Asian Federation of Natural Language Processing.

Saurı, R. and Badia, T. (2012). Spanish timebank 1.0. *LDC catalog ref. LDC2012T12*.

Saurí, R., Littman, J., Knippen, B., Gaizauskas, R., Setzer, A., and Pustejovsky, J. (2006). Timeml annotation guidelines. *Version*, 1(1):31.

Stenetorp, P., Pyysalo, S., Topić, G., Ohta, T., Ananiadou, S., and Tsujii, J. (2012). Brat: a web-based tool for nlp-assisted text annotation. In *Proceedings of the Demonstrations at the 13th Conference of the European Chapter of the Association for Computational Linguistics*, pages 102–107. Association for Computational Linguistics.

Verhagen, M., Sauri, R., Caselli, T., and Pustejovsky, J. (2010). Semeval-2010 task 13: Tempeval-2. In *Proceedings of the 5th international workshop on semantic evaluation*, pages 57–62.

Yaghoobzadeh, Y., Ghassem-Sani, G., Mirroshandel, S. A., and Eshaghzadeh, M. (2012). Iso-timeml event extraction in persian text. In *Proceedings of COLING 2012*, pages 2931–2944.

---

[6]mailto: pranavgoel25[at]gmail.com

Proceedings of the 16th Joint ACL-ISO Workshop Interoperable Semantic Annotation (ISA-16), pages 22–31
Language Resources and Evaluation Conference (LREC 2020), Marseille, 11–16 May 2020
© European Language Resources Association (ELRA), licensed under CC-BY-NC

Interoperable Semantic Annotation

Lars Hellan

Norwegian University of Science and Technology, Norway
lars.hellan@ntnu.no

Abstract

The paper presents an annotation schema with the following characteristics: it is formally compact; it systematically and compositionally expands into fullfledged analytic representations, exploiting simple algorithms of typed feature structures; its representation of various dimensions of semantic content is systematically integrated with morpho-syntactic and lexical representation; it is integrated with a 'deep' parsing grammar. Its compactness allows for efficient handling of large amounts of structures and data, and it is interoperable in covering multiple aspects of grammar and meaning. The code and its analytic expansions represent a cross-linguistically wide range of phenomena of languages and language structures. This paper presents its syntactic-semantic interoperability first from a theoretical point of view and then as applied in linguistic description.

Keywords: semantic annotation tags, typed feature structures, valence, semantic argument structure, situation structure, quantifier scope, Ga , Norwegian

1.   Introduction[1]

Semantic annotation can cover, amongst others, semantic argument structure; situation structure; quantifier scope; perspective of wording (transparent vs. oblique); anaphora; turns in discourse and types of moves or states within larger texts. Semantic annotation necessarily applies to linguistic expressions or texts, and the assigned content is often dependent on grammatical or lexical analysis, calling for *grammatically/lexically interoperable* annotation designs. This means that a natural format for semantic annotation is one where it interacts with grammatical or lexical representation more generally. In most areas the degree of complexity of the semantic representation, combined with the complexity of lexical or grammatical specification of the phenomena to which it is applied, is so high that it is reasonable to use a system of compact semantic *tagging*.

We here present a system of integrated morpho-syntactic and semantic tagging applicable to large constructs such as verb valence lexicons and corpora tagged for valence. The tagging system we present is an extension of the system Construction Labeling (CL) described and applied in Hellan and Dakubu 2010 and Dakubu and Hellan 2017. In this extended system, the CL code is mapped to a a Typed Feature Structure (TFS) formalism sustaining computational 'deep' parsers assigning both morphosyntactic and semantic analysis to the sentences parsed. The formalism of the system comes close to the HPSG formalism,[2] but with important exceptions (see below), and alternatives can be explored relative to other frameworks as well, such as, in all likelihood, LFG.[3]

The first part of the paper is devoted to the overall formal architecture of the system, in particular presenting its semantic components both inside of the TFS system and in the tagging formalism (sections 2-4). In the second part

(section 5) we describe how the overall tagging formalism can be employed in semantic specification in large resources such as valence lexicons and valence corpora, first addressing a valence lexicon and corpus for the West African language Ga (Kwa, spoken in Ghana), and then valence resources for Norwegian. In the third part (section 6) we mention possible extensions of the system from the argument structure domain to quantifier scope and other scopal phenomena.

2.   Annotation related to semantic argument structure of verbal constructions

The *Construction Labelling (CL)* code provides construction-level annotation tags which in one-line strings provide much of the information that could otherwise be expressed in multi-tier syntactic and semantic annotation. The strings are subject to semi-automatic consistency control, and can also be applied in valence specification in lexicons and in grammatical parsing. It has the added capacity of serving as types in a TFS system, enabling the consistency control and the parsing functionality. Following the overall left-to-right order indicated in (1), CL valency annotations are written as illustrated in (2):

(1)

head − valenceFrame − special properties of syntactic constituents − semantic roles of constituents − aspect, Aktionsart − situation type

(2)   *v-tr-suAg_obAffincrem-ACCOMPL*
[Ex. John ate the cake]

The string in (2) reads: 'a verb-headed transitive syntactic frame where the subject carries an agent role and the object an incrementally affected role, and the situation type expressed is 'accomplishment'.

The example (3) from Citumbuka (Bantu) instantiates verbal derivation underlying the expression of *causation*, illustrating interplay between morpho-syntax and semantics:

---

[1] I am grateful to the three reviewers for their helpful comments.
[2] On HPSG ('Head-Driven Phrase Structure Grammar), see Pollard and Sag 1994 and Copestake 2002.
[3] On LFG ('Lexical Functional Grammar'), see Bresnan (2001).

(3)

Mary wa-ka-mu-phik-**isk**-a		John	nchunga
Mary 1SM-Pst-1OM-cook-Caus-FV		John	beans
N	V	N	N
	vCaus-dbobCs		

'Mary made John cook beans'

The CL-string *vCaus* means that the head is a verb and has a causative morpheme, and *dbobCs* means that the construction is a double object construction 'derived' through causativization. The derivation can be further indicated through specifications of the arguments of the derived verb, in terms of their derivational histories, thus extending the formula *vCaus-dbobCs* to

(4)   *vCaus-dbobCs-suC-obCsu-ob2Cob*

where the added items read as follows:
    suC -   subject is created by Causativization
    obCsu -   object is derived ('demoted') from subject by Causativization
    ob2Cob -   second object is derived from object by Causativization

Expanding from what was said above (cf. (1)), each CL tag is a string consisting of, first, a label specifying POS of head of the construction and salient morphological marking (like *vCaus* in (3)), second, a label designating the overall structure of a construction (encoding notions like intransitive, transitive, ditransitive/double object, etc. (such as *dbobCs* in (3)), third a string of labels classifying features of the arguments such as the added tags above - first syntactic features and then semantic features -, and finally a string of labels for TAM features and situational content.

Whenever a putative CL string is composed, the labels of the string have to match with each other – for instance, if one label is *intr*, for 'intransitive', then there cannot be an argument label prefixed by *ob*, since *intr* is not defined for such a label. A processing mechanism enforcing such consistency is provided using a unification-based TFS system, in which the CL tag labels are defined as *types*. This TFS system is at the same time what underlies the automatic interoperability.

Information in such a system is generally exposed through Attribute Value Matrices (AVMs), where each AVM belongs to a type, and attributes are introduced (declared) according to the following conventions:

(5) *[A]* A given type introduces the same attribute(s) no matter in which environment it is used.

    [B] A given attribute is declared by one type only (but occurs with all of its subtypes).

Among the types in the present system are types for *grammatical functions* represented as values of the attribute '*GF*' (which constitutes an addition to the standard array of formal notions in HPSG) [4], and roles in *semantic argument structure* represented as values of the

---

[4] For discussion and motivation for the emplyment of GF notions in an HPSG-based formalism, see Hellan (2019a) and Hellan (2020).

---

attribute 'ACTNT' (see further in section 4 for types for *situation structure*). The type *gramfct* has subtypes declaring GF attributes such as 'SUBJ' and 'OBJ' (cf. (6a)), and the type *actnt* has subtypes declaring semantic participant attributes, such as 'ACT1' and 'ACT2' (cf. (6b)):

(6) a.   *gramfct*   b.   *actnt*
         /   \   /   \
    su-gf   *ob-gf*   *act1-rel*   *act2-rel*
    [SUBJ sign] [OBJ sign]   [ACT1 index]   [ACT2 index]
         \   /   \   /
          su-ob-gf   *act12-rel*

With such features as basis, one can represent, e.g., (3) as in (7), which is an AVM representing a *construction*. This involves a specification of grammatical functions and actants acting together, identified through the attributes GF and ACTNT, introduced at the level of constructions through a declaration '*cp* := *top* & [GF *gramfct*, ACTNT *actnt*]', where the type label *cp* stands for 'construction profile'. It has *dbobCs* as one of its subtypes, comprising the notion of *causation* through the PRED value 'cause' inside the ACTNT specification; the attribute 'D-BASE' stands for 'derivational base' (or 'input'):

(7)   AVM for double object construction with causative semantics and causative derivation (cf. (3)):

$$
dbobCs \begin{bmatrix}
\text{GF} \begin{bmatrix} \text{SUBJ} [\text{INDX } \boxed{1}] \\ \text{OBJ} [\text{INDX } \boxed{2}] \\ \text{OBJ2} [\text{INDX } \boxed{3}] \end{bmatrix} \\[3ex]
\text{ACTNT} \begin{bmatrix} \text{PRED } 'cause' \\ \text{ACT1 } \boxed{1} \\ \text{ACT2 } \boxed{6} \begin{bmatrix} \text{PRED } 'cook' \\ \text{ACT1 } \boxed{2} \\ \text{ACT2 } \boxed{3} \end{bmatrix} \end{bmatrix} \\[3ex]
\text{D-BASE } sign \begin{bmatrix} \text{GF} \begin{bmatrix} \text{SUBJ} [\text{INDX } \boxed{2}] \\ \text{OBJ} [\text{INDX } \boxed{3}] \end{bmatrix} \\ \text{ACTNT } \boxed{6} \end{bmatrix}
\end{bmatrix}
$$

We then outline how, in their capacity as types in the TFS grammar, CL labels define AVMs at the formal level of *constructions*. As subtypes of *cp*, definitions sustaining the type *tr* ('transitive') are shown in the following, achieved through a join of two *cp* subtypes, one defined with regard to GF, the other with regard to ACTNT:

(8)   *cp*
                          ⋰   ⋱
                 cpSuOb   *cpAct12*
              [GF *su-ob-gf*]   [ACTNT *act12-rel*]
                      \   /
$$
tr \begin{bmatrix}
\text{GF } su-ob-gf \begin{bmatrix} \text{SUBJ} [\text{INDX } \boxed{1}] \\ \text{OBJ} [\text{INDX } \boxed{2}] \end{bmatrix} \\[2ex]
\text{ACTNT } act12-rel \begin{bmatrix} \text{ACT1 } \boxed{1} \\ \text{ACT2 } \boxed{2} \end{bmatrix}
\end{bmatrix}
$$

tr is thus formally defined as a type of *construction*. Similar depths of specification are required for all CL labels.

When CL labels occur in a string, they *unify*. To illustrate with some types relevant also for English, the types to which the labels in (2) correspond are indicated in (9), and their unification is (10):

(9)
v - - - [HEAD *verb*]

tr - - - (cf. (8))

$suAg$ - - - $\left[\left[\text{GF}\left[\text{SUBJ}\left[\text{INDX } \boxed{1}\right]\right]\right]\left[\text{SIT}\left[\text{ACTOR } \boxed{1}\right]\right]\right]$

$obAffincrem$ - - - $\left[\text{GF}\left[\text{OBJ}\left[\text{INDX } \boxed{1}\right]\right]\right]\left[\text{SIT}\left[\text{AFFECTED } \boxed{1}\right]\right]$

ACCOMPL - - - [SIT *accomplishment*]

(10)
$$\begin{bmatrix} \text{HEAD } verb \\ \text{GF}\begin{bmatrix}\text{SUBJ}\left[\text{INDX } \boxed{1}\right] \\ \text{OBJ}\left[\text{INDX } \boxed{2}\right]\end{bmatrix} \\ \text{ACTNT}\begin{bmatrix}\text{ACT1 } \boxed{1} \\ \text{ACT2 } \boxed{2}\end{bmatrix} \\ \text{SIT } accomplishment\begin{bmatrix}\text{ACTOR } \boxed{1} \\ \text{AFFECTED } \boxed{2}\end{bmatrix}\end{bmatrix}$$

The semantic roles corresponding to the labels *suAg* and *obAffincrem* are represented in a space of semantics called *Situation Structure* ('SIT') through the attributes ACTOR and AFFECTED, both relevant within the situation type *accomplishment*; cf. section 4 below.

Returning to the label in (4), the AVMs for the 'derivational histories' will be as in (11), the unification with the structure for *dbobCs* is the structure in (7).

(11)

a. $suC\begin{bmatrix}\text{GF}\left[\text{SUBJ } sign\left[\text{INDX } \boxed{1}\right]\right] \\ \text{ACTNT}\begin{bmatrix}\text{PRED 'cause'} \\ \text{ACT1 } \boxed{1}\end{bmatrix}\end{bmatrix}$

b. $obCsu\begin{bmatrix}\text{GF}\left[\text{OBJ}\left[\text{INDX } \boxed{2}\right]\right] \\ \text{ACTNT}\begin{bmatrix}\text{PRED 'cause'} \\ \text{ACT2 } \boxed{6}\left[\text{ACT1 } \boxed{2}\right]\end{bmatrix} \\ \text{D-BASE } sign\begin{bmatrix}\text{GF}\left[\text{SUBJ}\left[\text{INDX } \boxed{2}\right]\right] \\ \text{ACTNT } \boxed{6}\end{bmatrix}\end{bmatrix}$

c. $ob2Cob\begin{bmatrix}\text{GF}\left[\text{OBJ2}\left[\text{INDX } \boxed{3}\right]\right] \\ \text{ACTNT}\begin{bmatrix}\text{PRED 'cause'} \\ \text{ACT2 } \boxed{6}\left[\text{ACT2 } \boxed{3}\right]\end{bmatrix} \\ \text{D-BASE } sign\begin{bmatrix}\text{GF}\left[\text{OBJ}\left[\text{INDX } \boxed{3}\right]\right] \\ \text{ACTNT } \boxed{6}\end{bmatrix}\end{bmatrix}$

Here each type represents the part of the whole AVM corresponding to the content of the (derived) subject, object, and second object ('ob2'). Unification presupposing feature compatibility, being the formal point illustrated here, the control of consistency in the CL string (4) is thereby inbuilt in the formalism. We have at the same time introduced two aspects of semantic analysis represented by the attributes ACTNT and SIT, to which we turn further below. First we consider semantic relations carried by structures internal to NPs.

3.   Annotation for semantic relations of nominal constructions

The sentence in (12) is a construction from Ga:[5]

(12)

Mi-yitso	mii-gba	mi
1S.POSS-head	PROG-split	1S
N	V	PN

"My head is aching." (literally: 'my head aches me')

Here we want to represent the subject as a possessive phrase, where the referent of the whole phrase is a (body)part of the specifier 'mi', and this specifier is also identical to the object; in terms of semantics, the situation as a whole has the label 'EXPERIENCE', the role of the subject is that of 'locus' of the experience, and the 'experiencer' is expressed by the object. In terms of the CL formalism this can be stated as follows:

(13)
v-tr-suPossp_suBPsuSpec_suSpecIDob-suLocus_obExp-EXPERIENCE

The part *suBPsuSpec* is a type representable as (14), where 'is-bodypart-of-rel' spells out 'BP', and the part *suSpecIDob* is spelled out as (15), where identical indices reflect the part 'ID':

(14)
$$suBPsuSpec\begin{bmatrix}\text{GF}\begin{bmatrix}\text{SUBJ}\begin{bmatrix}\text{INDX } \boxed{1} \\ \text{GF}\left[\text{SPEC}\left[\text{INDX } \boxed{2}\right]\right] \\ \text{ACTNT}\begin{bmatrix}\text{PRED 'is-bodypart-of-rel'} \\ \text{ACT1 } \boxed{1} \\ \text{ACT2 } \boxed{2}\end{bmatrix}\end{bmatrix}\end{bmatrix}\end{bmatrix}$$

(15)
$$suSpecIDob\begin{bmatrix}\text{GF}\begin{bmatrix}\text{SUBJ}\left[\text{GF}\left[\text{SPEC}\left[\text{INDX } \boxed{2}\right]\right]\right] \\ \text{OBJ}\left[\text{INDX } \boxed{2}\right]\end{bmatrix}\end{bmatrix}$$

Unification of (14) and (15) yields (16), adding the eventual contribution from the meaning specification of

---

[5] From Dakubu (Unpublished a).

the verb, and the semantic CL specifications, where 'locus' has a meaning close to 'stimulus' but in addition indicates the location of the 'stimulus':

(16)

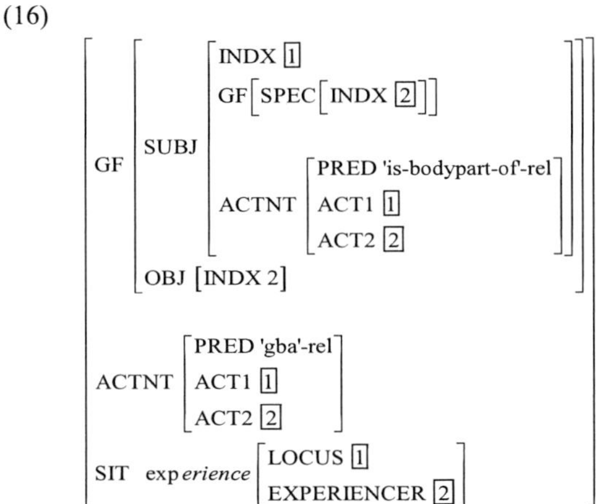

We now comment on 'Situation structure' as a semantic concept, and compare it with the attribute 'ACTNT'..

4. Situation Structure

A more detailed SIT-representation of a verb like *run* is given in (17). Here *run* is a situation type.

(17)

MOVER $\boxed{1}$ *running – partcpnt*

run — ACTOR $\boxed{1}$; MOVER $\boxed{1}$ *running – partcpnt* [ITERATN *zip – lock*, INCREM – DIM *horisontal*, PARTorORGAN *leg*, VELOCITY *fast*, MEDIUM *ground*]; DYN +; PROTR +

Types like these sit in an ontology of situational content as outlined in Hellan (2019a, b), where each label corresponds to a node in a situation type hierarchy. Figure 1 illustrates part of such a hierarchy (also obeying the conventions in (5)).

This hierarchy hosts both general situation types and types sorting under the notions 'Aspect' or 'Aktionsart', as developed in, e.g., Vendler 1967, Smith 1991,1997, Verkuyl 1996, and many others. Attributes declared by its types can have either '+/-' as their value, or types defined within another hierarchy, instantiated by *running-participant* in (17), whose attributes represent aspects of the behavior of a participant filling the outer attribute in question (such as 'MOVER' in (17)). *Run*, together with *walk,* count as subtypes of the type *actorLocomotion*, which, in joins with general types for reaching endpoints or going by via-points, also dominates situation types for 'running to' a certain point or 'running via' a certain point, as indicated in the figure.

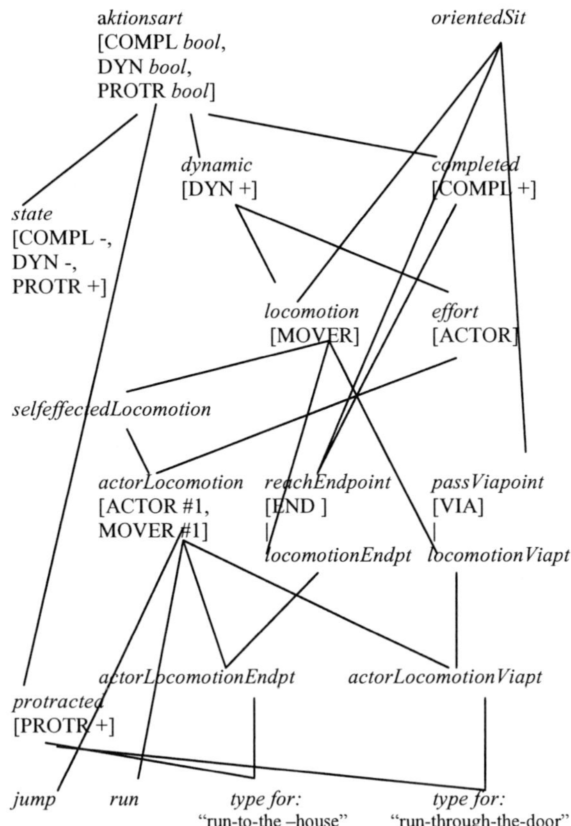

Figure 1. Partial Situation Type hierarchy

As an inheritance hierarchy, an attribute introduced for a given type will belong to all of its subtypes. Top types often introduce attributes with a value still unspecified, such as aktionsart, but once a value is set, that value holds for all the subtypes. In this way, for instance, the type *actorLocomotion* has the full structure (18), with the inherited values.

(18) *actorLocomotionEndpt* — ACTOR $\boxed{1}$; MOVER $\boxed{1}$; END; DYN +; COMPL +

A CL label can in principle relate to any node at any 'height' in such a hierarchy. For instance, the type *actorLocomotion* in Figure 1 corresponds to the CL label *MOTIONDIRECTED*, and its subtype *actorLocomotionEndpt* corresponds to MOTIONtoENDPT; thus, the Situation Structure assigned to a sentence like *They run to the town* will be (18), and a CL representation for the construction as such will be (19).

(19) v-intr-suDir-suEndpt-MOTIONtoENDPT

Labels such as *suAg* and *obExp* also refer into the SIT hierarchy, then into situation types sharing the attribute in question. Thus, when for instance *suMover* and

MOTIONDIRECTED occur in the same CL string, then the attribute MOVER is declared by a type also dominating *actorLocomotion*.

The expressiveness of this format of representation may be compared with formats of representation in Lexical Semantics using predicate-argument style notation, for instance considering the notation for lexical semantics developed in Jackendoff 1990, called '*Lexical Conceptual Structure' (LCS), (*see also Dorr 1993). Here a sentence like *John ran into the room* will have the representation (20), where the predicate 'GO' represents dynamic directional movement:

(20)
[GO ([JOHN]THING, [TO ([IN ([ROOM]THING)]PLACE)]PATH)]EVENT

Relative to this LCS formula, the type *actorLocomotion* corresponds to 'GO', and *reachEndpoint* corresponds to the predicate 'TO'. The dominance by *dynamic* corresponds to the bracket label 'EVENT', and *orientedSit* corresponds to 'PATH'. What in LCS corresponds to ACTOR in (18) is not stated in (20) but at an extra tier of representation displaying force relations, a bit like the function of *effort* in Figure 1. The formats thus seem to allow for comparison in a possibly tractable manner, and possibly with the conclusion that the information which can be displayed in them is essentially the same (both can in principle also be enriched to display more fine-grained information).

While the information of SIT thus in principle unfold the universe of what can be represented within approaches such as Lexical Semantics or Conceptual Semantics, the attributes defined within the attribute ACTNT are extremely few, and reflect only an enumeration of the arguments which are grammatically manifest in the sentence in question, and their numbering (as ACT1, ACT2, etc., up to maybe ACT4) only reflects an ordering between them particular to that sentence or predicate, based vaguely on a dimension of agentivity or 'proto-role', and respecting a conception of stages in a derivation. Thus, although the sentence in (3) has three syntactic arguments, the ACT-roles are just ACT1-ACT2 relative to the *cause*-predicate, and ACT1-ACT2 relative to the *cook*-predicate, as displayed in (7), in both cases such that what would be a subject in a closest paraphrase is ACT1. In the case of a passive construction, the role ACT1 will belong to the 'highest-ranking' item in the conceivable active form, which is again to say the subject in this active structure, so that the subject in the passive version may represent ACT2 or ACT3 as a role. This is a design familiar in formal grammars, corresponding to what is called 'Semantic Argument Structure' in Grimshaw (1992) and related work, to argument structure as common in Predicate Logic, and with a semi-shallow robustness which makes it suitable for 'Deep' computational grammars such as those based on HPSG, where the level of logical representation called 'Minimal Recursion Semantics' (MRS; cf. Copestake et al. 2005) displays sentential semantic content in this form. The CL code does not directly display ACTNT structure, but given the GF specifications of all items, and the formal tractability of derivational structure as illustrated in (4)-(7)-(11) for the Bantu derivational

form, the ACTNT roles of any derived sentence structure are tractable, and in plain non-derived structures the subject is the ACT1, the direct object the ACT2, and an indirect object the ACT3. For oblique objects one can use ACT4, ACT5, etc., or ACTobl.

Although superficially similar to the system using ARG1, ARG2, etc in PropBank,[6] the ACTNT system differs from that of PropBank in that none of the attributes ACT1, ACT2, etc represents a specific semantic value – ARG1 in PropBank, in contrast, is agent. In this way, semantic richness is represented in the SIT system, whereas the kind of semantics that very closely follows grammatical structure is represented in the ACTNT system.

Having now introduced the annotation system Construction Labeling, the components of the TFS to which it can be mapped, and in particular the semantic components, what we call the *grammatical interoperability* of the CL notation has been demonstrated. We now turn to uses and applications of the system.

5. Semantic annotation in valence lexicons and valence corpora

The CL annotation code is used in three types of applications – corpora, lexicons, and computational grammars, and in addition in the compilation of *language valence profiles*, which in a compact format represent the construction types and valence types available in a language.[7] We now describe the role of the semantic labels relative to such systems, first a construction and valence inventory of Ga, and then of Norwegian.

5.1 Situation types in a Ga construction and valence inventory

A valence resource for Ga was developed by Prof. Mary Esther Kropp Dakubu as an extension of the Toolbox lexicon underlying her Ga-English Dictionary Dakubu (2009). In this extension, valence specification using the CL code was added systematically, resulting in about 2000 entries such that each entry of a verb represents one valence frame. Each such entry is illustrated by a fully annotated sentence, which means that the lexicon is at the same time a valence corpus of about 2000 short sentences. An edited version of this resource is found at Ga Valence Profile in the downloadable text file Ga_verb_dictionary_for_digital_processing', cited as Dakubu (unpublished a), to which we refer in the following; a larger extension is available in Dakubu (unpublished b).

Ga makes little use of prepositions and adjectives, so that constructions involving nouns and verbs may be seen as playing a relatively large role, the latter for instance

---

[6] Cf. https://propbank.github.io/; Palmer et al. (2005).

[7] See Ga Valence Profile, and with examples, on Ga Appendix. For a valence profile for Norwegian, see Verbconstructions Norwegian - all types. Further examples are Valence Profile Kistaninya, Valence Profile English, and Gurene verb constructions. An inventory of CL tags in total is found at https://typecraft.org/tc2wiki/Construction_Label_tags.

through *multiverb expressions* subsuming *Serial Verb Constructions (SVCs)*, *Extended Verb Complexes (EVCs*) which are sequences of preverbs preceding a main verb, heading a clause by itself or partaking in an SVC), and *Verbid Constructions (ViD)*, where verb phrases play a role of adverbials.[8] The use of complex pre-nominal specifiers within noun phrases is another predominant feature, briefly summarized in terms of number of entries exhibiting them in Table 1 below, and exemplified in (12).

Table 1 Nominal specifications in terms of number of verb entry specifications

Bodypart relation	158
Identity relation	110
Subject headed by relational noun	99
Object headed by relational noun	690
Object's specifier headed by relational noun	29

The array of Situation Types used was conceived in parallel with the process of annotation of the data,[9] rather than being built on any pre-existing inventory. The frame types used in FrameNet[10] were consulted but found to be too English-biased for the purpose. As a result the situation types are at a somewhat general level, but also not very abstract – relative to types like those in Figure 1 they occupy the lower half, but not as far down as matching lexically-specific meanings; they thus may be said to classify *construction type meanings* rather than verb meanings. Table 2 renders the most frequently used type labels, ordered alphabetically and with indication of the number of entries exhibiting them:

Table 2 Situation Type labels most frequently applied.

ABSENT	29	MOTIONDIRECTED	55
ACQUISITION	29	PHENOMENON	29
CARETAKING	12	PLACEMENT	53
CAUSATIVE	23	POSTURE	7
CAUSED	17	PROPERTY	164
CLOSING	4	DYNAMIC-PROPERTY	13
COGNITION	83	PSYCHSTATE	23
COMMUNICATION	178	REMOVAL	47
COMPARISON	29	SENSATION	16
COMPLETED-MONODEVMNT	6	TRANSFER	47
CONTACT	56	USINGVEHICLE	5
CREATION	14		
CUTTING	19		
EJECTION	15		
EMOTION	29		
EXPERIENCING	45		
MAINTAINPOSITION	25		
MOTION	180		

With the set of 2000 entries classified by CL strings, one can investigate the frequency of frames used, the correspondence between syntactic and semantic structure, the clustering of certain valence types for sets of verbs (constituting 'Verb Classes', see below), and more. To exemplify, the layout of information illustrated in (21) indicates the entry ID, the full CL construction specification, and the gloss of the verb heading the construction. The ID links to a parallel display where the instantiating sentence is given. The entries exemplified all have the situation type MOTIONDIRECTED:

(21)

fa_212 := v-tr-obNomvL-suAg_obLoc-INCHOATION-MOTIONDIRECTED   (appx. gloss: "start up")

fo_338 := v-tr-obPostp-suAg_obPath-REFLEXIVE-MOTIONDIRECTED (appx. gloss: "turn around")

ke_737 := sv_suAspID-suAg-v2tr-v2pv1Pro-v2obLoc-MOTIONDIRECTED (appx. gloss: "proceed")

kɔ_757 := v-intr-suAg-MOTIONDIRECTED (appx. gloss: "climb")

kpeleke_841 := v-tr-obPostp_obSpecThAbst-suAg_obTh-MOTIONDIRECTED (appx. gloss: "land")

The glosses of the 55 entries with this situation type involve the following items as gloss of the head verb, listed by number of occurrence:

(22)

"go" – 12, "come" – 7, "push away" – 6, "arrive at" – 3, "land" – 3, "go before" – 3, "start" – 2, "run" – 2, "visit" – 2, "forget/leave" – 2, "push" – 2, "climb" – 2, "repent/turn away from" – 2, "travel" – 1, "turn around" – 1, "proceed" – 1, "depart" – 1, "strike" – 1, "paddle" – 1, "trail" - 1

For one thing, this illustrates that Situation Types and lexical meanings are distinct. For investigations into verb classes, such numbers, paired with the grammatical structures of the constructions involved, provide a good starting point. As for the grammatical structures involved in the 55 entries, most total strings are unique, only one applies to 5 entries, one to 3 entries, and three to 2 entries. However, the CL code allows one to compare also with regard to substrings, which allows for a flexible methodology of establishing correspondences in these domains.

The literature on Valency Classes (aka Verb Classes) starts with Levin 1993, which is an attempt to find correlations between verb meanings and the arrays of valency frames available for given verbs.[11] Levin's approach has been pursued for English during *VerbNet* at a large scale,[12] which is a resource featuring more than 6000 verbs divided into nearly 300 verb classes. In the *The Leipzig*

---

[8] See Dakubu 2004a,b, 2008, Dakubu et al. 2007.

[9] Conducted by Prof. Dakubu, with a few consultants.

[10] https://framenet.icsi.berkeley.edu/fndrupal/ 'Frame' in the FrameNet system corresponds to what we here call situation type.

[11] For instance, for the 'spray-load'-alternation verbs in English, as exemplified in *spray paint on the wall* vs *spray the wall with paint*, a characterizing feature is the expression of two incremental dimensions at the same time (here the amount of paint and the area of wall covered), whereby either one or the other can be expressed by an NP inducing completeness of that dimension, reflected in the alternating frames (the 'non-completed' dimension represented by the PP).

[12] http://verbs.colorado.edu/~mpalmer/projects/verbnet.html).

Valency Classes project (Malchukov and Comrie 2015) and the accompanying valency database ValPaL[13] the arrays of frames for 80 verb meanings are compared across 30 languages; here one uses English verbs as 'names' of verb meanings – for instance, the 'kill verb' is treated as a constant entity 'KILL' across the languages. This gives, for each of the 80 verbs, a view of the frames that the verb can take across these languages.

The current enterprise is mostly in the spirit of VerbNet, since we are dealing with a large number of verbs. Apart from size differences, what is particular to the present approach is the way in which it allows the annotation code to serve as a key instrument of representation. In the VerbNet verb entry illustrated in Figure 2 below, the syntactic specification consists of a dependency tree (not shown here) and a line combining POS and semantic role in an order matching the linear order in which the relevant constituents occur. In our approach, a syntactic format linked to the linear order of the constituents in the analyzed string is given in the example sentences, while the ordering within the CL string is independent of linear order in the examples. The CL syntactic code nevertheless comes close to representing a dependency analysis (and a full-fledged syntactic and semantic parse can in principle be called upon[14]). The display under SEMANTICS has a richness of content comparable to our Situation Structure, but closer in style to the predicate-argument structure exemplified in (20) than to the AVM format used here.

« Jessica loaded boxes into the wagon. »

SYNTAX: Agent VERB Theme { PREP } Destination

SEMANTICS:
HAS_LOCATION(e1 , Theme , ?Initial_Location)
DO(e2 , Agent)
MOTION(ee3 , Theme , Trajectory)
¬ HAS_LOCATION(ee3 , Theme , ?Initial_Location)
CAUSE(ee3 , e2)
HAS_LOCATION(e4 , Theme , Destination)

FORCE DYNAMICS: Volitional Apply FD representation

Figure 2 Copy from VerbNet view of 'spray-9.7' (March 27, 2020)

The design used in VerbNet has counterparts in most other valence-related applications,[15] so on a comparative note, we may say that the present analytic apparatus offers counterparts to all of the representations found in the standard applications. What the CL notation provides in addition is a compact one-line view of all of the relevant factors brought together, and an algorithm by which this compact notation is linked to the analytically full representations.

A further comparative aspect lies in the use of hierarchical

organization: FrameNet to a mild extent uses this for frames, i.e., situation structures, but not with the efficiency of TFS as illustrated in Figure 1. In return, though, a full system comprising all of the situation type labels in Table 2 (or the totality of the 140 types used) has not yet been constructed. VerbNet uses organization of entries like that for *spray-9.7* in Figure 2 such that a common meaning 'dominates' those structures that share that meaning. Such an organization can readily be provided also in the present notation. For instance, the array of entries for *ba* 'come' includes the following,

<ba_1, v-intr-suAg-MOTIONDIRECTED>
<ba_2, evSuAg-vintr-pv1obTh-MOTIONDIRECTED>
<ba_3, v-tr-obPostp-suAg_obLoc-MOTIONDIRECTED>
<ba_6, v-tr-suAg_obEndpt-MOTIONDIRECTED>
<ba_8, v-ditr-suAg_obTh_ob2Endpt-MOTIONDIRECTED>

which could be displayed as follows, keeping in mind that all labels unify, and hence a hierarchy (or ontology) can in principle be designed with any label as top node:

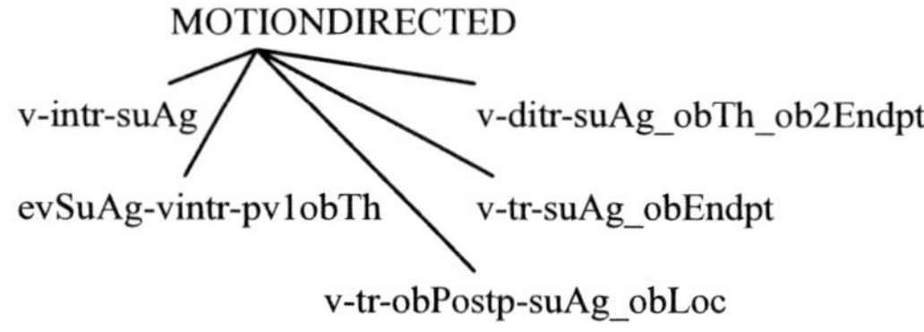

Figure 3 Hierarchical organization of entries for *ba* 'come' with *MOTIONDIRECTED* as common meaning

5.2 CL code in a verb valence lexicon and a valence corpus for Norwegian

A cluster of resources for Norwegian has been created where the CL code plays a pivotal role in (i) encoding the lexical types of verbs as represented in the HPSG-type computational grammar *Norsource*[16], (ii) constituting the valence specifications in a valence lexicon of about 13,000 valence entries, organized using the tags as lexical types coextensive with the verbal part of the grammar lexicon,[17] and (iii) serving as valence tags in a verb valence corpus generated by the grammar.[18] In the latter, valence and construction tags are thus assigned to verbs in 22,000 sentences, illustrated in Figure 4 below: here valence annotation labels supplement a standard IGT annotation,[19] with the CL notation accompanied by two other formats of valence labelling, 'SAS' for 'syntactic argument structure'

---

[13] http://valpal.info/

[14] Through a parser, cf. Hellan (2020).

[15] Among existing valence dictionaries are for instance: English:FrameNet; VerbNet; PropBank; German: Evalbu; Chech: Vallex; Polish: Walenty; respective urls:
https://framenet.icsi.berkeley.edu/fndrupal,
http://verbs.colorado.edu/~mpalmer/projects/verbnet.html,
https://ufal.mff.cuni.cz/czengvallex, http://hypermedia2.ids-mannheim.de/evalbu/, http://ucnk.ff.cuni.cz,
http://clip.ipipan.waw.pl/Walenty.

[16] *NorSource* (cf. Hellan and Bruland 2015) has been maintained since 2001. Code files are downloadable from GitHub: https://github.com/Regdili-NTNU/NorSource/tree/master.
[17] The valence lexicon, called *NorVal*, is under development, cf. Quasthoff et al. (2020). An earlier version can be seen at http://regdili.hf.ntnu.no:8081/multilanguage_valence_demo/multi valence, called *MultiVal*, described in Hellan et al. (2014), where four lexicons based on computational HPSG grammars for Norwegian, Ga, Spanish, Bulgarian are brought together using the same types of valence frame labels.
[18] Cf. Hellan et al. (2017, forthcoming).
[19] Using the glossing system and interface of TypeCraft (https://typecraft.org/; cf. Beermann and Mihaylov (2014)).

and 'FCT' for 'functional label'; the valence frames of both the main verb (*vite* ('know')) and the subordinate verb (*forbause* ('surprise')) are specified:

String: Jeg vet at hun forbauset Ola
Free translation: I know that she surprised Ola

Jeg	|vet vite	|at	|hun	|forbause forbause	|t	|Ola
1.SG.NOM	|PRES	|DECL	|3.SG.FEM	|	|PAST	
PN	|V	|COMP	|PN	|V		|Np

vite:	SAS:	NP+Sdecl
	FCT:	transWithSentCompl
	CL:	v-tr-obDECL
forbause:	SAS:	NP+NP
	FCT:	transitive
	CL:	v-tr

Figure 4 Sample representation of valence annotation in a valence corpus combined with morphological glossing

To the CL expressions, which here lack role and Situation Type labels, one could easily add such labels, but in the current state their absence reflects the cirumstance that most of the valence specifications in the underlying grammar, which uses CL code, do not have such specifications. Among reasons why this is so is that the introduction of semantic features in a large scale grammar is not only time consuming in linguistic respects but also requires the balancing of combinatorial complexities arising with the introduction of new dimensions of specification. Within limited domains like that of *location* and *direction* it has however been done, through the specification of lexical items and combinatory rules of the relevant kinds. Here a large part of the specifications are tied to prepositions and adverbs, so that for instance in the lexical specifications operative for the sentence *De løper til byen* ('they run to the town'), *løpe* is encoded as intransitive directional and *til* is encoded as an end-point preposition. The resulting parse will in Situation Type terms have the label MOTIONtoENDPOINT, while the verb by itself belongs to the type MOTIONDIRECTED. To the extent that a display like that in Figure 4 is generated through a grammar, thus, it cannot represent the verb as such as being of the type MOTIONtoENDPOINT. This illustrates a further factor by which a grammar-generated corpus can fail to be as specific as a 'hand-made' corpus. Still, the CL formalism being one where semantic specifications *can* be seamlessly added to the grammatical ones, it leaves room for incrementally adding such specifications in the corpus.

Figure 5 illustrates this interplay between verb and preposition. In the NorSource parse tree to the left one sees the critical specifications of the items *løpe* and *til*, and in the MRS to the right the specification 'Role: endpoint' is induced through the semantic specifications of the preposition and the verb together:

```
head-subject-rule
 de_perspron
  de
 telic-pp-mod-vp-rule
  pres-infl_rule
   løpe_intrdir_vlxm
    løper
  head-prep-comp-rule
   til_dirtel-end-p
    til
   sg_def_m_final-
full_irule
    sg-masc-def-noun-
lxm-lrule
     by_mascanim_nlxm
      byen
```

```
ltop=h0, index=e1
h3:de_pron_rel([arg0:x2])
h4:_pronoun_q_rel([arg0:x2, rstr:h5,
body:h6])
h7: løpe_v-intr_rel([arg0:e1,
arg1:x2])
h7: til_p-dirtel_rel([arg0:u8,
arg1:x2, arg2:x9, iarg:u10])
h11:_by_n_rel([arg0:x9])
h12:_def_q_rel([arg0:x9, rstr:h13,
body:h14])
< qeq(h5,h3), qeq(h13,h11) >
e1, sort=verb-act-specification,
sf=prop, e.tense=pres,
e.mood=indicative, e.aspect=semsort
x2, wh=-, png.ng.num=plur,
png.pers=thirdpers, role=mileage-obj
u8, sort=verb-act-specification
x9, wh=-, bounded=+,
png.ng.num=sing, png.ng.gen=m,
png.pers=thirdpers, role=endpnt
```

Figure 5 NorSource parse tree and MRS for *De løper til byen* ('they run to the town'), with encodings relevant for directionality in italic boldface. (Copied from the web demo http://regdili.hf.ntnu.no:8081/linguisticAce/parse on March 20, 2020.)

The MRS construction is based on what corresponds to the ACTNT component described in section 4 (but here with 'ARG' rather than 'ACT'), thus a fairly shallow level of semantic description, however with the possibility of specifying the ARG/ACT for semantic roles, which is done in the grammar, although at an earlier point.[20]

6.   Labeling for scope

Here we consider a possible extension of the CL style of specification to phenomena standardly analyzed in terms of *scope*. First addressing quantifier scope,[21] we may build on the CL designs used for NP internal structures, illustrated in section 3. In a sentence like (23), one commonly recognizes two scoping possibilities, for which the CL-style strings in (24) provide a labeling, with *QS* understood as 'quantifier out-scoping'; (a) represents *two men* as having wide scope, with *suQSob* read as 'subject outscoping object', and (b) represents *every book* as having wide scope:

(23)   Two men read every book.

(24)   a.   v-tr-suQSob

         b.   v-tr-obQSsu

In the more complex (25), plausible scope relations are probably restricted to those in (26), with *adj* interpreted as 'adjunct', here *every evening* (thus, any construal implying a man as reading a book over again counts as implausible):

(25)   Two men read every book every evening

(26)   a.   v-tr- suQSob_adjQSsu

         b.   v-tr-obQSsu_adjCSob

---

[20] Cf. Beermann and Hellan 2004, Hellan and Beermann 2005.

[21] See Bunt (2020) for an overview of issues relating to the annotation of quantifier scope.

A notation like this may be useful for corpus annotation with the goal of finding patterns as to when multiple scopings are possible. Given that syntactic subjects can probably by default be counted as outscoping everything that they c-command, the (a) versions of (24) and (26) may count as redundant. The link into the AVM formalism can follow the design of the feature structure input to MRS representations in HPSG grammars, as outlined in Copestake et al. 2005.

Although quantifier scoping is per se perhaps a strictly semantic matter, the participants in scoping relations are generally syntactically identifiable,[22] which makes the general design of the present notation possible.

Among phenomena manifest in a wider domain of configurations is 'reported speech', as studied (a) in their role in determining morpho-syntactic patterns across languages, for instance in phenomena like subjunctive mood and logophoricity,[23] and (b) in their role in various kinds of apparent analytic paradoxes in formal representation. A common denominator of many instances of both types is the choice of *whose construal* is reflected in the piece of text concerned: either the construal of the wording as that of the *speaker*, or the construal of the wording as that of one of the *participants*, mostly the *subject*. A typical example from the (b) domain is (27),

(27)   John thinks that the statue is taller than it is.

where the wording *taller than it is* is most reasonably attributed to the speaker, not to John. Exploring the annotation format used above, *speaker construal* relative to a text piece '...' can conceivably be annotated as 'spkCS...', with *spk* for 'speaker', and subject construal as 'suCS...', with *su* as before, and *CS* in both cases understood as *construal scope*. The fruitfulness of the format may depend in part on how easily what is indicated by '...' can be identified for given constructions. As exemplified in (13) above, the notation allows for the specification of paths 'down' into constituents, and in principle, as long as a text piece coincides with what can be syntactically motivated as a constituent, a path can be defined; (28) illustrates the point for *speaker construal* relative to the example in (27), for a path specification into the object clause's predicate (marked as *sc*, for 'secondary predicate').

(28)   spkCSobDECLsc

(This reads as: 'speaker has construal-scope over the secondary predicate of the declarative clause constituting the (matrix) object (counting "taller than it is" as secondary predicate).)

It will be a natural task to explore such extensions of the code, also transcending the sentence as annotation domain.[24]

---

[22] Wide scope readings of implicit arguments and null pronouns are not commonly encountered.

[23] Cf. Nikitina (2019).

[24] A medium of text representation where examples can be searched relative to *strings* of annotation code (as, e.g., in TypeCraft valence specifications, as exemplified in Figure 4), could allow for a search query such as 'suCSobDECL', which would lead to all examples annotated for subject construal into a

7. Conclusion

The semantic annotation system presented is an integral part of a grammatically complete annotation system, used both in corpus annotation, verb valence lexicons and formal and computational grammars. It is linked to a Type Feature Structure system sustaining formal grammars in general, and in the present system with a component of *Situation Structure* as an integral part. This component content-wise represents what is often referred to as lexical or conceptual semantics, but unlike most formal systems in this domain, the present version is constructed fully in terms of Typed Feature structures, whereby it has been fully integrated with the overall grammatical system. Apart from the formal interest in constructing such an architecture, the integration also gives formal expression to the circumstance that meaning, as the subject of semantics as a linguistic field, is inextricably carried by grammar, the co-construal of semantics with grammar thus being a desideratum of any formal framework of language. Thus, although representations within Situation Structure can be viewed by themselves, aspects which have a grammatical exponence can be represented with an explicit link to the exponence factor (where grammatical functions are main 'navigation points' relative to grammatical structure).

That being said, outlining the algorithmics of such a co-construal in principle is one thing, realizing it in a large scale representation of a language is another; our description of the resources for Ga suggest that this is fully possible. The Construction Labeling (CL) formalism for annotation can help in attaining significant coverage of linguistic material, as it can be used on a purely descriptive basis (thus not in tandem with formal analysis), and especially when done in parallel with (or posterior to) more elementary grammatical analysis and glossing. This is what has been demonstrated for Ga. For Norwegian we have demonstrated that the CL code can be used in an effective interplay between grammar, valence lexicon and valence corpus, providing language-wise full scale analytic structures to which situation structure semantic information can be incrementally added.

What has here been outlined resides partly in work done over the last decade, but with the formal integration of the CL system with the grammatical type representation as a novel step. With sentence analysis and sentence annotation being consolidated, we have indicated directions in which the annotation formalism can be brought into scopal analysis, and hopefully next into the analysis of larger text units representing further dimensions of analysis.

The compactness of the code facilitating the annotation of large corpora for valence- and construction type, and for the construction of large valence lexicons, this holds not only from the perspective of attaining complete coverage relative to a given language, but also from cross-linguistic perspectives concerning the presence of given construction-/valence types across languages. These are the main perspectives for the use of the annotation system into cross-linguistic construction-and-valence description and typology.

---

declarative clause, including those annotated with 'spkCSobDECLsc' and for other embedded constituents as well.

8. Bibliographical References

Beermann, Dorothee and Lars Hellan. 2004. A treatment of directionals in two implemented HPSG grammars. In Stefan Müller (ed) *Proceedings of the HPSG04 Conference*, Katholieke Universiteit Leuven. CSLI Publications /http://csli-publications.stanford.edu/

Beermann, Dorothee and Mihaylov, Pavel. 2014. Collaborative databasing and Resource sharing for Linguists. *Languages Resources and Evaluation* 48. Dordrecht: Springer, 1-23.

Bresnan, Joan. 2001. *Lexical Functional Grammar*. Oxford: Blackwell.

Bunt, Harry. 2020. Semantic Annotation of Quantification in Natural Language. Tilburg Centre for Creative Computing.

Copestake, Ann. 2002. *Implementing Typed Feature Structure Grammars*. CSLI Publications.

Copestake, Ann, Dan Flickinger, Ivan Sag and Carl Pollard. 2005. Minimal Recursion Semantics: An Introduction. *Journal of Research on Language and Computation*. 281-332.

Dakubu, M.E. Kropp, 2004a. The Ga preverb kɛ revisited. In Dakubu and Osam, eds., *Studies in the Languages of the Volta Basin* 2: 113-134. Legon: Linguistics Dept.

Dakubu, M.E. Kropp, 2004b. Ga clauses without syntactic subjects. *Journal of African Languages and Linguistics* 25.1: 1-40.

Dakubu, M.E. Kropp, 2008. Ga verb features. In Ameka and Dakubu eds., *Aspect and Modality in Kwa Languages*. Amsterdam & Philadelphia: John Benjamins Publishing Co. Pp. 91-134.

Dakubu, Mary Esther Kropp, 2009. *Ga-English Dictionary with English-Ga Index*. Accra: Black Mask Publishers.

Dakubu, Mary Esther Kropp. Unpublished a. 'Ga_verb_dictionary_for_digital_processing', accessed at https://typecraft.org/tc2wiki/Ga_Valence_Profile

Dakubu, Mary Esther Kropp. Unpublished b. Ga Verbs and their constructions. Monograph ms, Univ. of Ghana.

Dakubu, M.E.K., L. Hellan and D. Beermann. 2007. Verb Sequencing Constraints in Ga: Serial Verb Constructions and the Extended Verb Complex. In St. Müller (ed) *Proceedings of the 14th International Conference on Head-Driven Phrase Structure Grammar*. Stanford: CSLI Publications. (/http://csli-publications.stanford.edu/)

Dakubu, Mary Esther Kropp, and Hellan, Lars 2016. Verb Classes and Valency Classes in Ga. Presented at SyWAL II (Symposium on West African Languages), Vienna.

Dakubu, M.E. Kropp and Lars Hellan. 2017. A labeling system for valency: linguistic coverage and applications. In Hellan, L., Malchukov, A., and Cennamo, M (eds) *Contrastive studies in Valency*. Amsterdam & Philadelphia: John Benjamins Publ. Co.

Grimshaw, Jane. 1992. *Argument Structure*. Cambridge, Mass: MIT Press.

Hellan, Lars. 2019a. Construction-Based Compositional Grammar. March 2019. *Journal of Logic Language and Information*. DOI: 10.1007/s10849-019-09284-5

Hellan, Lars. 2019b. Situations in Grammar. In Essegbey, J., Kallulli, D. and Bodomo, A. (eds). *The grammar of verbs and their arguments: a cross-linguistic perspective*. Studies in African Linguistics. Berlin: R. Köppe.

Hellan, Lars. 2020. A computational grammar for Ga. LREC 2020, the RAIL workshop.

Hellan, Lars and Dorothee Beermann. 2005. Classification of Prepositional Senses for Deep Grammar Applications. In: Valia Kordoni and Aline Villavicencio (eds.). *Proceedings of the 2nd ACL-Sigsem Workshop on The Linguistic Dimensions of Prepositions and their Use in Computational Linguistics Formalisms and Applications*.

Hellan, Lars and M.E. Kropp Dakubu. 2010. *Identifying verb constructions cross-linguistically*. In *Studies in the Languages of the Volta Basin* 6.3. Legon: Linguistics Department, University of Ghana.

Hellan, L., D. Beermann, T. Bruland, M.E.K. Dakubu, and M. Marimon. 2014. *MultiVal*: Towards a multilingual valence lexicon. In Calzolari, Nicoletta et al. (eds.) Proceedings of the 9th International Conference on Language Resources and Evaluation (LREC 2014), pages 2785–2792, Reykjavík, Iceland. ELRA.

Hellan, Lars and Tore Bruland. 2015. A cluster of applications around a Deep Grammar. In: Vetulani et al. (eds) *Proceedings from The Language & Technology Conference* (LTC) 2015, Poznan.

Hellan, L., Beermann, D., Bruland, T., Haugland, T., and Aamot, E. 2017. Creating a Norwegian valence corpus from a deep grammar. In: Vetulani et al. (eds) *Proceedings from The Language & Technology Conference* (LTC) 2017, Poznan.

Jackendoff, Ray. 1990. *Semantic Structures*. MIT Press.

Malchukov, Andrej L. & Comrie, Bernard (eds.) 2015. *Valency classes in the world's languages*. Berlin: De Gruyter Mouton. 2015.

Nikitina, Tatyana. 2019. The mysteries of reported speech. Workshop on *Reported discourse across languages and cultures*. LLACAN, CNRS; Paris.

Palmer, Martha, Dan Gildea, Paul Kingsbury, The Proposition Bank: A Corpus Annotated with Semantic Roles *Computational Linguistics Journal, 31:1*, 2005.

Pollard, Carl and Ivan Sag. 1994. *Head-driven Phrase Structure Grammar*. Chicago Univ. Press.

Quasthoff, Uwe, Lars Hellan, Erik Körner, Thomas Eckart, Dirk Goldhahn, Dorothee Beermann. 2020. Typical Sentences as a Resource for Valence. LREC 2020.

Smith, Carlota. 1991, 1997. *The parameter of aspect*. Dordrecht: Kluwer.

Vendler, Zeno. 1967. *Linguistics in Philosophy*. Ithaca, NY: Cornell Univ. Press.

Verkuyl, Henk. 1996. *A Theory of Aspectuality*. Cambridge University Press.

9. Language Resource References

CL code: Construction Label tags
Norwegian valence corpus:
https://typecraft.org/tc2wiki/Norwegian_Valency_Corpus
Multilingual valence resource :
http://regdili.hf.ntnu.no:8081/multilanguage_valence_demo/multivalence
Ga valence profile and lexicon files:
https://typecraft.org/tc2wiki/Ga_Valence_Profile

Proceedings of the 16th Joint ACL-ISO Workshop Interoperable Semantic Annotation (ISA-16), pages 32–35
Language Resources and Evaluation Conference (LREC 2020), Marseille, 11–16 May 2020
© European Language Resources Association (ELRA), licensed under CC-BY-NC

Transfer of ISOSpace into a 3D Environment for Annotations and Applications

Alexander Henlein, Giuseppe Abrami, Attila Kett, Alexander Mehler
Goethe University
Frankfurt am Main 60323, Germany
{henlein, abrami, mehler}@em.uni-frankfurt.de, attila.kett@stud.uni-frankfurt.de

Abstract

People's visual perception is very pronounced and therefore it is usually no problem for them to describe the space around them in words. Conversely, people also have no problems imagining a concept of a described space. In recent years many efforts have been made to develop a linguistic scheme for spatial and spatial-temporal relations. However, the systems have not really caught on so far, which in our opinion is due to the complex models on which they are based and the lack of available training data and automated taggers. In this paper we describe a project to support spatial annotation, which could facilitate annotation by its many functions, but also enrich it with many more information. This is to be achieved by an extension by means of a VR environment, with which spatial relations can be better visualized and connected with real objects. And we want to use the available data to develop a new state-of-the-art tagger and thus lay the foundation for future systems such as improved text understanding for Text2Scene Generation.
Keywords: ISOSpace, ISOTimeML, Unity3D, Annotation, Virtual Reality

1. Introduction

Humans have a strong spatial perception. This is reflected not only in how well people can adapt to new spatial environments, but also in their language (Haun et al., 2011).
In recent years there have been increased efforts to create a linguistic model for these spatial references. This led to new linguistic models, like ISOSpace (ISO, 2014a) and SceneML (Gaizauskas and Alrashid, 2019) and new tasks, such as Spatial Role Labeling (Kordjamshidi et al., 2010) or SpaceEval (Pustejovsky et al., 2015). Nevertheless, these annotation schemes have not really been able to establish themselves in applications so far. This could be due to the models' complexity, the availability of annotated training data and the lack of automated taggers. There were indeed approaches to apply such models to image descriptions (Pustejovsky and Yocum, 2014), but to our knowledge there were no efforts to transfer the corresponding annotation schemes into three-dimensionality. For the latter, the language model would be particularly interesting, for example, to reconstruct scenes from speech and text three-dimensionally.
In this paper we present our project plan on a 3D VR framework that addresses the problems mentioned above and offers a direct application. In Section 2 we describe the models and systems we refer to in our project, and in Section 3 we explain how we build on these models to create a framework that supports both annotation and application of these language models.

2. Related Work

In recent years, much work has been spent on the development of linguistic models for the semantic understanding of language. The largest of these is probably the Semantic Annotation Framework (SemAF), published under ISO/TC 37/SC 4/WG 2 Semantic Annotation. This consists of individual modules that relate to specific semantic units and are compatible with each other (Ide and Pustejovsky, 2017, Chapter 4). The most widespread model of SemAF is ISO-

TimeML (Pustejovsky et al., 2010; ISO, 2012a), a scheme for the annotation of time and time dependencies of events based on TimeML (Pustejovsky et al., 2005). Such dependencies are important for text understanding, because without them text contents can hardly be fully understood (Ide and Pustejovsky, 2017, p. 942). There is also a model that focuses more on spatial and spatial-temporal structures, the ISOSpace (Pustejovsky et al., 2011; ISO, 2014a). The focus is on spatial and spatial-temporal relations between (spatial) entities and the connection via motion events. Spatial Entities are marked and connected to each other via different spatial connections. QSLinks (Qualitative Spatial Links) are for topological relations, OLinks (Orientation Links) for non-topological relations and MoveLinks for movements of entities in space. This scheme was the basis of SpaceEval (Pustejovsky et al., 2015) and was successfully applied to image descriptions to differentiate between content and structural statements (Pustejovsky and Yocum, 2014). ISOSpace in particular is being further improved (ISO, 2019) and serves as a basis for more specialized models, such as SceneML (Gaizauskas and Alrashid, 2019) for scene descriptions. In addition, SemAF contains schemata such as Semantic Roles (ISO, 2014b), Dialog Acts (ISO, 2012b) and other modules are under development, e.g. QuantML (Bunt et al., 2018).

As the requirements for the annotation of text contexts are constantly changing, flexible and dynamic annotation environments are required to enable the efficient annotation of complex situations. This challenge is addressed by TEXT-ANNOTATOR (Abrami et al., 2019), a browser-based and therefore platform-independent annotation tool for collaborative multi-modal annotation of texts. Using TEXTANNO-TATOR, NER annotations can be created in texts in a short execution time as well as the annotation of rhetorical (Helfrich et al., 2018), time, propositional and even argument structures can be graphically visualised and executed. Furthermore, texts can be linked to ontological resources (e.g. Wikipedia, Wikidata, Wiktionary) and the annotations are

His [**room**]$_{p1}$, a proper [**room**]$_{p1}$ for a human being, only somewhat too small, lay quietly [**between**]$_{ss1}$ the four well-known [**walls**]$_{se1}$. [**Above**]$_{ss2}$ the [**table**]$_{se2}$, [**on**]$_{ss3}$ which an unpacked collection of [**sample cloth goods**]$_{se3}$ was spread out, hung the [**picture**]$_{se4}$ which he had [**cut out**]$_{m1}$ of an illustrated [**magazine**]$_{se6}$ a little while ago and [**set in**]$_{m2}$ a pretty gilt [**frame**]$_{se7}$.

QSLINK(p1, se1, ss1, between)
QSLINK(se3, se2, ss3, EC)
OLINK(se3, se2, ss3, above)
OLINK(se4, se2, ss2, above)
MOVELINK(m1, se4, se6, se4)
MOVELINK(m2, se4, se4, se7)

Figure 1: On the left side a (simplified) annotation of an abridged section of Kafka's: The Metamorphosis according to the ISOSpace (2014) scheme. On the right side a 3D representation. Each entity in the text is linked to the corresponding 3D object from ShapeNetSem and we linked the two clothing to one object group. The relationship between the table and the room is not explicitly mentioned, but is implied by the placement of the table in the room.
p: place, *se*: spatial entity, *ss*: spatial signal, *m*: move event.
QS/OLINK(*figure, ground, signal, relation*). MOVELINK(*move, mover, source, goal*).

managed in different annotation views based on user and group-based permissions (Gleim et al., 2012). As a result, TEXTANNOTATOR is capable of creating a real-time calculation of an inter-annotator agreement based on classes defined in the annotation task (Abrami et al., 2020b).

Since humans are spatially anchored not only in their actions and perception but also in their linguistic behavior (Bateman, 2010; Bateman et al., 2010), this led to new efforts to spatially translate annotations by means of virtual reality. One of these projects is VANNOTATOR (Spiekermann et al., 2018), a system for the annotation of linguistic and multi-modal information units, implemented in Unity3D[1]. VANNOTATOR is a platform for use in various scenarios such as visualization and interaction with historical information (Abrami et al., 2020a) or the annotation of texts and the linking of texts and images with 3D objects (Mehler et al., 2018). Since VANNOTATOR integrates TEXTANNOTATOR and thus makes the annotation spectrum of the latter available in VR, annotations in VANNOTATOR can be performed collaboratively (in workgroups) as well as simultaneously.

3. Our Current Project

ISOSpace is a very expressive model, but its complexity makes it difficult to use it as a basis for annotation. Work is not made easier when 3D information is annotated on a 2D surface. This becomes particularly clear in the annotation of spatial relations between entities, where, e.g., in the case of SpaceEval data, the inter-annotator agreement was only 33% for QSLinks and 39% (Pustejovsky et al., 2015) for OLinks. These are hardly values that guarantee high data quality. Here an extended visualization, as our project aims at, could significantly support these annotation tasks.

---

[1] https://unity.com/

To this end, our aim is to integrate ISOSpace and other SemAF models such as ISOTimeML into TEXTANNOTATOR. Since TEXTANNOTATOR is based on UIMA (*Unstructured Information Management Applications*) (Ferrucci and Lally, 2004), its annotation schemes are defined as UIMA TYPE SYSTEM DESCRIPTORS (TSD). Before the ISO models can be used in UIMA, they have to be transferred to TSD. This is the first step towards collaborative annotation in a visually supporting interface. The annotation can then be enriched by TEXTANNOTATOR embedded into VANNOTATOR. This enables spatial annotations with a 3D interface in VR. In addition, spatial entities can be directly linked to 3D objects via a large number of categorized objects from ShapeNet (Chang et al., 2015), the slightly deeper annotated objects from ShapeNetSem (Savva et al., 2015), objects annotated using VoxML notation (Pustejovsky and Krishnaswamy, 2016) (under development) or via abstract representations (as exemplified in Figure 1). Simply by placing the objects in space, conclusions can be drawn about the relationships between them (and thus also about QSLinks and OLinks) because the information bandwidth of annotation acts in VR is much larger than with pure text annotation. For example, if a book is placed on the desk in VR, the corresponding QSLink and OLink can be set automatically with their relevant attributes. Such concrete pictorial representations are not always unambiguous, but in conjunction with the corresponding sentence, classifiers can be trained to solve this (Hürlimann and Bos, 2016). This can also be extended to MoveLinks, which are set automatically when, for example, the book is carried through the room and placed on a shelf. Or the annotator can follow a direction described in the text in the VR environment. Such actions are much more natural and easier for humans to perform than abstract annotations in a 2D display. Missing links can thus be more easily identified and in some

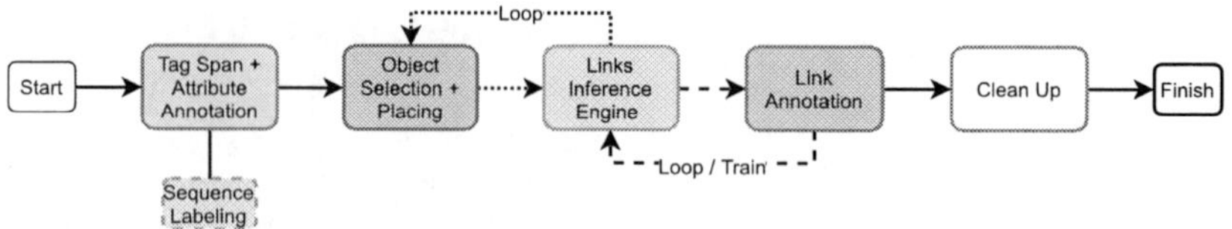

Figure 2: Workflow for ISOSpace Annotation. Blue borders stand for the original annotation steps (Pustejovsky et al., 2015). Red filled for VR support and orange for machine learning support. Span tagging can be supported with a sequence labeling system. And the link inference engine learns through annotations.

cases automatically predicted and attributed, e.g., by examining transitive relations. Such support has also been successfully applied to the annotation of the TimeML standard (Setzer et al., 2005; Verhagen et al., 2006; Verhagen, 2007). The underlying workflow is shown in Figure 2.

A central challenge will be the underspecification of scene descriptions. Related issues concern descriptions containing negations. Though we do not yet have a solution to solve the problems involved, we assume that by combining spatial experience in VR with annotation services provided by annotators, for example, underspecified reference relations can be annotated by exploring additional information with regard to the annotators' positions in relation to referred objects. In examples such as "There is no book on the table" a corresponding book object can be highlighted to indicate the negation (as done, e.g., in WordsEye (Coyne and Sproat, 2001)). In the case of underspecified relations, as expressed in examples of the sort of "The pencil is next to the book", there is the possibility of assigning relative or variable positions to objects (so that they take up tipping states in the visualization).

The next step is the stepwise extension of our annotation system by further (e.g. ISOTimeML) and future (e.g. QuantML (Bunt et al., 2018)) SemAF modules. In this way we create a multi-modal, virtualized annotation system capable of mapping text to abstract or concrete spatial representations of a very broad complexity.

The available ISOSpace data will then be used to develop and train taggers that automatically perform or largely support this annotation. The taggers can support annotators with annotation suggestions, which the annotators then only have to accept or minimally correct.

TEXTANNOTATOR is already actively used for annotating historical text data in the BIOfid project[2]. These annotations (Ahmed et al., 2019) will be extended in the near future to include ISOSpace, ISOTimeML, SemAF-SR and probably also QuantML.

Such in-depth annotations could form the still missing basis for Text2Scene systems (Coyne and Sproat, 2001), which in turn should be able to provide a much deeper understanding of spatial language than previous systems that focus primarily on key words (e.g. (Chang et al., 2017; Ma et al., 2018). Application areas could be, for example: Reconstructing events from multiple texts (based on Twitter, news reports, etc.), visualizing descriptions of accidents (Johansson et al., 2005) or crime scenes or 3D visualizations of text content to clarify certain relations (e.g. intersections of biographical life paths). This could also help to identify weaknesses of

the ISOSpace model, such as missing information relevant for spatial annotation. A problem that could occur is that RCC (Region Connection Calculus) (Randell et al., 1992) for representing topological relations of regions is not sufficient to represent 3D spaces. One reason is that it does not refer to a specific dimension (Renz, 2002).

4. Conclusion

We argued that ISOSpace, despite its expressiveness, has not yet reached the application density that is essential to provide training data for tools for automatically annotating spatial language. To fill this gap, we plan to integrate ISOSpace into VANNOTATOR to enable 3D annotations of spatial language. This will also include other SemAF models in order to ultimately provide the data basis for the creation of Text2Scene systems.

5. Acknowledgements

The support by the *Stiftung Polytechnische Gesellschaft* (SPTG) is gratefully acknowledged. And many thanks to all reviewers for their comments, suggestions, hints and references. These were very helpful and we will incorporate much of this in our future work.

6. Bibliographical References

Abrami, G., Mehler, A., Lücking, A., Rieb, E., and Helfrich, P. (2019). TextAnnotator: A flexible framework for semantic annotations. In *Proc. of ISA-15*, May.

Abrami, G., Mehler, A., Spiekermann, C., Kett, A., Lööck, S., and Schwarz, L. (2020a). Educational technologies in the area of ubiquitous historical computing in virtual reality: Finding new ways to teach in a transformed learning environment. In Linda Daniela, editor, *New Perspectives on Virtual and Augmented Reality*. Taylor & Francis. in press.

Abrami, G., Stoeckel, M., and Mehler, A. (2020b). TextAnnotator: A UIMA based tool for simultaneous and collaborative annotation of texts. In *Proc. of LREC 2020*, LREC 2020. accepted.

Ahmed, S., Stoeckel, M., Driller, C., Pachzelt, A., and Mehler, A. (2019). BIOfid Dataset: Publishing a german gold standard for named entity recognition in historical biodiversity literature. In *Proc. of CoNLL 2019*.

Bateman, J. A., Hois, J., Ross, R., and Tenbrink, T. (2010). A linguistic ontology of space for natural language processing. *Artificial Intelligence*, 174(14):1027–1071.

Bateman, J. A. (2010). Language and space: A two-level semantic approach based on principles of ontological engineering. *Int J Speech Tech*, (1):29–48.

---

[2] https://www.biofid.de/en/

Bunt, H., Pustejovsky, J., and Lee, K. (2018). Towards an ISO standard for the annotation of quantification. In *Proc. of LREC 2018*.

Chang, A. X., Funkhouser, T., Guibas, L., Hanrahan, P., Huang, Q., Li, Z., Savarese, S., Savva, M., Song, S., Su, H., Xiao, J., Yi, L., and Yu, F. (2015). ShapeNet: An information-rich 3D model repository. Technical Report arXiv:1512.03012 [cs.GR].

Chang, A. X., Eric, M., Savva, M., and Manning, C. D. (2017). SceneSeer: 3D scene design with natural language. *arXiv preprint arXiv:1703.00050*.

Coyne, B. and Sproat, R. (2001). WordsEye: An automatic text-to-scene conversion system. In *Proc. of SIGGRAPH 2001*, pages 487–496.

Ferrucci, D. and Lally, A. (2004). UIMA: An architectural approach to unstructured information processing in the corporate research environment. *Natural Language Engineering*, (3-4):327–348.

Gaizauskas, R. and Alrashid, T. (2019). SceneML: A proposal for annotating scenes in narrative text. In *Workshop on ISA-15*, page 13.

Gleim, R., Mehler, A., and Ernst, A. (2012). SOA implementation of the eHumanities Desktop. In *Proc. of the Workshop on SOAs for the Humanities: Solutions and Impacts, Digital Humanities 2012*.

Haun, D. B., Rapold, C. J., Janzen, G., and Levinson, S. C. (2011). Plasticity of human spatial cognition: Spatial language and cognition covary across cultures. *Cognition*, (1):70–80.

Helfrich, P., Rieb, E., Abrami, G., Lücking, A., and Mehler, A. (2018). TreeAnnotator: Versatile visual annotation of hierarchical text relations. In *Proc. of LREC 2018*.

Hürlimann, M. and Bos, J. (2016). Combining lexical and spatial knowledge to predict spatial relations between objects in images. In *Proc. of CVPR 2016*, pages 10–18.

Ide, N. and Pustejovsky, J. (2017). *Handbook of linguistic annotation*. Springer.

ISO. (2012a). Language resource management — Semantic annotation framework (SemAF) — Part 1: Time and events (SemAF-Time, ISO-TimeML). Standard ISO/IEC TR 24617-1:2012.

ISO. (2012b). Language resource management — Semantic annotation framework — Part 2: Dialogue acts. Standard ISO/IEC TR 24617-2:2012.

ISO. (2014a). Language resource management — Semantic annotation framework (SemAF) — Part 7: Spatial information (ISO-Space). Standard ISO/IEC TR 24617-7:2014.

ISO. (2014b). Language resource management — Semantic annotation framework — Part 4: Semantic roles (SemAF-SR). Standard ISO/IEC TR 24617-4:2014.

ISO. (2019). Language resource management — Semantic annotation framework (SemAF) — Part 7: Spatial information (ISO-Space). Standard ISO/IEC TR 24617-7:2019.

Johansson, R., Berglund, A., Danielsson, M., and Nugues, P. (2005). Automatic text-to-scene conversion in the traffic accident domain. In *IJCAI*, volume 5, pages 1073–1078.

Kordjamshidi, P., Moens, M.-F., and van Otterlo, M. (2010). Spatial Role Labeling: Task definition and annotation scheme. In *Proc. of LREC 2010*, pages 413–420.

Ma, R., Patil, A. G., Fisher, M., Li, M., Pirk, S., Hua, B.-S., Yeung, S.-K., Tong, X., Guibas, L., and Zhang, H. (2018). Language-driven synthesis of 3D scenes from scene databases. In *SIGGRAPH Asia 2018 Technical Papers*, page 212. ACM.

Mehler, A., Abrami, G., Spiekermann, C., and Jostock, M. (2018). VAnnotatoR: A framework for generating multimodal hypertexts. In *Proc. of HT 2018*.

Pustejovsky, J. and Krishnaswamy, N. (2016). VoxML: A visualization modeling language. *arXiv preprint arXiv:1610.01508*.

Pustejovsky, J. and Yocum, Z. (2014). Image annotation with ISO-Space: Distinguishing content from structure. In *Proc. of LREC 2014*, pages 426–431. ELRA.

Pustejovsky, J., Ingria, B., Sauri, R., Castano, J., Littman, J., Gaizauskas, R., Setzer, A., Katz, G., and Mani, I. (2005). The specification language TimeML. *The language of time: A reader*, pages 545–557.

Pustejovsky, J., Lee, K., Bunt, H., and Romary, L. (2010). ISO-TimeML: An international standard for semantic annotation. In *Proc. of LREC 2010*.

Pustejovsky, J., Moszkowicz, J. L., and Verhagen, M. (2011). ISO-Space: The annotation of spatial information in language. In *Proc. of the Sixth Joint ISO-ACL SIGSEM Workshop on ISA*, pages 1–9.

Pustejovsky, J., Kordjamshidi, P., Moens, M.-F., Levine, A., Dworman, S., and Yocum, Z. (2015). SemEval-2015 Task 8: SpaceEval. In *Proc. of SemEval 2015*, pages 884–894.

Randell, D. A., Cui, Z., and Cohn, A. G. (1992). A spatial logic based on regions and connection. *KR*, pages 165–176.

Renz, J. (2002). A canonical model of the region connection calculus. *Journal of Applied Non-Classical Logics*, (3-4):469–494.

Savva, M., Chang, A. X., and Hanrahan, P. (2015). Semantically-enriched 3D models for common-sense knowledge. *CVPR 2015 Workshop on Functionality, Physics, Intentionality and Causality*.

Setzer, A., Gaizauskas, R., and Hepple, M. (2005). The role of inference in the temporal annotation and analysis of text. *Language Resources and Evaluation*, 39(2-3):243–265.

Spiekermann, C., Abrami, G., and Mehler, A. (2018). VAnnotatoR: A gesture-driven annotation framework for linguistic and multimodal annotation. In *Proc. of AREA 2018 Workshop*, AREA.

Verhagen, M., Knippen, R., Mani, I., and Pustejovsky, J. (2006). Annotation of temporal relations with Tango. In *LREC*, pages 2249–2252.

Verhagen, M. (2007). Drawing TimeML relations with TBox. In *Annotating, Extracting and Reasoning about Time and Events*, pages 7–28. Springer.

Proceedings of the 16th Joint ACL-ISO Workshop Interoperable Semantic Annotation (ISA-16), pages 36–48
Language Resources and Evaluation Conference (LREC 2020), Marseille, 11–16 May 2020
© European Language Resources Association (ELRA), licensed under CC-BY-NC

Annotation-based Semantics

Kiyong Lee

Korea University
Seoul, Korea
ikiyong@gmail.com

Abstract

This paper proposes a semantics *ABS* for the model-theoretic interpretation of annotation structures. It provides a language *ABSr* that represents *semantic forms* in a (possibly λ-free) type-theoretic first-order logic. For semantic compositionality, the representation language introduces two operators $\oplus$ and $\oslash$ with some subtypes for the conjunctive or distributive composition of semantic forms. *ABS* also introduces a small set of logical predicates to represent semantic forms in a simplified format. The use of *ABSr* is illustrated with some annotation structures that conform to ISO 24617 standards on semantic annotation such as ISO-TimeML and ISO-Space.

Keywords: annotation structure, semantic forms, logical predicates, conjunctive or disjunctive composition

1.   Introduction

This paper has two aims: [i] to formulate a semantics, called *Annotation-based Semantics* (*ABS*), for the model-theoretic interpretation of annotation structures and [ii] to recommend it as a semantics for ISO 24617 standards on semantic annotation frameworks such as ISO-TimeML (ISO, 2020) or ISO-Space (ISO, 2020). As a semantics for these annotation frameworks, *ABS* has two roles. One role is to validate the abstract syntax that formally defines each annotation framework in set theoretic terms (Bunt, 2010). The other is to interpret the annotation structures that are generated by, or conform to, a relevant annotation framework (see (Lee, 2018) and (Pustejovsky et al., 2019)).

ABS is a structurally simple semantics, consisting of [i] a representation language *ABSr* and [ii] a finite set of logical predicates that are used in *ABSr*, but are defined as part of a model structure like meaning postulates or word meanings as introduced by Carnap (1947 1956) and Montague (1974), as shown in Figure 1, and further developed by Dowty (1979) and Pustejovsky (1995).

The rest of the paper develops as follows: Section 2 provides some motivations for *ABS*. Section 3 describes the basic design of *ABS*. Section 4 defines the type-theoretic first-order predicate logic-based representation language *ABSr*. Section 5 breifly outlines some characteristics of an interpretation model structure for *ABS*. Section 6 shows how the composition rules of *ABSr* apply to the annotation structures that conform to some of the ISO 24617 standards on semantic annotation. Section 7 introduces some related works and discuses the convertibility of semantic forms of *ABS* to DRSs or λ-formulas. Section 8 makes some concluding remarks.

2.   Motivation for *ABS*

The main motivation of *ABS* is to lighten the burden of automatically generating intermediary interpretations, called *semantic forms* or *logical forms*, of semantic annotation structures for both human and machine learning or understanding. For this purpose, *ABS* and its representation language *ABSr* introduce two minor operational modifications into the two well-established and model-theoretically interpretable representation languages, the type-theoretic λ-calculus, used for Montague Semantics (MS) (Montague,

1974), and Kamp and Reyle (1993)'s Discourse Representation Theory (DRT). The representation language *ABSr* of *ABS* is designed to to be free from λ-operations, especially involving higher-order variables, by replacing the operation of substitution through the λ-conversion with an equation solving approach (see Lee (1983)), or to convert its semantic forms into visually more readable Discourse Representation Structures (DRSs) preferably without introducing embedded or stacked structures into them. From a theoretical point of view, neither *ABS* nor *ABSr* is totally different from Bunt (2020b) or his earlier efforts to develop an annotation-based semantics with the interpretation function I to convert or annotation structures, defined in abstract (set-theoretic) terms, to DRSs based on Kamp and Reyle (1993)'s Discourse Representation Theory (DRT). From a practical point of view, *ABS* is characterized by dividing the task of interpreting annotation structures between the representation of simpler or *abbreviated* semantic forms and their interpretations enriched with lexical meaning in the form of meaning postulates that constrain the set of possible interpretation model structures.

Based on a type-theoretic first-order predicate logic (*FOL*), *ABSr* is augmented with [i] a small set of operators and [ii] a set of logical predicates. As is developed in Section 3, for any **a** that refers to the abstract specification of an annotation structure or its substructures, either an entity or a link structure, preferably through its ID, the operator σ maps **a** to a semantic form $\sigma(\mathbf{a})$, represented in a first-order logic, while the two non-Boolean operators $\oplus$ and $\oslash$, with their finer-grained subtypes of *merging*, each relate $\sigma(\mathbf{a})$ to another semantic form, constrained by their semantic type. Without much depending on the particular syntactic analysis of each input, these operators combine, in a compositional manner, the pieces of information conveyed by each annotation structure or its substructures into a model-theoretically interpretable logical form, called *semantic form*, in *FOL*. Besides the Boolean connectives in *FOL*, these non-Boolean operators are needed to combine semantic forms that are not of type t (sentential type) as bridges that connect annotation structures to logical forms: for instance, to combine $\sigma(Fido)$ of individual entity type e with $\sigma([runs(e) \wedge agent(e, x)])$ of type $e \rightarrow (v \rightarrow t)$ without using λ-operations in an overt way.

As is elaborated in Section 3, ABS also introduces a small set of *logical predicates* into its representation language *ABSr* and treats them as meaning postulates that constrain a model structure (see Montague (1974) and Dowty (1979)). There are at least two reasons for the introduction of a small set of logical predicates. One reason is *representational simplicity*: it can, for instance, represent the semantic form of the past tense of a verb in English as **past**(e), where **past** is a predicate to be defined as part of an interpretation model and e is a variable of type v for eventualities, instead of introducing one of its definitions, which is the most common one $[\tau(e) \subseteq t \wedge t \prec n]$ into the semantic form. This semantic form requires the introduction of a real-time function τ from events to times, two temporal relations, those of inclusion $\subseteq$ and precedence $\prec$, and the notion of the present time n. Furthermore, it is a straightforward process to translate an entity structure like **event**(e1, ran, *pred*:run, *tense*:past) into a semantic form $[run(e_1) \wedge \mathbf{past}(e_1)]$.

Another reason is *representational flexibility*. *ABS* can first choose an appropriate definition or meaning from a set of possible definitions given in a model structure and then decide on an appropriate model M and an assignment g that together satisfy a semantic form like $[run(e_1) \wedge \mathbf{past}(e_1)]$. This would be the case particularly if the past tense needs to be interpreted in a deictic or situational sense, as discussed by Partee (1973) and Quirk et al. (1985).

ABS upholds the principle of minimalism and partiality in its representation. It does not aim nor claim to treat the total interpretation of natural language expressions. Being based on a restricted set of markables in data, either textual or audio-visual, and their annotation, the task of annotation and that of its semantics such as *ABS* are bound to be restrictive: the semantics can be either simple or complex depending on what needs to be annotated. The granularity or complexity of semantic forms only depends on that of the input annotation structures and their substructures. The granularity of perceiving and constructing these structures, especially involving spatio-temporal information, is controlled or modulated through common-sense logic by the need of their applications, as is discussed by Miller and Shanahan (1999) and Gordon and Hobbs (2017)).

3. Basic Design

3.1. Basic Assumptions

The main characteristics of *ABS* are the following. First, *ABS* is based on annotation work, making use of the semantic annotation of coumminicative linguistic data for their semantic interpretation. Without relying on a pre-defined syntax, it manipulates minimally what is encoded in annotation structures and their substructures and converts these structures to logical forms that can be interpreted model-theoretically. *ABS* is, for instance, designed to support spatio-temporal annotation by validating the abstract syntax of ISO-Space (ISO, 2020), as proposed and outlined by Lee (2016), Lee (2018), and Lee et al. (2018) as well as ISO-TimeML (ISO, 2012) and Pustejovsky et al. (2010).

Second, *ABS* only provides *partial* information on a restricted set of markables for semantic annotation. Unlike ordinary semantics like Montague Semantics (Montague, 1974) or even Minimal Recursion Semantics (Copestake et al., 2005), *ABS* is not a general semantics that attempts to treat all aspects of language in an abstract way.

Third, *ABS* leaves much of the information *unspecified*. It allows, for instance, some variables to occur unbound in well-formed semantic forms, as in the interval temporal logic of Pratt-Hartmann (2007), while their scoping is left unspecified till the last stage of composing semantic forms or being interpreted (model-theoretically), unless the scope is specified as part of annotation. As a result, the semantic type of semantic forms is partially non-deterministic: it can be interpreted either as of type t potentially denoting a proposition or a truth-value or of a functional type $\alpha \rightarrow t$, where α is a well-defined type, denoting a set of individual objects or of higher-order objects.

Fourth, *ABS* introduces a small set of predicates such as **past** and **perfective** for the specification of tense and aspect. It can also introduce the predicates **holds** and **occurs**, as defined in Allen (1984) and others, for the event-type dependent temporal anchoring into semantic forms. All these predicates that occur in semantic forms are defined as part of an interpretation model or leaving room for various uses of grammatical concepts or their contextually dependent interpretations.

Being based on annotations, *ABS* must deal with complex issues in semantic annotation such as quantification, for instance, as raised by Bunt (2020a) and Bunt (2020b) or the meaning of determiners that include numerals as in "two donkeys" in language in general. It may also have to deal with the structure and substructures of eventualities, especially dealing with dynamic motions, as discussed in Mani and Pustejovsky (2012). The complexity or granularity of *ABS* thus totally depends on that of annotation structures or the type of annotations.

In addition, *ABS* upholds a couple of well-established basic assumptions as its theoretical basis:

1. Semantics is constrained by a type theory (Montague semantics: Montague (1974) and Dowty et al. (1981))

2. Events are viewed as individuals (Neo-Davidsonian semantics: Davidson (1979), Davidson (2001), Parsons (1990), Pustejovsky (1995))

3. Variables are linked to discourse referents (Discourse representation theory: Kamp and Reyle (1993))

3.2. Metamodel

Figure 1 shows the general design of *ABS*, which consists of (1) a representation language *ABS* and (2) an interpretation model M with logical predicates defined.

ABS is an annotation-based semantics, meaning that its representation language *ABSr* translates each **a** of the abstract specification of entity or link structures that constitute annotation structures to a well-defined semantic form $\sigma(\mathbf{a})$. *ABS* then interprets each semantic form $\sigma(\mathbf{a})$ with respect to a model M, a list D of definitions of logical predicates, and an assignment g of values to variables, $[\![\sigma(\mathbf{a})]\!]^{M,D,g}$. Each $\sigma(\mathbf{a})$ in *ABSr* is an expression of first-order logic, but each of the logical predicates that my occur in $\sigma(\mathbf{a})$ may be defined in terms of higher-order logic as part of the model structure.

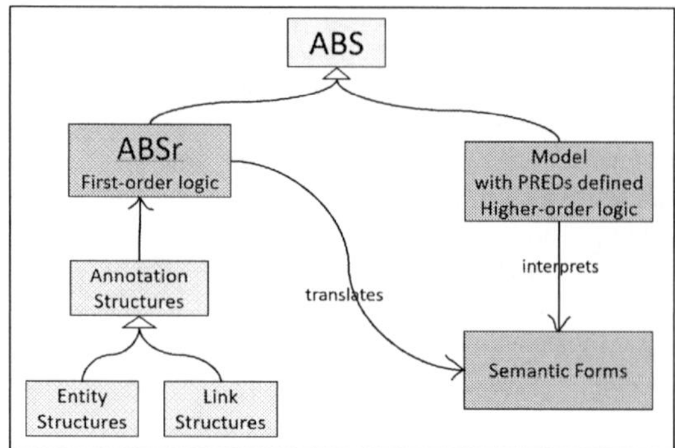

Figure 1: metamodel of *ABS*

4. Syntax

ABSr subsumes a type-theoretic first-order predicate logic (*FOL*). This means: [i] every well-formed (semantic) form in *ABSr* is assigned one of the types, as specified in 4.1, and [ii] every well-formed formula in *FOL* is well-formed and of type t (having a truth-value) in *ABSr*.

4.1. Basic and Functional Types

ABS adopts the system of semantic types which Kracht (2002) and Pustejovsky et al. (2019) have developed. They extend the list of basic types from Montague (1974)'s basic set of types $\{e, t\}$ to an enlarged list, as specified in (1).

(1) Extended List of Types:
    [i] Basic Types:
    a. t, the type of truth-values
    b. e, the type of individual entities
    c. v, the type of eventualities
    d. i, the type of time points
    e. p, the type of spatial points
    f. m, the type of measures
    g. int, the type of intervals
    h. vec, the type of vectors[1]
    [ii] Functional Types:
    h. If α and β are any types, then $\alpha \rightarrow \beta$ is a type.

Type constructors such as $\rightarrow$ are introduced to define *functional types*: e.g., $e \rightarrow t$, $v \rightarrow t$, $i \rightarrow t$, $p \rightarrow t$ or $e \rightarrow (e \rightarrow t)$. Eventuality descriptions such as *run* or *love* are of type $v \rightarrow t$, which is abbreviated to $\mathcal{E}$ (see Pustejovsky (1995)), while the same symbol $\mathcal{E}$ is also used as as a symbol for a variable ranging over a set of eventualities or instances of an eventuality. The functional type $p \rightarrow t$, denoting a set of spatial points, is often represented by a type r of regions[2] I may call these functional types $\mathcal{E}$ and r *pseudo-basic types*, for they are seldom analyzed as functional types.

As introduced by Pustejovsky et al. (2019), path types are defined on the basis of the type of intervals int, which is defined $[0, 1] \subset R$, where R is a set of reals. A path π will be that function $int \rightarrow p$, which indexes locations on the

path to values from the interval [0,1] (see Pustejovsky et al. (2019)). A vector path π_v can also be defined as $int \rightarrow vec$. An event path π_v will be defined as $v \rightarrow \pi_v$ as the function from eventualities to the vector path.

Kracht (2002) and Pustejovsky et al. (2019) also introduce the group operator $\bullet$ to form group types, for example, $p^\bullet$ for the group of spatial points. Link (1998) introduces two symbols * and * and prefixes them to a predicate P to generate the group predicate $^*P$ and the plural predicate $^\star P$, both based on the predicate P.

Corresponding to each of the IDs of annotation structures or its substructures, entity or link structures, and of each of the types as defined in (1), there is a list of variables. Some of them are listed below:

Categories[3]	Ids	Types	Variables
annotation	a_1,...	t	$a_1, ...$
entity	x_1,...	e	$x, x_1, ...$
		v	$s, e, e_1, ...$
event	e_1,...	$\mathcal{E}, e \rightarrow t$	$\mathcal{E}, ...$
timex3	t_1,...	$\mathcal{I}, i \rightarrow t$	$t, t_1, ...$
place	pl_1,...	$r, p \rightarrow t$	$l, l_0, ...$
path	p_1,...	$\pi_v, int \rightarrow p$	$p, p_1, ...$
event-path	ep_1,...	π_ϵ	$v \rightarrow \pi_v$
measure	me_1,...	m	$m, m_1, ...$
link	l_1,...	t	

Table 1: IDs, variables, and types

The list of variables is just a conventionally used list. To be precise, for each entity structure E that confirms to a recognized annotation scheme such as ISO-TimeML or ISO-Space, a variable is defined as a pair $<var{:}\tau>$, where var is a variable and τ is a type. Conventionally, any lowercase Latin characters such as x, y, etc. or e and s are used as variable for any one of the basic types provided that its type is specified: for example, $x{:}<var, p \rightarrow t>$ to use x as a variable ranging over regions of type r, or $p \rightarrow t$. Uppercase Latin characters or special characters like $\mathcal{E}$ are used for functional types: $\mathcal{E}$ is a variable for eventuality descriptions such as what is denoted by a verb like "run". Note that $run(e)$ is of type t, while the eventuality description run is of type $v \rightarrow t$ and its argument e is a variable of eventuality type v.[4]

4.2. Syntax Proper

The part of *ABSr* that introduces the *merge* operators and their use is defined by $Syntax_{absR}$. This syntax specifies what constitutes *ABSr* and how its constituents are formed. Some preliminary remarks are made before specifying the syntax of *ABSr*.

4.2.1. Preliminary Remarks

Just like any language, the representation language *ABSr* is a language that consists of a non-empty set of strings of character symbols. Each of such character strings in

---

[1] (g) and (h) are my own additions to the list of basic types.

[2] See Mani and Pustejovsky (2012) for the discussion of 3.2.2 regions as primitive objects vs. 3.2.3 regions as sets of points.

[4] Here, it is a bit confusing to use e as standing for a basic type for individual entities and use it as referring to an eventuality of type v: e.g. $[run_{v \rightarrow t}(e_v) \wedge \mathbf{agent}(e, x)]_{e \rightarrow (v \rightarrow t)}$.

ABSr is called a *semantic form* because it serves as an intermediary form for the model-theoretic interpretation of annotation structures. Further to clarify what *ABSr* is, I make some technical remarks.

Remark 1: Mapping σ For any **a** that refers to the *abstract specification* of each of the entity or link structures which together constitute an annotation structure, independent of how these structures are represented, σ maps **a** to a semantic form in *ABSr*. $\sigma(\mathbf{a})$ is read as "the semantic form of **a**" in *ABSr* and is a *well-formed form* (wff) of *ABSr*. $\sigma(\mathbf{a})$ is considered independent of the format that represents it, but has to check the abstract syntax that validates the abstract specification **a**. Hence, **a** must be the same as the interpretation function I that is introduced in Bunt (2020b) and Bunt (2020a).

Remark 2: Model-theoretic Interpretation   The symbol $[\![\ ]\!]$ is used to represent a (model-theoretic) denotation. Given any semantic form $\sigma(\mathbf{a})$ in *ABSr*, its denotation with respect to a model M, an assignment g of values to variables, and a set D of definitions for **logical predicates** is represented by $[\![\sigma(\mathbf{a})]\!]^{M,g,D}$.

Remark 3: Typing   *ABSr* is a type-based language. Hence, every well-formed (semantic) form A and any c of its constituents such as variables in *ABSr* is assigned a type. The type τ of A or c is represented as a pair: e.g., $<A{:}\tau>$, $<c{:}\tau>$, $<var{:}\tau>$, or as a subscript to A or one of its constituents: A_τ, c_τ or x_e.

4.2.2.   Formulation of Syntactic Rules

Like the syntax of an ordinary language, $Syntax_{absR}$ consists of a vocabulary and a set of formation rules, as specified in (2).

(2) $Syntax_{absR} = <V,R>$ such that
a. V is a vocabulary that includes binary *merge* operators $\{\oplus, \oslash\}$ over the set of semantic forms in *ABSr* and their subtypes, and
b. R is a set of composition rules for merging, as formulated in (7).

There are two sorts of well-formed semantic forms (swff) in *ABSr*: basic and composed, each defined by a rule in R, a list of rules, in (4.2.3) and (7).

4.2.3.   Atomic Semantic Forms

Atomic semantic forms are defined by Rule A.

(3) **Rule A** for Atomic semantic forms:
For any abstract specification $\mathbf{a}_{Ec}$ of an entity structure E of category c,[5] and a type τ associated with *cat*, $\sigma(\mathbf{a}_{Ec})_\tau$ is a well-formed form of type τ in *ABSr*.

Remark 4: $\mathbf{a}_{Ec}$ in $\sigma(\mathbf{a}_{Ec})_\tau$ is replaced by the ID of Ec.

Following DRT (Kamp and Reyle, 1993), the new occurrences of variables in a semantic form are registered.

(4) **Rule A.1** for Variable Registry:
Any variable that is newly introduced to $\sigma(\mathbf{a}_{Ec})$ is listed in the preamble: i.e., $\Sigma_{var:type}\sigma(\mathbf{a}_{Ec})$.
Note: These variables may not be registered if they can be recognized contextually.

The variables in the preamble $\Sigma_{var:type}$ are treated as *discourse referents*, to which each occurrence of the variables in $\sigma(\mathbf{a}_{Ec})$ is bound.
Consider an example, annotated as in (5):

(5)   a. Fido ran$_{w2}$ away$_{w3}$.

b. Annotation(id=a5)
event(e1, w2-3, *pred*:run, *tense*:past)

c. Semantic form:
$\sigma(e1_e)_\alpha := \{e_1{:}e\}[run(e_1)_t \wedge past(e_1)_t]_\alpha$
where ":=" is a meta-symbol standing for "is".

Some notes are needed here. (1) For now temporally, the type of $\sigma(e1)$ is left unspecified: it is only marked with α, whereas the type of e_1 in the registry is specified as the individual type e. (2) The ID "e1" in $\sigma(e1)$ does not refer to the entity structure of category **event**, but its abstract specification that conforms to the abstract syntax of the relevant annotation scheme. (3) The representation of $\Sigma_{var:type}\sigma(\mathbf{a}_{Ec})$ is exactly the same as DRS except that $\sigma(e1)$ in *ABSr* is typed, as in Bos et al. (2017)'s Groningen Meaning Bank (GMB). The semantic form in (5) can be converted to a type-based DRS except that the type of the entire DRS is not specified.

(6)

$e_1{:}e$
$run(e_1)_t$
$past(e_1)_t$

4.2.4.   Composed Semantic Forms

The current version of *ABSr* introduces two *merge* operators, $\oplus$ and $\oslash$, and their subtypes each marked with a different superscript to represent the merging of (1) two semantic forms or (2) a pair of semantic forms with a functor-like semantic form. The second type of merging is motivated by the treatment of tripartite link structures of the form $<\eta, E, \rho>$, where ρ is a type of relation between an entity η and a set E of entities, in *ABSr*.

These operators are non-Boolean connectives. They are needed to be able to merge semantic forms of type other than the truth-type t. More operators may need to be introduced to treat finer-grained compositions, especially involving the semantics of determiners that include generalized quantifiers, plurals, and the merging of scopes. As suggested by Bunt (personal communication), different symbols will be introduced to represent various subtypes of composition.[6]

For the formulation of composition rules, it is assumed that these rules hold for any well-formed semantic forms A_α, B_β, and C_γ, each of which is typed as α, β, and γ, respectively. For these semantic forms, there are two major types

---

[5]In a concrete syntax, this category is often called *tag* or *element*.

[6]Bunt (2020b), for instance, introduces the *scope merge operator* $\oplus^s$ and the *possessive scoped merge operator* $\oplus^{ps}$.

of composition, conjunctive ($\oplus$) and distributive ($\oslash$), and then their subtypes:

(7) Types of composition:
Conjunctive composition ($\oplus$):
Rule 1^{bo} Boolean conjunctive composition ($\oplus^{bo}$)
Rule 1^{fa} Functional conjunctive composition ($\oplus^{fa}$)
Rule 1^{sub} Substitutive conjunctive composition by substitution ($\oplus^{sub}$)
Rule 1^{eq} Equative conjunctive composition by equation solving ($\oplus^{eq}$)
Disjunctive composition ($\oslash$):
Rule 2 Disjunctive composition ($\oslash$)
Rule 2^{int} Intensional disjunctive composition ($\oslash^{int}$)
Rule 2^{imp} Implicational disjunctive composition ($\oslash^{imp}$)

Rule 1^{bo} **Boolean conjunctive composition** ($\oplus^{bo}$) is the most common type of composition, as formulated in

(8) **Rule 1**^{bo}: Boolean conjunctive composition:
a. $[A_t \oplus^{bo} C_t]_\alpha := [A_t \wedge C_t]_t$
b. $[\{A_t, B_t\}_\alpha \oplus^{bo} C_t] := [[A_t \wedge B_t]_t \wedge C_t]$

Rule 1^{bo} applies to most of the annotation structures in ISO-TimeML (ISO, 2012), ISO-Space (ISO, 2020), and ISO standard on semantic role annotation (ISO, 2014). For illustration, consider (9):

(9) a. Fido is barking.

b. Entity Structures:
entity(x1, w1, *type*:dog, *form*:nam)
event(e1, w2-3, *pred*:bark, *tense*:present, *aspect*:progressive)

c. Link Structure:
srlink(e1, x1, agent)

The annotation of text fragment (9a) consists of a list of entity structures in (b) and a link structure (c) over them. Here, **srlink** specifies the semantic role of the participant x_1 as an **agent** participating in the event e_1 of barking, as illustrated in (10).

(10) a. Semantic forms of the entity structures:
$\sigma(x1)_t := \{x_1{:}e\}[dog(x_1) \wedge \textbf{named}(x_1, Fido)]$
$\sigma(e1)_t := \{e_1{:}v\}[bark(e_1) \wedge \textbf{presProg}(e_1)]$

b. Semantic form of Semantic role link:
$\sigma(srlink)_t$
$:= \{x_1{:}e, e_1{:}v\}$
$[\{\sigma(x1)_t, \sigma(e_1)_t\} \oplus^{bo} agent(e_1, x_1)_t]$
$:= \{x_1{:}e, e_1{:}v\}$
$[[\sigma(x1)_t \wedge \sigma(e_1)_t] \wedge agent(e_1, x_1)_t]$
$:= \{x_1{:}e, e_1{:}v\}$
$[[dog(x_1) \wedge \textbf{named}(x_1, Fido)] \wedge$
$[bark(e_1) \wedge \textbf{presProg}(e_1)] \wedge agent(e_1, x_1)]$

c. Semantic form of annotation structure:
$\sigma(a_9)$
$:= \{x{:}e, e{:}v\}\sigma(srlink)$

by Variable renaming and binding
$:= \{x{:}e, e{:}v\}[bark(e) \wedge \textbf{presProg}(e)] \wedge$
$\textbf{agent}(e, x)]$

Rule 1^{fa} **Functional conjunctive composition** reflects the functional application of a functor applying to its argument(s) in Montague Semantics (Montague, 1974) or (Dowty et al., 1981). Rule 1^{fa} is formulated in (11):

(11) Rule 1^{fa} Functional conjunctive composition:
a. $[A_\alpha \oplus^{fa} C_{\alpha \to t)}] := [A_t \wedge C_t]$
or
b. $[\{A_\alpha, B_\beta\}] \oplus^{fa} C_{\beta \to (\alpha \to t)}] := [[A_t \wedge B_t] \wedge C_t]$

Example (9) can be analyzed in terms of a functor-argument analysis by assigning a functional type $\alpha \to t$, where α is a type, to the type of each of the annotation structures.

(12) a. Semantic forms of the entity structures:
$\sigma(x1)_{e \to t}$
$:= \{x_1{:}e\}[dog(x_1) \wedge \textbf{named}(x_1, Fido)]$
$\sigma(e1)_{v \to t}$
$:= \{e_1{:}v\}[bark(e_1) \wedge \textbf{presProg}(e_1)]$

b. Semantic form of Semantic role link:
$\sigma(srlink)$
$:= \{x_1{:}e, e_1{:}v\}$
$[\{\sigma(x1)_{e \to t}, \sigma(e_1)_{v \to t}\} \oplus^{fa}$
$\textbf{agent}(e_1, x_1)_{(v \to t) \to ((e \to t) \to t)}]$
$:= \{x_1{:}e, e_1{:}v\}$
$[[\sigma(x1)_t \wedge \sigma(e_1)_t] \wedge \textbf{agent}(e_1, x_1)_t]$
$:= \{x_1{:}e, e_1{:}v\}$
$[[dog(x_1) \wedge \textbf{named}(x_1, Fido)]_t$
$\wedge [bark(e_1) \wedge \textbf{presProg}(e_1)]_t \wedge$
$\textbf{agent}(e_1, x_1)_t]_t$

c. Semantic form of annotation structure:
$\sigma(a_9)$
$:= \{x{:}e, e{:}v\}\sigma(srlink)$
$:= \{x{:}e, e{:}v\}$
$[[dog(x) \wedge \textbf{named}(x, Fido)]$
$\wedge [bark(e) \wedge \textbf{presProg}(e)] \wedge \textbf{agent}(e, x)]$
by Variable renaming and binding

The functional composition with the operator $\oplus^{fa}$ is equivalent to the functional application in λ-calculus, as shown by (13):

(13) a. Arguments:
$\sigma(x1)_{e \to t}$
$:= \lambda x_1[dog(x_1) \wedge \textbf{named}(x_1, Fido)]$
$\sigma(e1)_{v \to t}$
$:= \lambda e_1[bark(e_1) \wedge \textbf{presProg}(e_1)]$

b. Funtor for Semantic role link applying to the two arguments in (a):
$\sigma(srlink)$
$:= [\lambda Q[\lambda P[P(x_1) \wedge Q(e_1) \wedge$
$\textbf{agent}(e, x)](\sigma(e_1))](\sigma(x_1))]$

By applying four λ-conversions to (13b), we obtain the same result as (12c). One noticeable problem with the functional application in λ-calculus is the placing of the arguments in the right order when the functor applies to them.

Rules 1^{sub} and 1^{eq}, subtypes of conjunctive composition, are needed when one of the inputs to links is treated as of some basic or pseudo basic type. Consider the same example (9) but with a different semantic treatment:[7]

(14) a. $\sigma(x1)_e := fido_e$
$\sigma(e1)_{v \to t}$
$:= \{e_1{:}v\}[bark(e_1) \wedge \mathbf{presProg}(e_1)]$

b. $\sigma(srlink3)$
$:= \{e_1{:}v\}$
$[\{\sigma(x1)_e, \sigma(e1)_{v \to t}\} \oplus^{sub}$
$\mathbf{agent}(e_1, x_1)_{(v \to t) \to (e \to t)}]$
$:= \{e_1{:}v\}$
$[\sigma(e1)_t \wedge \mathbf{agent}(e_1, fido)_t]$
$:= \{e_1{:}v\}$
$[[bark(e_1) \wedge \mathbf{presProg}(e_1)]_t \wedge$
$\mathbf{agent}(e_1, fido)]$

The substitution simply replaces some occurrences of a variable with something like a name *fido*.

The equation solving composition ($\oplus^{eq}$) also deals with basic types like names or measures. There is no substitution, but something like $fido_e$ turns into an equation that does not carry kinds of information other than what is stated, as shown in (15):

(15) a. $\sigma(x1)_e := \{x_1{:}e\}[x_1{=}fido_e]_t$

b. $\sigma(e1)_t$
$:= \{e_1{:}v\}[bark(e_1) \wedge \mathbf{presProg}(e_1)]$

c. $\sigma(srlink4)$
$:= \{x_1{:}e, e_1{:}v\}$
$[\{\sigma(x1)_e, \sigma(e_1)_t\} \oplus^{eq} \mathbf{agent}(e_1, x_1)_t]$
$:= \{x_1{:}e, e_1{:}v\}$
$[[\sigma(x_1) \wedge \sigma(e_1)_t] \wedge \mathbf{agent}(e_1, x_1)_t]$
$:= \{x_1{:}e, e_1{:}v\}$
$[[x_1{=}fido] \wedge [bark(e_1) \wedge \mathbf{presProg}(e_1)]_t \wedge$
$\mathbf{agent}(e_1, x_1)]$

d. $\sigma(a_9) := \sigma(srlink4)$

Now by the rule of substitution of identicals in FOL, we have:

(16) $\{e_1{:}v\}$
$[[bark(e_1) \wedge \mathbf{presProg}(e_1)] \wedge \mathbf{agent}(e_1, fido)]$

Unlike the equation solving approach proposed here, Kamp and Reyle (1993) represents names like Fido as $Fido(x)$ of type t in DRSs. This is acceptable but fails to apply the substitution of identicals. Note also that the equation solving approach can be extended to basic types other than entity type e.

Rule 2 Distributive Composition ($\oslash$):
$[\{A_\alpha, B_\beta\} \oslash C_{\beta \to (\alpha \to t)}] := [A'_t \to_c B'_t]_t,$
where $\to_c$ refers to an implication the type of which needs to be specified for each case and A' and B' are minimal modifications of A and B.

---

[7]In practice, the semantic treatment of names is much more complicated than treating it merely for its referential use. Kamp and Reyle (1993) treat names like "John" as a predicate, thus representing it as *John(x)* in a DRS.

The conjunctive operator $\oplus$ and its subtypes generate truth-functional conjunctions. In contrast, the distributive operator $\oslash$ possibly with its subtypes generates non-conjunctive relations of implication the type or meaning of which needs further analysis.

4.3. Additional Illustrations

Rule 1^{fa} Functional conjunctive composition with ($\oplus^{fa}$) applies to link structures that relate non-basic type entity structures. Consider example (17)

(17) a. John died$_{w3}$ last$_{w3}$ year$_{w4}$.

b. Annotation (id=a$_{17}$):
Entity structure:
$\mathbf{event}$(e1,w2, *pred*:die, *tense*:past)
$\mathbf{timex3}$(t1,w3-4, *type*:date, *value*:2019-XX-XX)
Link structure:
$\mathbf{tlink}$(e1,t1, isIncluded(e1,t1))

(18) a. Semantic form of entity structures:
$\sigma(e1) := \{e_1\}[die(e_1) \wedge \mathbf{past}(e_1)]$
$\sigma(t1) := \{t_1\}[year(t_1{,}2019)]$

b. Semantic form of temporal link structure:
$\sigma(tlink)$
$:= \{e_1, t_1\}[\{\sigma(e1)_{v \to t}, \sigma(t1)_{i \to t}\}$
$\oplus^{fa} \mathbf{occurs}(e_1, t_1)_{(i \to t)((v \to t) \to t)}]$
$:= \{e_1, t_1\}[[\sigma(e1)_t \wedge \sigma(t1)_t] \wedge \sigma(tlink)_t]$
$:= \{e_1, t_1\}[[die(e_1) \wedge \mathbf{past}(e_1)] \wedge year(t_1{,}2019)$
$\wedge \mathbf{occurs}(e_1, t_1)]$

c. Semantic form of annotation structure:
$\sigma(\mathbf{a}_{17})$
$:= \{e, t\}\sigma(tlink)$
$:= \{e, t\}[die(e) \wedge \mathbf{past}(e) \wedge year(t{,}2019)$
$\wedge\mathbf{occurs}(e, t)]$

Rule 1^{eq} Equation solving ($\oplus^{eq}$) applies to the annotation structures that contain names or other basic types. Consider an example taken from Pustejovsky et al. (2019) that introduce the semantics of ISO-Space.

(19) a. [$\mathbf{Gothenburg}_{pl1}$] is [$\mathbf{in}_{s1}$] [$\mathbf{Sweden}_{pl2}$].
b. [[Gothenburg]] = G, $<G{:}p \to t>$
c. [[Sweden]] = S, $<S{:}p \to t>$
d. [[in]] = $\lambda y \lambda x[in(x, y)]$, $<in{:}r \to (r \to t)>$
e. $in(G, S)$

The treatment of a spatial relation given in (19d,e) fails to indicate which location stands for x and which for y. In fact, one of the difficulties with λ-operation is where to place its arguments. Example (19) can be treated more explicitly with Rule 1^{eq} equation solving.

(20) a. $\sigma(pl1)_t := \{x\}[x{=}G]$, $<x{:}p \to t>$

b. $\sigma(pl2)_t := \{y\}[y{=}S]$, $<y{:}p \to t>$

c. $\sigma(\mathbf{qslink})_t$
$:= \{x, y\}[\{[x{=}G]_t, [y{=}S]\} \oplus^{eq} in(x, y)]$
$:= \{x, y\}[[[x{=}G]_t \wedge [y{=}S]_t] \wedge in(x, y)]$

With the rule of substitution of identicals, we then obtain the same result $in(G, S)$, as given in (19e).

Rule 2 Distributive composition with the operator $\oslash$ applies to subordination or quantification constructions. Consider example (21), called *equi-NP construction*.[8]

(21)   a. $\text{John}_{x1,w1}$ $\text{wants}_{e1,w2}$ to $\text{teach}_{e2,w4}$ on Monday.

         b.   Annotation (id = a_{21}):
            Entity structures:
            entity(x1, w1, *form*:John)
            event(e1, w2, *pred*:want, **theme**(e1,e2))
            event(e2, w4, *pred*:teach, **agent**(e2,x1))
            Subordination link structure:
            slink(e1, e2, modal)[9]

Pustejovsky et al. (2005) annotated the subordination relation between two events, $want(e_1)$ and $teach(e_2)$ as being *modal*. Montague Semantics, in contrast, treats it as a relation between the intensional predicate *want* and the property of teaching. However, the intensionality of the predicate *want* in the main clause requires Rule 2^i with an operator $\oslash^i$, a subtype of disjunctive composition for *intensional* cases like $\sigma(a_{21})$.

(22)   a.   Semantic forms of the entity structures:
$$\sigma(x1)_t := \{x_1\}[x_1{=}John]$$
$$\sigma(e1)_{\mathcal{E}}, \text{where } \mathcal{E}{=}(v \to t),$$
$$:= \{e_1, e_2\}[want(e_1) \wedge \textbf{theme}(e_1, e_2)]$$
$$\sigma(e2)_{e \to (\mathcal{E} \to t)}$$
$$:= \{x_1, e_2\}[teach(e_2) \wedge \textbf{agent}(e_2, x_1)]$$

         b.   Semantic form of the subordination link structure:
$$\sigma(slink)_t$$
$$:= \{x_1, e_1, e_2\}[\{\sigma(e_1)_{\mathcal{E}}, \sigma(e_2)_{e \to (\mathcal{E} \to t)}\} \oslash^i$$
$$(\sigma(e_1), \sigma(e_2))_{(e \to (\mathcal{E} \to t)) \to (\mathcal{E} \to t)}]$$
$$:= \{x_1, e_1, e_2\}[\sigma(e_1)_t \to^{int} \sigma(e_2)_t]$$
$$:= \{x_1, e_1, e_2\}[[want(e_1) \wedge \textbf{theme}(e_1, e_2)]$$
$$\to^i ([go(e_2) \wedge \textbf{agent}(e_2, x_1)])]$$

         c.   Semantic form of the whole annotation structure:
$$\sigma(a_{21}) := \sigma(slink)_t$$

The semantic form $\sigma(a_{21})$ shows that the predicate *want* has the event e_2 as its **theme** and that the **agent** of the predicate *go* in the subordinated complement is John. The non-Boolean connective $\to^{int}$ connects the semantic forms of the two components of the subordination construction (21) involving the *intensional* predicate *want*. The connective $\to^i$ needs to be defined as part of a model structure with a tentative definition as in (23):

(23)   Definition of $\to^{int}$ (tentative)
     Given a model M for a modal logic with a set W of possible worlds W that includes the actual world w_0 and an *intentional* world w_i accessible from w_0, and two semantic forms, ϕ and ψ, of type t,
$$[\![\phi \to^i \psi]\!]^{M,w_0}{=}1 \text{ iff}$$
$$[\![\psi]\!]^{M,w_i}{=}1 \text{ provided } [\![\phi]\!]^{M,w_0}{=}1.$$

This means that the eventuality of "teaching (on Monday)" is or becomes realized in the mind (intended world) of the experiencer *John* only.

---

[8] Annotation $\textbf{a}_{21}$ is simplified to focus on the subordination link (**slink**).

[9] This example is taken from Pustejovsky et al. (2005), p. 553.

5.   Model-theoretic Interpretation

5.1.   General

Semantic forms are subject to a model-theoretic interpretation. Each well-formed semantic form $\sigma(a)$ of an annotation structure $\mathbf{a}$ is interpreted with respect to a model M and an assignment g of values to variables. $[\![\sigma(\mathbf{a})]\!]^{M,g}$ is then understood as the interpretation or denotation of $\sigma(\mathbf{a})$. The structure of each model M depends on the kind of semantic annotation. For the interpretation of temporal annotation, for instance, a set of times T and a set of temporal relations such as the precedence relation $\prec$ over T become a part of its model structure. Furthermore, the construction of such a model is constrained by some possible uses or definitions of logical predicates, called *meaning postulates*, as is discussed in 5.2.1.

5.2.   Interpretation of unbound occurrences of variables

There may be some unbound occurrences of variables in well-formed semantic forms of *ABSr*. By Rule A.1 for Variable Registry, these variables may be either bound to the discourse referents registered before the semantic form of each of the substructures of an annotation structure or bound existentially when their scope is explicitly specified. Or else they can be interpreted with the assignment g as if they were bound existentially.

5.2.1.   Meaning Postulates as Constraints

ABS makes use of logical predicates as part of the (object) representation language to simplify the representation of semantic forms or make it flexible to accommodate different interpretations. These predicates, marked in boldface, in *ABSr* are defined possibly in terms of higher-order logic as part of the model structure.

The predicate **past** is, for instance, introduced to represent the tense of an event as in (24):

(24)   a. $[walk(e) \wedge \textbf{past}(e)]$

         b.   instead of $[walk(e) \wedge e \subseteq t \wedge t \prec n]$

as in Kamp and Reyle (1993, page 521). Then its definition is given in (25) as part of an interpretation model structure.

(25)   Truth Definition of Predicate **past**:
     Given an event e, a runtime function τ from events to times, a time t, and the present time n, as specified in a model structure M,
     $\textbf{past}(e)$ is true with respect to a model M if and only if $\tau(e) \subseteq t$ and $t \prec n$.

The predicate **past** may be defined differently to accommodate its deitic or situational use (see Partee (1973) or Quirk et al. (1985)).

Aspectual features such as *present perfect* and *progressive* are also encoded into annotations just as they are. Consider a case of the present perfect aspect in (26).

(26)   a.   Mia [has visited]$_{e1}$ Boston.

         b.   Annotation (id=a_{26}):
            event (e1, w2-3, *pred*:visit, *tense*:present,
                aspect: perfect)

c. Semantic Form:
$$\sigma(e1) := [visit(e_1) \wedge \mathbf{presPerfect}(e_1)]$$

Semantic form (26c) is then interpreted by the definition of **presPerfect** given as part of a model structure. Otherwise, its representation gets complicated similar to DRS, for instance. Here is an example from Cann et al. (2009).

(27) a. The plant has died.

b. $\{a, e, t, n, r, s, u\}$

$$e \subseteq t$$
$$t \leq n$$
$$r = n$$
$$\textit{Result-from'}(e, s)$$
$$s \bigcirc r$$
$$\textit{Die'}(e, u)$$
$$u = a$$
$$\textit{Plant'}(u)$$
$$\textit{Dead'}(s, u)$$

ABSr, in contrast, yields the following representation:

(28) a. The plant has died.

b. Annotation:
entity(x1, w2, *type*:plant)
event(e1, w4, *pred*:die, *tense*:present,
    aspect:perfct)
srlink(e1,x1, theme)

c. Semantic Forms:
$$\sigma(x_1) := plant(x_1)$$
$$\sigma(e_1) := [die(e_1) \wedge \mathbf{presPerfect}(e_1)]$$
$$\sigma(srlink)$$
$$:= [\{\sigma(x_1)_t, \sigma(e_1)_t\} \oplus^{bo} \mathbf{theme}(e_1, x_1)_t]$$
$$\sigma(26)$$
$$:= \{e, x\}[die(e) \wedge \mathbf{presPerfect}(e) \wedge$$
$$\mathbf{theme}(e, x)]$$

The interpretation of $\sigma(e_1)$ in (28c), for instance, requires the truth-conditional definition of **presPerfect**(e) that reflects those notions of the perfective aspect encoded in DRS (27b) above.

Furthermore, the proposed way of treating tense, aspect, and other complex predicates allows different interpretations or uses of them. Those predicates that constitute part of the representation language of semantic forms in *ABSr*, however, require truth-definitions or *meaning postulates* that constrain and define a set of admissible model structures (see Carnap (1947 1956; Montague (1974; Dowty (1979)).

6. Applications

6.1. Boolean Conjunctive Composition

ISO-Space (ISO, 2020) introduces the movement link (**movelink**) to annotate motions involving paths. The predicate **traverses** associated with motions is one of the logical predicates that need to be defined in the model structure of *ABS*. It can also be illustrated how the semantic forms involving motions and paths can be derived through Rule 1^{bo} Boolean conjunctive composition, as is demonstrated in (29).

(29) a. Marakbles:
Mia$_{x1,w1}$ arrived$_{m1,w2}$ $\emptyset_{ep1}$ in Boston$_{pl1,w4}$ yesterday.

b. Annotation (id=a$_{29}$):
Entity structures:
entity(x1,w1, *type*:person, *form*:nam)
motion(m1,w2, *pred*:arrive, *type*: transition,
    tense:past)
eventPath(ep1,∅, *start*:unspecified, *end*:pl1,
    trigger(m1,ep1))
place(pl1,w4, *type*:city, *form*:nam)
Movement link structure:
movelink(*figure*:x1, *ground*:ep1,
    relType:traverses)

Each markable is identified with an ID associated with its category and anchored to a word. Motions, as denoted by verbs like `arrive`, trigger a path, called *event-path*. This path is marked with a null category or non-consuming tag $\emptyset$ because it is not associated with any non-null string of words.

(30) a. Semantic forms of entity structures:
$$\sigma(x1)_t := [person(x_1) \wedge named(x_1, Mia)]$$
$$\sigma(m1)_t := [arrive(m_1) \wedge past(m_1)]$$
$$\sigma(ep1)_t := [start(\pi, \gamma(l_0)) \wedge end(\pi, l_1)$$
$$\wedge \mathbf{triggers}(m_1, \pi)]$$
$$\sigma(pl1)_t := [named(l_1, Boston) \wedge city(l_1)]$$

b. Semantic form of the movement link structure:
$$\sigma(movelink)$$
$$:= [\{\sigma(x1)_t, \sigma(ep1)_t\} \oplus^{bo} \mathbf{traverses}(x, \pi)_t]$$
$$:= [[[person(x_1) \wedge named(x_1, Mia)]$$
$$\wedge [start(\pi, \gamma(l_0)) \wedge end(\pi, l_1)$$
$$\wedge \mathbf{triggers}(m_1, \pi)]$$
$$\wedge [named(l_1, Boston) \wedge city(l_1)]]$$
$$\wedge \mathbf{traverses}(x, \pi)]$$

c. Annotation structure:
$$\sigma(a_{29})$$
$$:= \{x_1, \pi_1, l_0, l_1, m_1\}\sigma(movelink)$$
$$=: \{x, \pi, l_0, l_1, m\}$$
$$[[[person(x) \wedge named(x, Mia)]$$
$$\wedge [start(\pi, \gamma(l_0)) \wedge end(\pi, l_1)$$
$$\wedge \mathbf{triggers}(m, \pi)]$$
$$\wedge [named(l_1, Boston) \wedge city(l_1)]]$$
$$\wedge \mathbf{traverses}(x, \pi)]$$

All of the semantic forms that are derived through various links have been shown to undergo Rule 1^{bo} Boolean conjunctive composition only. This was illustrated with **srlink** for semantic role labeling, **tlink** for temporal anchoring, **qslink** for the location of regions, and **movelink** for the annotation of motions involving their movers and event-paths.

6.2. Distributive Composition for Conditionals

Besides its subtype $\oslash^{int}$ for intensional subordinate constructions, the distributive composition can have other subtypes. Here I introduce Rule 2^{imp} with the operator $\oslash^{imp}$ for the case of implication. The word *if* in English triggers a conditional sentence which is often interpreted as a truth-functional implication in Propositional Logic. Given two well-formed formulas ϕ and ψ, the conditional formula $[\phi \rightarrow \psi]$ is treated as a well-formed formula in Propositional Logic and interpreted truth-functionally as being false only if ϕ is true but ψ is false. Although the interpretation of conditionals in ordinary language is more complex than the truth-functional interpretation just given, (31) and (32) illustrate how *if*-constructions are annotated and how their semantic forms are represented in a tripartite structure.

(31) Data:

    If it rains tomorrow, then the picnic will be canceled.

(32) a. Annotation of Antecedent (id=a_{32a}):
    event($e1$, w3, *pred*: rain)
    timex3($t1$, w4, *type*:date, *value*:2020-02-04)
    tlink(tl1, $e1$, $t1$, isIncluded)

    b. Annotation of Consequent (id=a_{32b}):
    event($e2$, w7, *pred*: picnic)
    event($e3$, w10, *pred*: beCanceled, *tense*:future,
        theme:e2)
    timex3($t2$, $\emptyset$, *type*:date, *value*:unspecified)
    tlink(tl2, $e3$, $t2$, isIncluded)

    c. Subordination link:
    slink(*antecedent*:a1, *consequent*:a2, conditional)

Based on annotation (32), we obtain the semantic forms, as shown in (33):

(33) a. Semantic forms of antecedent:
$$\sigma(e1)_t := [rain(e1)_t]$$
$$\sigma(t1)_t := [date(t_1) = 2019\text{-}02\text{-}04]_t$$
$$\sigma(tl1)$$
$$:= [\{\sigma(e1)_t, \sigma(t1)_t\} \oplus^{(\ bo)} occurs(e_1, t_1)_t]$$
$$:= [[rain(e_1) \wedge date(t_1, 2019\text{-}02\text{-}04)]$$
$$\wedge occurs(e_1, t_1)]_t$$

    b. Semantic form of consequent:
$$\sigma(e2)_t := [picnic(e_2)]$$
$$\sigma(e3)_t := [beCanceled(e_3) \wedge theme(e_3, e_2)]$$
$$\sigma(t2)_t := \gamma(t_2)^{10}$$
$$\sigma(tl2)$$
$$:= [\{\sigma(e3)_t, \sigma(t2)_t\} \oplus^{bo} occurs(e_3, \gamma(t_2))_t]$$
$$:= [[[beCanceled(e_3) \wedge theme(e_3, e_2)]$$
$$\wedge \gamma(t_2)] \wedge occurs(e_3, \gamma(t_2))]_t$$

    c. Semantic form of conditional:
$$\sigma(slink)$$
$$:= [\{\sigma(tl_1)_t, \sigma(tl_2)_t\} \oslash^{imp}$$
$$implies(\sigma(tl_1), \sigma(tl_2))_{t \rightarrow (t \rightarrow t)}]$$
$$:= [\sigma(tl_1) \rightarrow \sigma(tl_2)]$$
$$:= [[rain(e_1) \wedge date(t_1, 2019\text{-}02\text{-}04)$$
$$\wedge \textbf{occurs}(e_1, t_1)]_t \rightarrow [[beCanceled(e_3)$$
$$\wedge theme(e_3, e_2) \wedge \textbf{future}(e_3)] \wedge \gamma(t_2)$$
$$\wedge \textbf{occurs}(e_3, \gamma(t_2))_t]]$$

$^{10}\gamma$ is a function that assigns a time to a deitic temporal expression or a contextually determinable unspecified time.

    d. $\sigma(a_{32b})$
$$:= \{e_1, e_2, e_3.t_1, \gamma(t2)\}\sigma(slink)$$
$$[[rain(e_1) \wedge date(t_1, 2019\text{-}02\text{-}04)$$
$$\wedge \textbf{occurs}(e_1, t_1)]_t \rightarrow [[beCanceled(e_3)$$
$$\wedge theme(e_3, e_2) \wedge \textbf{future}(e_3)] \wedge \gamma(t_2)$$
$$\wedge \textbf{occurs}(e_3, \gamma(t_2))_t]]$$

With respect to the operator $\oslash^{imp}$, the semantic form of the antecedent, $\sigma(tl1)$, is understood to be the restrictor R and that of the consequent, $\sigma(tl2)$, is the nuclear scope N, while the relation of implication between them is represented by the operator $\rightarrow$.

7. Comparison

7.1. Related Work

There have been several theoretical works showing how annotation structures can be interpreted and a variety of large-scale computational efforts to implement them for computational applications. Some of them are annotation-based semantics in one way or another.

Hobbs and Pustejovsky (2003) develop a semantics for TimeML (Pustejovsky et al., 2005), based on the OWL-time ontology. They provide a fine-grained way of annotating and interpreting various temporal relations. *ABS* is designed to accommodate the OWL-time ontology in defining its logical predicates related to temporal annotation.

Katz (2007) introduces a denotational semantics that directly interprets TimeML annotation structures represented in XML. The model structure proposed in Katz (2007) becomes part of the temporal model structure for *ABS*.

Bunt (2007) and Bunt (2011) introduce a semantics for semantic annotation. This eventually develops into a semantics based on the abstract syntax of a semantic annotation scheme. Bunt (2020a) and Bunt (2020b) have developed QuantML, a markup language for quantification, that can apply to the annotation and interpretation of a full-range of features related to quantification such as the definiteness, involvement or collectivity (distributivity) of entities or scope ambiguity involving quantifiers and eventualities.

Lee (2008) and Lee (2011) follow the OWL-time ontology and a compositional approach to work on temporal annotations with an extensive use of λ-operations. It shows some degree of complexity in the use of λ-operations when they are recursively embedded, for it requires to raise the order of variables as the embedding gets deeper.

One of the reasons for introducing *ABSr* is to avoid recursive embedding and substitutions (see Hausser (2015)). For now, *ABSr* has Rule 1^{sub} Substitutive conjunctive composition, but this should be deleted eventually except for the illustration of rudimentary annotations involving names and other basic types. Database Semantics (DBS) (Hausser, 2006) provides a theoretical foundation for the understanding of language analysis and generation without recursions and substitutions, but with the associative linear processing of language. This has motivated the design of *ABS* to some extent.

Then there are other types of semantics that present different ways of representing meaning in language. Banarescu et al. (2013) introduce AMR (the Abstract Meaning Representation) to represent the semantic roles mainly based on

PropBank in a logical format, PENNMAN format, or directed graph structure. He (2018) also introduces a way of annotating semantic roles, which is called *Shallow Semantics*, without relying on pre-defined syntactic structures but introducing syntax-independent span-based neural models or labelled span-graph networks (LSGNs).

Based on syntax-free annotations, *ABSr* is also syntax-independent. Its current representation format is strictly linear but needs to move onto a graphic mode for visual purposes. The composition rules of *ABSr* are constrained by type matching and also syntax-independent unlike Moens and Steedman (1988)'s categorial grammar or Kamp and Reyle (1993)'s DRSs. Dobnik et al. (2012) and Dobnik and Cooper (2017) introduce a type theory with records to constrain semantic representations and their manipulations in language processing. Their type system, especially related to spatial perception, will properly orient the spatio-temporal annotation of ISO-Space and meaning representation through *ABS*. The earlier work of Pustejovsky (2001) on type construction also lays a basis for the type theory of *ABS* for a finer-grained treatment of entities and eventualities.

For the computational applications of semantic annotations, the Gronigen Meaning Bank (GMB) (Bos et al., 2017) is very much related to the basic motivation of *ABS* in efforts to modify the classical version of DRT by making its syntax based on a (Montagovian) type systems consisting of two types, e and t, and by translating DRSs into a first-order logic only, for instance, while deleting so-called *duplex conditions* in DRSs. The basic design of the Parellel Meaning Bank (PMB) also adopts DRT as its formalism for meaning representation while adopting Combinatory Categorial Grammar as its syntax. Since it applies to multilingual annotation, *ABS* can make use of it when the ISO standards on semantic annotation are extended to multilingual annotations, especially for the purposes of multilingual translations.

Nevertheless, the theoretical framework of *ABS* and its representation language is conservative in practice, being essentially based on the λ-calculus and the graphic representation of Kamp and Reyle (1993)'s DRT. This will be shown in the ensuing Subsection 7.2.

7.2. Convertibility

The composition of semantic forms is constrained by their semantic types. These types simply reflect those in Montague semantics (Montague, 1974) and (Dowty et al., 1981) and also the extended type theory by Kracht (2002) and Pustejovsky et al. (2019), thus making all these semantic forms isomorphic to those λ-constructions in λ-calculus. If such a typing of the semantic forms of annotation structures is ignored or if each of the semantic forms is treated as being of type t, then these semantic forms can easily be converted to DRSs (Kamp and Reyle, 1993).

There is an option to choose a type-theoretic semantics or not. *ABS* allows both but prefers to choose a type-theoretic semantics to constrain its representation language *ABSr*, while enriching its interpretation model structure, as shown in Figure 2.[11]

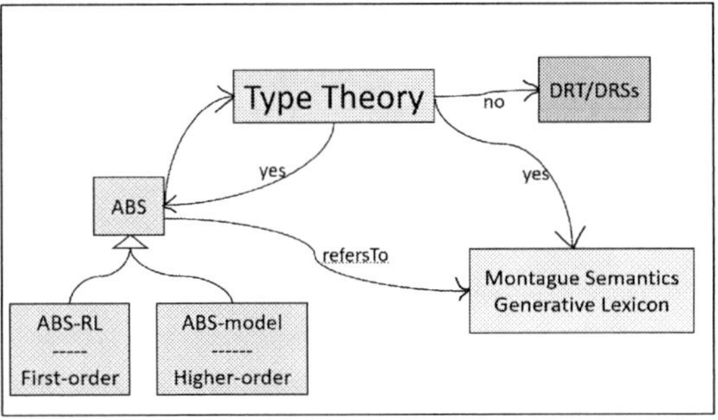

Figure 2: Options: Type-theoretic or Not

If a type theory is adopted, then the logical predicates can be defined in terms of type-theoretic higher-order logic. In *ABS*, the choice of a theory depends on the treatment of unbound variables and unspecified types. *ABS* treats logical forms with occurrences of unbound variables as well-formed semantic forms. Individual (or predicate) variables may occur unbound in well-formed semantic forms, as in the interval temporal logic of Pratt-Hartmann (2007).[12] Here is an example with a markable `"visited"`$_{e_1}$:

(34) a. Data:
Mia$_{x1}$ visited$_{e_1}$ Berlin, New York, [last year]$_{t1}$.

b. Annotation (id=a$_{5.unbound}$):
    Entity structures:
event(e1, m1, *pred*:visit, *tense*:past)
timex3(t1, m2, *type*:gYear, *value*:2019)
    Link structure:
tlink(e1, t1, isIncluded)

c. Semantic Forms:
$\sigma(e1)_\alpha := \{e_1\}[visit(e_1) \wedge past(e_1)]$
$\sigma(t1)_\beta := \{t_1\}[gYear=(t_1, 2019)]$
$\sigma(tlink)_\gamma$
$:= \{e_1, t_1\}[\{\sigma(e1), \sigma(t1)\} \bigcirc \mathbf{occurs}(e_1, t_1)]$

Each of the semantic forms in (34c) contains some variables which are registered in its preamble. In *ABSr*, these variables can be bound in two different ways, either by the existential quantifier or by the λ-operator. The assignment of a type to each semantic form depends on which way these (registered) variables are bound. The type of each semantic form is:

- Case 1: either of type t (truth-value carrying) as if the unbound variables were bound by the existential quantifier $\exists$:
i.e., $\exists\{e\}[visit(e) \wedge past(e)]$ (type t)

- Case 2: or of some functional type (predicate) as if the unbound variables were bound by the λ-operator:
i.e., $\lambda e[visit(e) \wedge past(e)]$ (type $v \rightarrow t$)

---

[11] Although Figure 2 indicates that DRT/DRSs are not based on

a type theory, the DRT formalism adopted by Bos et al. (2017) is based on a type theory.

[12] *ABS* has no predicate variables.

Depending on which case is chosen, the semantic form of a link like $\sigma(tlink)$ in (34c) undergoes a different rule of composition.

Case 1 allows the conversion of semantic forms in *ABS* to DRSs.

(35) Case 1:
Rule 1 Boolean conjunctive composition
a. $\sigma(tlink)$
$:= [\{\sigma(e_1)_t, \sigma(t_1)_t\} \oplus^{bo} occurs(e_1, t_1)_t]$
$:= \{e, t\}[[visit(e) \wedge past(e)] \wedge gYear(t, 2019) \wedge occurs(e, t)]$
b. $\sigma(a_{34}) = \sigma(tlink)$

As shown in (35), Case 1 Boolean conjunctive composition ($\oplus^{bo}$) can easily be converted to an equivalent DRS.

(36) Case 1 in DRS:

$e\ t$
visit(e)
past(e)
gYear(t,2019)
occurs(e,t)

Although the application of Rule 1^{bo} Boolean conjunctive composition is type-constrained, there is no such a constraint on the derivation of DRSs.

Case 2 allows the conversion of semantic forms in *ABSr* to well-formed forms in λ-calculus as in Montague Semantics (Montague, 1974). For the illustration of Case 2, consider example (34), as was just given:

(37) Case 2:
Rule 2 Functional conjunctive composition ($\oplus^{fa}$):
a. $\sigma(tlink)_t$
$:= [\{\sigma(e_1)_\mathcal{E}, \sigma(t_1)_I\} \oplus^{fa} occurs(e_1, t_1)_{I \to (\mathcal{E} \to t)}]$
$:= [[visit(e_1) \wedge past(e_1)] \wedge gYear(t_1, 2019) \wedge occurs(e_1, t_1)]$
b. $\sigma(a_{34}) = \sigma(tlink)_t$

The semantic form $\sigma(tlink)$ in (37) is treated of a functional type, $I \to (\mathcal{E} \to t)$, where I is $i \to t$ and $\mathcal{E}$ is $v \to t$. Then the semantic forms $\sigma(e1)$ and $\sigma(t1)$ are treated as arguments of $\sigma(tlink)$ such that they are of types $\mathcal{E}$ (set of eventuality descriptions) and I (set of time points), respectively.

In the process of the Boolean conjunctive composition, the unbound occurrences of the variables are anchored to the discourse referents e and t, as in DRS, or existentially quantified, while adjusting their variable names accordingly.

As for the case of the functional conjunctive composition, the whole process is understood as if all the semantic forms were subject to a series of λ-conversions as in (38):

(38) λ-operations:
a. $\sigma(e_1)_{v \to t} := \lambda e_1[visit(e_1) \wedge past(e_1)]$
b. $\sigma(t_1)_{i \to t} := \lambda t_1[gYear(t_1, 2019)]$
c. $\sigma(tlink)_t :=$
$\lambda T \lambda \mathcal{E} \exists\{e, t\}[\mathcal{E}(e) \wedge T(t) \wedge occurs(e, t)]$
$\qquad (\sigma(e_1))(\sigma(t_1))$
$:= \exists\{e, t\}[\sigma(e1)(e) \wedge \sigma(t1)(t)]$

$:= \exists\{e, t\}[[visit(e) \wedge past(e)] \wedge gYear(t, 2019) \wedge occurs(e, t)]$

It should again be stated that the derivation of semantic forms in *ABSr* does not undergo such λ-operations. The application of Rule 2 Functional conjunctive composition is only implicitly understood to undergo such operations. Unlike semantic forms that involve λ-operations, the application of the $\oplus^{fa}$ in *ABSr* does not introduce predicate variables of a higher-order, but individual variables of the first order only. This keeps *ABSr* to remain at the level of first-order.

8.   Concluding Remarks

As in other parts of ISO 24617 standards on semantic annotation, this paper has a gap in dealing with the semantics of entities and determiners that include generalized quantifiers. Specifically, this paper fails to fully accommodate the new developments on quantification that have been made by Bunt (2020a) and Bunt (2020b).

ABS aims to lighten the burden and possible complexity of generating semantic annotation structures. It would be an ideal situation if semantic annotation structures could have every piece of relevant semantic information encoded into them and be interpreted directly without relying on any intermediate auxiliary representation scheme. But the task of generating such annotation structures and interpreting them directly should easily run into enormous cost and complexity.

ABS is an annotation-based semantics that converts annotation structures to semantic forms for their (model-theoretic) interpretation. For the representation of these semantic forms, *ABS* provides a simple representation language, a type-theoretic first-order logic without the overuse of λ-operations. This language makes use of a small set of *logical* predicates, such as referring to semantic roles or event and time structures and types, that are defined as part of an interpretation model. The meta-language that defines these logical predicates may be of a higher-order logic.

To follow the principle of semantic compositionality, *ABS* introduces two types of composition with the conjunctive $\oplus$ and distributive $\oslash$ operators and their subtypes over the semantic forms of annotation structures that consist of entity and link structures. Most, if not all, of the link structures in ISO-TimeML and ISO-Space only require conjunctive composition, while quantificational, plural constructions or some subordinated constructions such as the *if-then* construction may undergo distributive (selective) composition.

There are two major types of conjunctive composition: the Boolean type $\oplus^{boo}$ and the functional type $\oplus^{fa}$. Then the functional type has two subtypes, one by substitution $\oplus^{sub}$ and the other by equation solving $\oplus^{eq}$. Annotation structures that are isomorphic to non-embedded structures in Kamp and Reyle (1993)'s DRSs are considered as undergoing the process of Boolean conjunctive composition. In contrast, those annotation structures that match λ-structures in Montague Semantics (Montague, 1974) undergo the functional conjunctive composition. This distinction is not very significant, for the semantic forms of most of the annotation structures undergo the process of Boolean conjunctive composition only.

This is the first version of *ABS*. It requires to be further tested against a variety of larger data and annotation structures. This should be the case especially for the distributive composition involving complex semantic structures.

9. Acknowledgements

Thanks to Jae-Woong Choe, Chongwon Park, and James Pustejovsky for their reading the preliminary draft with invaluable comments and to the four anonymous reviewers for their detailed constructive comments. I am very much indebted to Harry Bunt for his laborious work to help improve the final submission for publication. I thank them all, but do not claim that all these reviewers agree with my proposal or that I have fully succeeded in accommodating their comments and suggestions.

10. Bibliographical References

Allen, J. F. (1984). Towards a general theory of action and time. *Artifical Intelligence*, 23:123–54.

Banarescu, L., Bonial, C., Cai, S., Georgescu, M., Griffitt, K., Hermjakob, U., Knight, K., Koehn, P., Palmer, M., and Schenider, N. (2013). Abstract meaning representationf or sembanking. In *Proceedings of the 7th Linguistic Annotation Workshop and Interoperability with Discourse*, pages 178–186, Sofia, Bulgaria, August.

Bos, J., Basile, V., Evang, K., Venhuizen, N. J., and Bjerva, J. (2017). The Groningen Meaning Bank. In Nancy Ide et al., editors, *Handbook of Linguistic Annotation*, pages 463–496. Springer, Berlin.

Bunt, H. (2007). The semantics of semantic annotations. In *Proceedings of the 21st Pacific Asia Conference on Language, Information and Computation*, pages 13–28, Seoul, Korea. The Korea Society for Language and Information.

Bunt, H. (2010). A methodology for designing semantic annotation languages exploiting semantic-syntactic isomorphisms. In Alex C. Fang, et al., editors, *Proceedings of the Second International Conference on Global Interoperability for Language Resources (ICGL20100)*, pages 29–46, City University of Hong Kong, Hong Kong.

Bunt, H. (2011). Introducing abstract syntax + semantics in semantic annotation, and its consequences for the annotation of time and events. In Eunryoung Lee et al., editors, *Recent Trends in Language an Knowledge Processing*, pages 157–204. Hankookmunhwasa, Seoul.

Bunt, H. (2020a). Annotation of quantification: the current state of ISO 24617–12. In Harry Bunt, editor, *Proceedings of the 16th Joint ISO–ACL/SIGSEM Workshop on Interoperable Semantic Annotation*, pages 1–13, May. A satellite workshop at LREC 2020, May 11–15, 2020, Marseille, France (postponed due to COVID–19).

Bunt, H., (2020b). *Semantic Annotation of Quantification in Natural Language*. TiCC/Department of Cognitive Science and Artificial Intelligence, Tilburg University, Tilburg, 2nd edition, February. TiCC TR 2020-2.

Cann, R., Kempson, R., and Gregoromichelaki, E. (2009). *Semantics: An Introduction to Meaning in Language*. Cambridge University Press, Cambridge.

Carnap, R. (1947, 1956). *Meaning and Necessity: A Study in Semantics and Modal Logic*. The University of Chicago Press, Chicago, 2nd edition.

Copestake, A., Flickinger, D., Sag, I., and Pollard, C. (2005). Minimal recursion semantics: an introduction. *Journal of Research on Language and Computation*, pages 281–332.

Davidson, D. (1979). The logical form of action sentences. In N. Rescher, editor, *The Logic of Decision and Action*, pages 81–120, Pittsburgh. University of Pittsburgh Press. Reprinted in Davidson (2001).

Davidson, D. (2001). *Essays on Actions and Events*. Oxford University Press, Oxford, 2nd edition.

Dobnik, S. and Cooper, R. (2017). Interfacing language, spatial perception and cognition in type theory with records. *Journal of Language Modelling*, 5(2):273–301.

Dobnik, S., Cooper, R., and Larsson, S. (2012). Modelling language, action, and perception in type theory with records. In D. Duchier et al., editors, *Constraint Solving and Language Processing - 7th International Workshop on Constraint Solving and Language Processing, CSLP 2012*, Orelans, France, September. Revised Selected Papers, number 8114 in Publications on Logic, Language and Information (FoLLI), Springer, Berlin, Heidelberg, 2013.

Dowty, D. R., Wall, R. E., and Peters, S. (1981). *Introduction to Montague Semantics*. D. Reidel, Dordrecht.

Dowty, D. R. (1979). *Word Meaning and Montague Grammar: The Semantics of Verbs and Times in Generative Semantics and in Montague's PTQ*. D. Reidel, Dordrecht.

Gordon, A. S. and Hobbs, J. R. (2017). *A Formal Theory of Common Sense Psychology: How People Think People Think*. Cambridge University Press, Cambridge.

Hausser, R. (2006). *A Computational Model of Natural Language Communication: Interpretation, Inference, and Production in Database Semantics*. Springer, Berlin.

Hausser, R. (2015). From montague grammar to database semantics. *Language and Information*, 19(2):1–16. available at *lagrammar.net*.

He, L. (2018). *Annotating and Modeling Shallow Semantics Directly from Text*. Dissertation of doctor of philosophy in computer science and engineering, University of Washington.

Hobbs, J. and Pustejovsky, J. (2003). Annotating and reasoning about time and events. In *Proceedings of AAAI Spring Symposium on Logical Formalizations of Common Sense Reasoning*, Stanford, CA, March. Reprinted in Mani et al. (eds), 2005, pages 301-315.

ISO, (2012). *ISO 24617-1 Language resource management - Semantic annotation framework - Part 1: Time and events*. International Organization for Standardization, Geneva. Working group: ISO/TC 37/SC 4/WG 2 semantic annotation.

ISO, (2014). *ISO 24617-4 Language resource management - Semantic annotation framework - Part 4: Semantic roles (SemAF-SR)*. International Organization for Standardization, Geneva. Working group: ISO/TC 37/SC 4/WG 2 semantic annotation.

ISO, (2020). *ISO 24617-7 Language resource management - Semantic annotation framework - Part 7: Spatial information*. International Organization for Standardization, Geneva, 2nd edition. Working group: ISO/TC 37/SC 4/WG 2 semantic annotation.

Kamp, H. and Reyle, U. (1993). *From Discourse to Logic: Introduction to Modeltheoretic Semantics of Natural Language, Formal Logic and Discourse Representation Theory*. Kluwer Academic Publishers, Dordrecht.

Katz, G. (2007). Towards a denotational semantics for TimeML. In Frank Schilder, et al., editors, *Annotating, Extracting and Reasoning about Time and Events*, pages 88–106, Berlin. Springer.

Kracht, M. (2002). On the semantics of locatives. *Linguistics and Philosophy*, 25:157–232.

Lee, K., Pustejovsky, J., and Bunt, H. (2018). Revising ISO-Space and the role of the movement link. In Harry Bunt, editor, *Proceedings of the 14th Joint ACL–ISO Workshop on Interoperable Semantic Annotation (ISA-14): COLING 2018 Workshop*, pages 35–44, Santa Fe, New Mexico, U.S.A, August.

Lee, K. (1983). Equation solving. In Chungmin Lee et al., editors, *Language, Information and Computation*, pages 14–26. Taehaksa, Seoul.

Lee, K. (2008). Formal semantics for interpreting temporal annotation. In Piet van Sterkenburg, editor, *Unity and Diversity of Languages*, pages 97–108, Amsterdam. John Benjamins Publishing Co. Invited talk at the 18th Congress of Linguists, held in Seoul on July 21–26 2008.

Lee, K. (2011). A compositional interval semantics for temporal annotation. In Eunryoung Lee et al., editors, *Recent Trends in Language an Knowledge Processing*, pages 122–156. Hankookmunhwasa, Seoul.

Lee, K. (2016). An abstract syntax for ISO-Space with its `<moveLink>` reformulated. In Harry Bunt, editor, *Proceedings of the LREC 2016 Workshop ISA-12 – 12th Joint ACL-ISO Workshop on Interoperable Semantic Annotation*, pages 28–37, Portorož, Slovenia, May.

Lee, K. (2018). Revising ISO-Space for the semantic annotation of dynamic spatial information in language. *Language and Information*, 22.1:221–245.

Link, G. (1998). *Algebraic Semantics in Language and Philosophy*. CSLI Publications, Stanford, CA.

Mani, I. and Pustejovsky, J. (2012). *Interpreting Motion: Grounded Representations for Spatial Language*. Oxford University Press, Oxford.

Miller, R. and Shanahan, M. (1999). The event-calculus in classical logic — alternative axiomatizations. *Electronic Transactions on Artificial Intelligence*, 3(1):77–105.

Moens, M. and Steedman, M. (1988). Temporal ontology and temporal reference. *Computational Linguistics*, 14(2):15–28.

Montague, R. (1974). *Formal Philosophy: Selected Papers of Richard Montague*. Yale University Press, New Haven and London.

Parsons, T. (1990). *Events in the Semantics of English: A Study in Subatomic Semantics*. The MIT Press, Cambridge, MA.

Partee, B. H. (1973). Some structural analogies between tenses and pronouns in English. *The Journal of Philosophy*, 80(18):601–9. Reprinted in *Compositionality in Formal Semantics: Selected Papers by Barbara H. Partee*, Malden, MA: Blackwell. pp. 50–58.

Pratt-Hartmann, I. (2007). From TimeML to interval temporal logic. In Harry Bunt, editor, *Proceedings of the Seventh International Workshop on Computational Semantics*, pages 111–180, Tilburg, the Netherlands. Tilburg University.

Pustejovsky, J., Ingria, R., Saurí, R., o, J. C., Littman, J., Gaizauskas, R., Setzer, A., Katz, G., and Mani, I. (2005). The specification language TimeML. In James Pustejovsky Inderjeet Mani et al., editors, *The Language of Time*, pages 545–557. Oxford University Press, Oxford.

Pustejovsky, J., Lee, K., Bunt, H., and Romary, L. (2010). ISO-TimeML: An international standard for semantic annotation. In Harry Bunt, editor, *Proceedings of LREC 2010*, Valletta, Malta, May. LREC 2010.

Pustejovsky, J., Lee, K., and Bunt, H. (2019). The semantics of ISO-Space. In Harry Bunt, editor, *Proceedings of the 15th Joint ACL – ISO Workshop on Interoperable Semantic Annotation (ISA-15)*, pages 46–53, Gothenburg, Sweden, May. International Workshop on Computational Semantics (IWCS 2029).

Pustejovsky, J. (1995). *The Generative Lexicon*. The MIT Press, Cambridge, MA.

Pustejovsky, J. (2001). Type construction and the logic of concepts. In Pierrette Bouillon et al., editors, *The Language of Word Meaning*, pages 91–135. Cambridge University Press, Cambridge, UK.

Quirk, R., Greenbaum, S., Leech, G., and Svartvik, J. (1985). *A Comprehensive Grammar of the English Language*. Longman, London and New York, January.

Proceedings of the 16th Joint ACL-ISO Workshop Interoperable Semantic Annotation (ISA-16), pages 49–58
Language Resources and Evaluation Conference (LREC 2020), Marseille, 11–16 May 2020

Annotating Croatian Semantic Type Coercions in CROATPAS

Costanza Marini, Elisabetta Ježek
University of Pavia Department of Humanities
Corso Strada Nuova, 65, 27100 Pavia PV
costanza.marini93@gmail.com, jezek@unipv.it

Abstract
This short research paper presents the results of a corpus-based metonymy annotation exercise on a sample of 101 Croatian verb entries – corresponding to 457 patters and over 20,000 corpus lines – taken from CROATPAS (Marini & Ježek, 2019), a digital repository of verb argument structures manually annotated with Semantic Type labels on their argument slots following a methodology inspired by Corpus Pattern Analysis (Hanks, 2004 & 2013; Hanks & Pustejovsky, 2005). CROATPAS will be made available online in 2020. Semantic Type labelling is not only well-suited to annotate verbal polysemy, but also metonymic shifts in verb argument combinations, which in Generative Lexicon (Pustejovsky, 1995 & 1998; Pustejovsky & Ježek, 2008) are called Semantic Type coercions. From a sub lexical point of view, Semantic Type coercions can be considered as exploitations of one of the *qualia* roles of those Semantic Types which do not satisfy a verb's selectional requirements, but do not trigger a different verb sense. Overall, we were able to identify 62 different Semantic Type coercions linked to 1,052 metonymic corpus lines. In the future, we plan to compare our results with those from an equivalent study on Italian verbs (Romani, 2020) for a crosslinguistic analysis of metonymic shifts.

Keywords: Semantic Type coercion, Croatian, metonymy

1.   Introduction

If we look at the lexicon in its whole, it is possible to identify systematic alternations of meaning that apply not only to single lexical instances but entire classes of words, i.e. patterns of so-called *regular polysemy* (Apresjan, 1973). Some common alternations are *author/work*; *product/producer*; *event/food* or *container/content*.

When dealing with these alternations, however, it is necessary to distinguish between *metonymic* and *inherent polysemy*. In *metonymic shifts*, meaning is extended by conceptual contiguity and a change of referent is required, since one entity is used to denote another which is conceptually associated with it (Ježek, 2016: 59). This is the case, for instance, of the alternation *container/content*, exemplified by sentences such as "I would have eaten the whole fridge", where *fridge* actually stands for the food it contains.

In the case of *inherent polysemy*, on the other hand, there is no sense extension nor change of referent, but only one ontologically complex entity. This is the case, for instance, of alternations such as *information source/ artifact* as in "The book I am reading weighs one kilo" (Pustejovsky & Ježek, 2008: 185), where the lexical item *book* can be understood at the same time as the information it contains and a heavy object. The possibility for more than one of the senses of a complex entity to be activated simultaneously is called *co-predication* and is a prerogative of inherently polysemous words.

In this paper, we are going to present the first results of a metonymy annotation exercise on a sample of Croatian verbs taken from the Croatian Typed Predicate Argument Structures resource (CROATPAS, Marini & Ježek, 2019) (see section 2.1). Since the resource rests on Generative Lexicon Theory (Pustejovsky, 1995 & 1998; Pustejovsky & Ježek, 2008), metonymies are annotated and analysed as Semantic Type Coercions (see section 2.2). The set of semantic labels used for the annotation and the sample choice are covered in section 2.3 and 2.4, respectively.

2.   Methodology

2.1   The CROATPAS resource

CROATPAS (Marini & Ježek, 2019) – short for Croatian Typed Predicate Argument Structure resource – is a digital dictionary of Croatian verbs focusing on verbal polysemy, which is currently being developed at the University of Pavia[1] next to its Italian sister project TPAS (Ježek et al., 2014). CROATPAS consists in a repository of verb valency structures whose argument slots have been manually annotated with a set of semantic labels called Semantic Types (henceforth *SemTypes*), following a corpus-based lexicographic methodology inspired by Corpus Pattern Analysis (CPA, Hanks, 2004 & 2013; Hanks & Pustejovsky, 2005).

From a theoretical point of view, CPA rests on the Theory of Norms and Exploitations (TNE, Hanks 2004 & 2013), which differentiates between two types of word uses: conventional ones – the *norms* – and deviations from such norms – the *exploitations*. When applying CPA, lexicographers traditionally focus on identifying normal word usage by mapping standard meanings onto their syntagmatic patterns of use.

In CROATPAS, our CPA-inspired methodology consists in the following four steps: 1) sampling 250 random concordances from a representative corpus of Standard Croatian for each verb entry, namely the Croatian Web as Corpus (Ljubešić & Klubička, 2014); 2) manually disambiguating its different senses and 3) associating the right SemTypes to the argument slots found in each sense-bound valency structure. The fourth and last step is only possible thanks to our editing environment SKEMA, which is connected to the Croatian Web as Corpus through the *Sketch Engine* corpus management platform (Kilgarriff et al., 2014) and enables annotators to create *patterns* for each retrieved verb sense, such as the ones in Figure 1.

---

[1] Its first release will contain approximately 200 Croatian verb entries and will be accessible by 2020 on the website of University of Pavia: https://cla.unipv.it/?page_id=53723.

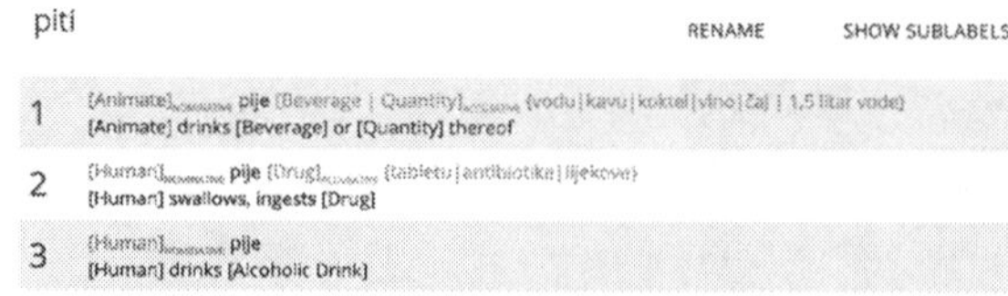

Figure 1: The first 3 patterns from the Croatian verb *piti* (English, *to drink*)

As you can see from the patterns above, the first sense of the Croatian verb *piti* (English, *to drink*) is the most obvious one, namely that of an [Animate] *drinking* a [Beverage]. However, if a [Human] is told to be drinking a [Drug] – such as a pill or antibiotics (Croatian, *tabletu* and *antibiotike*) – then he or she is simply *ingesting* or *swallowing* them. Finally, if we talk of a [Human] drinking (without specifying any direct object), he or she is by default *ingesting an alcoholic drink*.

2.2   Annotating Semantic Type Coercions

In addition to verbal polysemy, CROATPAS also allows lexicographers to annotate metonymic arguments by adding specific sub patterns to existing verb senses (see Figure 2).

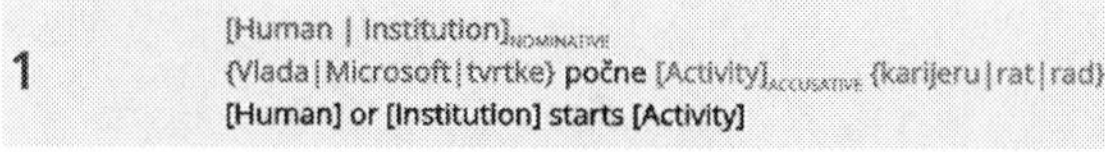

Figure 2: Pattern 1 and its metonymic sub pattern 1.1.m from the Croatian verb *početi* (English, *to begin*)

Despite involving the same verb sense as pattern 1, the metonymic sub pattern 1.1.m is linked only to those concordance lines where there is a mismatch in the SemType of the direct object: namely [Document] instead of [Activity]. This mismatch signals that a metonymic shift is taking place, which in Generative Lexicon Theory takes the name of Semantic Type coercion (Pustejovsky & Ježek, 2008; Ježek & Quochi, 2010). In order to explain this concept, let us look at a couple of sentences provided by Pustejovsky (1995: 115-6) starring a good translational equivalent of the Croatian verb *početi*, namely:

(1) *John began reading a book.*
(2) *John began a book.*

In sentence (1), the verb's second argument – i.e. *reading a book* – denotes an [Activity], whereas in sentences (2) it denotes a [Document] – *a book*. We call Semantic Type Coercion the compositional mechanism which enables us to reconstruct the semantics of the second direct object by forcing – i.e. *coercing* – [Document] into an [Activity] denotation. As pointed out by Ježek & Quochi (2010: 1465), coercion always involves an attested Source Type (e.g. [Document]) which is coerced into a Target Type to fit the verb's selectional requirements (e.g. [Activity]). The shift can involve any argument slot and is graphically represented as follows: [Document] → [Activity].

2.2.1   *Qualia* Exploitation

This being said, if we look at Semantic Type Coercions from a sub lexical point of view, they can be considered exploitations[2] of one of the available *qualia* roles associated with the Source Type not satisfying the verb's selectional requirements (Pustejovsky & Ježek, 2008: 195).

Qualia structure is one of the four levels of representation involved in the computational apparatus of Generative Lexicon (Pustejovsky, 1995 & 1998) and it consists of the four most important semantic properties of any lexical item: its Formal, Constitutive, Telic and Agentive *qualia*. The term *qualia* comes from Latin and is the plural of the word *quale*, which means "what kind?".

$$
\begin{bmatrix}
\text{sandwich(x)} \\
\text{CONST} = \{\text{bread,...}\} \\
\text{FORMAL} = \text{physform(x)} \\
\text{TELIC} = \text{eat(P,w,x)} \\
\text{AGENTIVE} = \text{make\_activity(z,x)}
\end{bmatrix}
$$

Figure 3: The *qualia* structure of the noun *sandwich* (Pustejovsky & Ježek, 2008: 185)

As we can see in Figure 3, the Constitutive *quale* consists of all the parts that make up the entity we are dealing with – in this case, the sandwich's ingredients. The Formal *quale* answers to the question "What sort of thing is this?" – in this case, a [Physical Entity]. The Telic *quale* – from the Greek word *télos*, i.e. *end* – expresses the function of the entity denoted by our lexical item – which, for a sandwich, is being eaten. Last but not least, the Agentive *quale* specifies the entity's origin.

If we look at the metonymic sub pattern 1.1.m from Figure 2 under this new light, the Semantic Type Coercion [Document] → [Activity] can be interpreted as an exploitation of either the Telic *quale* "reading" or the Agentive quale "writing", both associated with the qualia structure of any document, since we write so that others can read. It will be the broader context to assign the correct interpretation.

2.3   The System of Semantic Type labels

The list of SemTypes used in CROATPAS is taken from the Italian TPAS resource (Ježek et al., 2014) and belongs to the TPAS ontology (Ježek, 2019), a hierarchically organised set of labels originating from the Brandeis Shallow Ontology (Pustejovsky et al., 2004) currently containing 180 bracketed labels, such as [Human], [Document], and so forth.

Despite looking like ontological categories, SemTypes are semantic classes obtained by "manual clustering and generalization over sets of lexical items found in the argument positions" in valency structures taken from large corpora (Ježek et al, 2014: 891). They are thus able to mirror the way humans talk about entities, states and events through language.

According to Generative Lexicon, SemTypes can be divided into three groups depending on their internal structure:

---

[2] Be aware that term *exploitation* in this paper may refer to two different frameworks: in section 2.1 it falls within Hank's Theory of Norms and Exploitations, while in section 2.2.1 and 2.3 we generally use it in the expression "*qualia* exploitation", which pertains to Generative Lexicon terminology.

1) *Natural Types* referring to natural concepts characterised only by a Formal and a Constitutive *quale*, e.g. [Animal] or [Natural Landscape Feature];

2) *Artifactual* or *Tensor Types* denoting man-made entities usually possessing also a Telic and an Agentive *quale* to express their purpose and origin, e.g. [Beverage];

3) *Complex Types* characterised by multiple Semantic Types clustered together and normally used to denote inherently polysemous lexical items, e.g. [Institution].

If Tensor Types are characterised by an asymmetrical structure linking their head SemType to a component of its *qualia* structure, as in [Beverage ⊗ Telic Activity (*drinking*)], Complex Types are generally internally symmetrical, as in the case of [Institution = Human Group • Abstract Entity]. Since a dot is used to link together their components, Complex Types are also called Dot Objects.

Artifactual Types are those usually instantiating metonymic shifts via Qualia Exploitation whereas, Complex Types can either allow for *co-predication* or, when only one of their senses is used, for Dot Exploitation. Since differentiating between Qualia Exploitation and Dot Exploitation is not always clear-cut, the TPAS ontology (Ježek, 2019) keeps track of all acknowledged Complex Types by treating them as cases of *multiple inheritance*, i.e. by anchoring them to multiple positions within the SemType hierarchical system as in Figure 4, where [Institution] inherits from both [Abstract Entity] and [Human Group].

Figure 4: The top-level of the TPAS system (Ježek 2019)

2.4 Verb choice

The verb sample[3] we concentrated on for this metonymy annotation study consists of 44 Croatian aspectual verb pairs[4] and 13 biaspectual verbs taken from the CROATPAS resource (Marini & Ježek, 2019), for a total of 101 verb entries linked to 457 different patterns.

Half of the sample is made up of the Croatian translational equivalents of a sample of Italian verbs known to trigger Semantic Type Coercions, the so-called *coercive verbs* analysed by Ježek & Quochi (2010); while the other half are the Croatian translational equivalents of a selection of Italian verbs belonging to the language's fundamental vocabulary (FO), i.e. a group of 2,000 words with the highest frequency counts covering about 90% of all Italian written and spoken text (Chiari & De Mauro, 2014: 113). All Croatian translational equivalents were selected consulting the Zanichelli Italian/Croatian bilingual dictionary *Croato compatto* (Aleksandra Špikić, 2017).

3. Results

As a result of our metonymy annotation exercise, we were able to enrich the 457 patterns stored in CROATPAS adding 106 metonymic sub patterns. The metonymic corpus lines justifying these sub patterns are 1,052, a number which is already included in the over 22,000 annotated corpus lines currently linked to the resource.

Patterns	Sub patterns	Tagged corpus lines	Metonymic corpus lines
457	106	22,052	1,052

Table 1: Patterns, sub patterns and corpus lines

This being said, the Reader should keep in mind that the number of metonymic sub patterns does not equal the number of identified Semantic Type coercions (see Appendix 2 for the full inventory). Since different metonymic shifts can occur in the same pattern and even in the same argument slot, we decided to encode them – when possible – within the same sub pattern, as in Figure 5.

Figure 5: Pattern 1 from the verb *slušati* (English, *to listen*) and its metonymic sub pattern 1.1.m

As we can see above, 5 different Semantic Type coercions are nested within the same sub pattern, namely [Musical Composition] → [Sound], [Activity] → [Sound], [Human = Singer | Composer] → [Sound], [Human Group: Band] → [Sound] and [Sound Maker] → [Sound]. Each of them counts as an instance of the Semantic Type Coercion they stand for, which might have other instances in other sub patterns. All of the coercion instances above occur on the direct object slot of pattern 1 of the verb *slušati* (English, *to listen to*) and are justified by corpus examples such as

---

[3] See Appendix 1 for a complete list of all the CROATPAS verbs in our sample, together with their TPAS counterparts and English equivalents. In the Italian list, the verbs *sentire* and *guidare* appear twice because we decided to create entries for more than one of their Croatian translational equivalents, namely *čuti* (to hear) and *osjećati/osjetiti* (to feel) for the first, *voditi/provoditi* (to lead) and *voziti* (to drive) for the second. On the other hand, one of the verbs from the original list of Ježek & Quochi (2010) has not been taken into account because its Croatian translational equivalent was deemed too polysemous, namely *ići* (Italian, *recarsi*; English *to go*).

[4] Since Croatian is a Slavic language, we usually deal with verb pairs made up of a perfective and imperfective variant, for instance *piti/popiti* (imperfective/perfective - English, *to drink*). All variants are treated and annotated as independent verb entries, in order to collect corpus-based evidence to evaluate to what extent verb meaning depends on aspectual differences.

the ones in Figure 6. We are going to focus on the three highlighted ones.

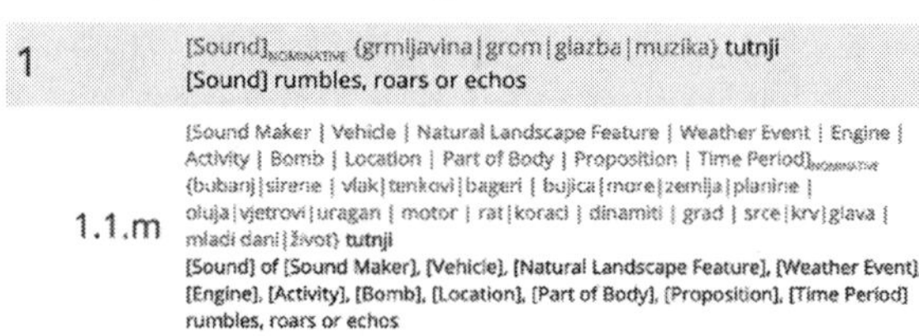

Figure 6: Corpus lines linked to sub pattern 1.1.m of the CROATPAS verb entry *slušati* (English, *to listen to*)

In the sentence *"U rodilištima bebe slušaju Mozarta i Vivaldija"* (English, *"In maternity wards, babies listen to Mozart and Vivaldi"*), we have two examples of the classic metonymy *author/work*, which in our framework translates to the Semantic Type coercion [Human = Composer] → [Sound]. The same applies to *"Slušam neki metal bend"* (English, *"I am listening to a certain metal band"*), where it is not the group but the music they play that is being listened to, thus giving rise to the coercion [Human Group: Band] → [Sound]. Finally, in *"Slušam korake izgubljenih ljubavnika"* (English, *"I listen to the footsteps of lost lovers"*), the direct object we should be "listening to" is *footsteps*, a lexical item that according to our ontology can be labelled as an [Activity]. However, it is only the [Sound] of said activity which can be heard, thus justifying the coercion [Activity] → [Sound].

3.1 The most frequent Semantic Type coercions

In our annotation exercise, we managed to identify a total of 179 Semantic Type coercions of 62 different kinds (see Appendix 2 for the full list). Table 2 portrays the 15 most frequent coercions in our inventory. Since we did not extract the number of corpus lines each Semantic Type coercion is exemplified by, the figures in the third column report the *coercion instances*, i.e. the amount of times each coercion appears in a different sub pattern or in a different argument slot within the same sub pattern.

Rank	Semantic Type Coercion	Coercion instances
1	Area > Human Group	25
2	Area > Institution	21
3	Area > Human Group: Football Team	6
4	Artifact > Activity	6
5	Business Enterprise > Road Vehicle	6
6	Musical Composition > Sound	6
7	Concept > Human Group	5
8	Sound Maker > Sound	5
9	Activity > Sound	4
10	Beverage > Activity	4
11	Building > Activity	4
12	Event > Location	4
13	Food > Activity	4
14	Bomb > Sound	4
15	Document > Activity	3

Table 2: Our 15 most frequent Semantic Type coercions

As we can see from the data, the most frequently annotated Semantic Type coercion in our sample happens to be [Area] → [Human Group], which makes up for 25 out of the 179 attested occurrences of our 62 different Semantic Type Coercions. As for the second and the third most frequent coercions, we can say that they not only share the same Source Type as the most frequent one, but their Target Types are also somewhat hierarchically related, since [Human Group] is one of the constituents of the Complex Type [Institution] and [Football Team] is a hyponym of [Human Group]. The metonymic sub pattern 2.1.m in Figure 7 encoding the Semantic Type coercion [Area] → [Human Group: Football Team] will give us an idea of how this specific coercion works.

<table>
<tr><td>2</td><td>[Human = Football Team]_{NOMINATIVE} ugosti [Human Group = Football Team]_{ACCUSATIVE} {reprezentaciju | američku skupinu}
[Human Group = Football Team] plays, in their home city or country, against other [Human Group = Football Team]</td></tr>
<tr><td>2.1.m</td><td>[Area]_{NOMINATIVE} {Zadar | Hrvatska} ugosti [Area]_{ACCUSATIVE} {Pulu | Srbiju}
[Human Group = Football Team] coming from [Area] plays, in their home city or country, against [Human Group = Football Team] coming from other [Area]</td></tr>
</table>

Figure 7: Pattern 2 and its metonymic sub pattern 2.1.m from the Croatian verb *ugostiti* (English, *to host*)

When saying a sentence like *"Hrvatska će ugostiti Srbiju u četvrtfinalu"* (which translates to *"Croatia will host Serbia for the quarter final"*), the SemType [Area] is coerced into a [Football Team], since what the speaker actually means is that the Croatian national team will play against the Serbian one, and not the respective geographical areas.

3.2 The most *coercive* Croatian verbs

The CROATPAS verbs giving rise to the most Semantic Type coercions are the following: *tutnjati* (English, *to rumble*) with 11 coercions to be traced back to only 2 observed patters; *odjekivati* (English, *to echo*) with 10 coercions and only 3 patterns; *okrenuti* (English, *to turn*) with 9 SemType coercions and 16 patterns, followed by both the perfective and imperfective variant of the Croatian equivalent of *to listen* – namely *slušati* and *poslušati* – both with 3 recorded senses and 9 metonymic sub patterns each.

Since after these first five verbs the number of SemType coercions drastically diminishes to 5 or less for the rest of the sample, it is not unreasonable to suggest that *verbs of hearing* are particularly well suited to trigger metonymic shifts within their valency structure. To give an idea of the mechanisms at play in these sound-focused coercions, take a look at Figure 8.

<table>
<tr><td>1</td><td>[Sound]_{NOMINATIVE} {grmljavina | grom | glazba | muzika} tutnji
[Sound] rumbles, roars or echos</td></tr>
<tr><td>1.1.m</td><td>[Sound Maker | Vehicle | Natural Landscape Feature | Weather Event | Engine | Activity | Bomb | Location | Part of Body | Proposition | Time Period]_{NOMINATIVE} {bubanj | sirene | vlak | tenkovi | bageri | bujica | more | zemlja | planine | oluja | vjetrovi | uragan | motor | rat | koraci | dinamiti | grad | srce | krv | glava | mladi dani | život} tutnji
[Sound] of [Sound Maker], [Vehicle], [Natural Landscape Feature], [Weather Event], [Engine], [Activity], [Bomb], [Location], [Part of Body], [Proposition], [Time Period] rumbles, roars or echos</td></tr>
</table>

Figure 8: Pattern 1 and its metonymic sub pattern 1.1.m from the Croatian verb *tutnjati* (English, *to rumble*)

As we can see, pattern 1.1.m lists all the SemTypes of the entities whose sound can rumble, roar or echo (e.g. [Vehicle], [Weather Event], [Engine], [Sound Maker]…) and provides also some particularly well-suited examples between square brackets, such as *vlak* (English, *train*), *oluja* (English, *storm*) and motor (English, *engine*). In all of these instances, a *qualia* role of the entity in object position is exploited and coerced into a [Sound], like in the case of *sirene* (English, *sirens*), whose Telic *quale* is "producing a sound".

3.3 Semantic Type coercions and clause roles

If we look at the clause roles where Semantic Type coercions take place (see Table 3), we can see that approximately half of the observed metonymic shifts take place in the subject slot, nearly 40% involves the verb's direct object and 14% indirect complements.

Argument slots	Coercion instances	Coercion %
Subject	85	47.5 %
Object	69	38.5 %
Indirect complements	25	14 %
Total	179	100 %

Table 3: Semantic Type Coercions by clause roles

Even though subjects, objects and indirect complements are not equally distributed across the verb sample, the percentages in Table 2 still demonstrate that all argument slots can be good candidates for metonymies to take place.

3.4 Source Types and Target Types

As previously mentioned, Semantic Type Coercions can also be analysed in terms of Source Type and Target Type (Ježek & Quochi: 2010). As we could have already guessed from the most coercive verbs mentioned in section 3.2, the most frequent Target Type is [Sound], which appears in 39 Semantic Type coercions instances out of 179. The second most frequent Target Type is [Human Group] (30 instances), followed by [Activity] (29) and [Institution] (20), which – if considered as a hyponym of [Human Group] – would actually cause the latter to become the most frequent Target Type overall.

As for Source Types, as it was to be expected from the data in Table 2, the most frequent Type is [Area], appearing in 53 coercion instances, followed by [Human] (16 instances) and both [Activity] and [Business Enterprise] at 11. Since [Event] – hypernym of [Activity] – is used as Source Type in 7 more Semantic Type coercions, it might be worth looking at an example. We are talking, for instance, of alternations like [Activity] → [Sound], which are triggered by words such as *korake* (English, *steps*) when used as direct objects of verbs such as *slušati* (English, *to listen*).

4. Conclusions

In this paper, we have presented the first results of a metonymy annotation exercise on a sample of 101 Croatian verb entries taken from the semantic resource CROATPAS (Marini & Ježek, 2019), a digital repository of verb argument structures manually annotated with Semantic Type labels on their argumental structure. At present, the resource contains 457 patterns and 106 metonymic sub patterns. The overall number of annotated corpus lines is 22,052, of which 1,052 are linked to the 106 metonymic sub patterns they provide evidence for. We explained the mechanism underlying how metonymy works in our chosen framework and provided an overview of the set of semantic labels we used, together with a clarification of our verb choice. Our results show that [Area] → [Human Group] proves to be our most frequent Semantic Type Coercion, appearing 25 out of 179 times. Sound verbs such

as *tutnjati* (English, *to rumble*), *odjekivati* (English, *to echo*) and *slušati/poslušati* (English, *to listen*) position themselves amongst the most coercive verbs in the sample: a result supported also by the fact that the most frequent Target Type, appearing in 39 coercion instances out of 179, is [Sound]. On the other hand, the most frequent Source Type is [Area], a finding which agrees with the data on the most frequent Semantic Type coercions overall. From a tentative analysis of clause role predisposition to Semantic Type Coercion, all argument slots seem to be able to enable the shift. In order to give a stronger claim to our results and evaluate the CROATPAS resource, we plan on involving other annotators and devise a task to measure the degree of Inter Annotator Agreement. Once evaluated, we believe that our inventory of manually annotated metonymic corpus lines could be used as training data to develop an automatic metonymy recognition method. Current on-going work is focussed on comparing our results with an equivalent annotation performed in the TPAS resource on the set of Italian verbs which corresponds to the first half of our Croatian sample (Romani, 2020). We expect this comparison to provide crosslinguistic insights on the linguistic and cognitive basis of metonymic shifts.

5. References

Apresjan, Y.D. (1973). Regular polysemy. In: *Linguistics*, 142, pp. 5-32.

Chiari, I. & De Mauro, T. (2014). The New Basic Vocabulary of Italian as a Linguistic Resource. In: *Proceedings of the 1st Italian Conference on Computational Linguistics (CLiC-it)*. Pisa, Italy.

Hanks, P. (2004). Corpus Pattern Analysis. In: *Proceedings of the 11th EURALEX International Congress*. Lorient, France.

Hanks, P. (2013). *Lexical Analysis: Norms and Exploitations*. Cambridge: The MIT Press.

Hanks, P. & Pustejovsky, J. (2005). A Pattern Dictionary for Natural Language Processing. In: *Revue française de linguistique appliquée*, 10 (2), pp. 63-82.

Ježek, E. (2016). *The lexicon: An introduction*. Oxford: Oxford University Press.

Ježek, E. (2019). Sweetening Ontologies Cont'd: Aligning bottom-up with top-down ontologies. In: *Proceedings of CREOL 2019*. Graz, Austria.

Ježek, E. & Quochi, V. (2010). Capturing Coercions in Texts: A First Annotation Exercise. In: *Proceedings of the 7th conference on International Language Resources and Evaluation (LREC)*. Valletta, Malta.

Ježek, E., Magnini, B., Feltracco, A., Bianchini, A., Popescu, O. (2014). T-PAS: A resource of Typed Predicate Argument Structures for linguistic analysis and semantic processing. In: *Proceedings of the 9th conference on International Language Resources and Evaluation (LREC)*. Reykjavik, Iceland.

N. Ljubešić & F. Klubička (2014). {bs, hr, sr} WaC – web corpora of Bosnian, Croatian and Serbian. In: *Proceedings of the 9th Web as Corpus Workshop*, pp. 29–35.

Kilgarriff, O., Baisa, V., Bušta, J., Jakubíček, M., Kovar, V., Michelfeit, J., Rychlý, P., Suchomel, V. (2014). The Sketch Engine: ten years on. In: *Lexicography 1(1)*, pp. 7-36.

Marini, C. & Ježek, E. (2019) CROATPAS: A Resource of Corpus-derived Typed Predicate Argument Structures for Croatian. In: *Proceedings of the 6th Italian Conference on Computational Linguistics (CLiC-it)*. Bari, Italy.

Pustejovsky, J. (1995). *The Generative Lexicon*. Cambridge: The MIT Press.

Pustejovsky, J. (1998). The semantics of lexical underspecification. In: *Folia Linguistica* 32.

Pustejovsky, J. & Ježek, E. (2008). Semantic Coercion in Language: Beyond Distributional Analysis. In: *Italian Journal of Linguistics*, vol. 20, pp. 181-214.

Romani, E. (2020). *Searching for Metonymies in Natural Language Text. A corpus-based study on a resource for Italian for Verbs*. BA Thesis, University of Pavia.

Špikić, A. (2017). *Croato compatto: dizionario croato/italiano e italiano/croato*, Zanichelli: Bologna.

Appendix 1:

The Croatian verb entries from CROATPAS used for our Semantic Type Coercion exercise[5]

	CROATPAS	TPAS	English translations
1	bacati/baciti	lanciare	to throw
2	čitati/pročitati	leggere	to read
3	čuti	sentire*	to hear
4	čuvati/očuvati	conservare	to preserve
5	dirati/dirnuti	toccare	to touch
6	djelovati	agire	to act
7	dočekivati/dočekati	accogliere	to welcome
8	dolaziti/doći	arrivare	to arrive
9	dovršavati/dovršiti	completare	to complete
10	gostiti/ugostiti	ospitare	to accommodate
11	informirati	informare	to inform
12	isključivati/isključiti	escludere	to exclude
13	jesti/pojesti	mangiare	to eat
14	kontaktirati	contattare	to contact
15	kriti/sakriti	nascondere	to hide
16	liječiti/izliječiti	curare	to heal
17	napredovati	avanzare	to advance
18	obavještavati/obavijestiti	avvisare	to apprise
19	objašnjavati/objasniti	precisare	to specify
20	objavljivati/objaviti	annunciare	to announce
21	odjekivati/odjeknuti	echeggiare	to echo
22	okretati/okrenuti	girare	to turn
23	organizirati	organizzare	to organise
24	osjećati/osjetiti	sentire*	to feel
25	osnovati/osnivati	fondare	to found
26	padati/pasti	cadere	to fall
27	parkirati	parcheggiare	to park
28	piti/popiti	bere	to drink
29	početi/započeti	cominciare	to commence
30	podvrgnuti	sottoporre	to submit

---

[5] Verbs marked by an asterisk (*) appear twice.

31	pokušavati/pokušati	tentare	to try
32	posjećivati/posjetiti	visitare	to visit
33	posuđivati/posuditi	prestare	to lend
34	preferirati	preferire	to prefer
35	prekidati/prekinuti	interrompere	to interrupt
36	preporučivati/preporučiti	consigliare	to advise
37	približavati/približiti	avvicinare	to approach
38	pripadati/pripasti	appartenere	to belong
39	raditi/uraditi	funzionare	to work
40	rezervirati	riservare	to book
41	slijetati/sletjeti	atterrare	to land
42	slušati/poslušati	ascoltare	to listen
43	snimati/snimiti	riprendere	to shoot
44	spasavati/spasiti	salvare	to save
45	stizati/stići	raggiungere	to reach
46	tutnjati	rimbombare	to rumble
47	tužiti/optužiti	accusare	to accuse
48	ubijati/ubiti	uccidere	to kill
49	ujedinjavati/ujediniti	unire	to unite
50	upravljati	dirigere	to manage
51	uzlaziti/uzaći	salire	to rise
52	voditi/provoditi	guidare*	to lead
53	voziti	guidare*	to drive
54	zaključivati/zaključiti	concludere	to conclude
55	završavati/završiti	finire	to finish
56	žderati/požderati	divorare	to devour
57	zvati/pozvati	chiamare	to call

Appendix 2:

The complete list of the Semantic Type Coercions resulting from our annotation exercise[6]

Rank	Semantic Type Coercion	Raw frequency
1	Area > Human Group	25
2	Area > Institution	21
3	Area > Human Group: Football Team	6
4	Artifact > Activity	6
5	Business Enterprise > Road Vehicle	6
6	Musical Composition > Sound	6
7	Concept > Human Group	5
8	Sound Maker > Sound	5
9	Activity > Sound	4
10	Beverage > Activity	4
11	Building > Activity	4
12	Event > Location	4
13	Food > Activity	4
14	Bomb > Sound	3
15	Document > Activity	3
16	Document > Narrative	3
17	Event > Sound	3
18	Activity > Food	2
19	Activity > Information	2
20	Activity > Location	2
21	Artwork > Activity	2
22	Business Enterprise > Flying Vehicle	2
23	Business Enterprise > Location	2
24	Container > Beverage	2
25	Engine > Sound	2
26	Flying Vehicle > Human	2
27	Food > Flavour	2
28	Human > Document	2

[6] The Coercions ranked 58 (*srce* > Sound) and 59 (*suze* | *smijeh* | *smiješak* > Emotion) do not have a proper Source Types but only source lexical items due to the fact that they belong to idiomatic patterns. In the first case, *srce* (English, *heart*) can be coerced into a sound since hearts usually have a heartbeat. As for the second case, although the words *suze* (English, *tears*), *smijeh* (English, *laughter*) and *smiješak* (English, *smile*) are all coerced into the emotions they typically represent, they cannot be grouped into a shared SemType since some of them are [Physical Entities] (e.g. *suze*), while others are [Activities] (e.g. *smijeh* and *smiješak*).

29	Human > Flying Vehicle	2
30	Human > Information	2
31	Human > Information: Advice	2
32	Human > Road Vehicle	2
33	Human > Sound	2
34	Human > Speech Act	2
35	Human Group > Sound	2
36	Part of Language > Sound	2
37	Physical Entity > Activity	2
38	Proposition > Sound	2
39	Route > Activity	2
40	Activity > Asset: Victory	1
41	Area > Activity: Car Race	1
42	Asset > Money Value	1
43	Business Enterprise > Food	1
44	Container > Food	1
45	Deity > Information: Advice	1
46	Device > Asset	1
47	Human > Musical Composition	1
48	Human > Part of Language	1
49	Institution > Money Value	1
50	Location > Activity	1
51	Location > Sound	1
52	Metal > Asset: Award	1
53	Musical Instrument > Sound	1
54	Natural Landscape Feature > Sound	1
55	Part of Body > Sound	1
56	Part of Language > Activity	1
57	Physical Entity > Smell	1
58	*srce* > Sound	1
59	*suze	smijeh	smiješak* > Emotion	1
60	Time Period > Sound	1
61	Vehicle > Sound	1
62	Weather Event > Sound	1

Proceedings of the 16th Joint ACL-ISO Workshop Interoperable Semantic Annotation (ISA-16), pages 59–66
Language Resources and Evaluation Conference (LREC 2020), Marseille, 11–16 May 2020
© European Language Resources Association (ELRA), licensed under CC-BY-NC

A Consolidated Dataset for Knowledge-based Question Generation using Predicate Mapping of Linked Data

Johanna Melly[*]

Cortexia S.A.
Route de Vevey 105a
1618 Châtel-Saint-Denis
Switzerland
johanna@melly.me

Gabriel Luthier

HEIG-VD / HES-SO
Route de Cheseaux 1, CP 521
1401 Yverdon-les-Bains
Switzerland
gabriel.luthier@heig-vd.ch

Andrei Popescu-Belis

HEIG-VD / HES-SO
Route de Cheseaux 1, CP 521
1401 Yverdon-les-Bains
Switzerland
andrei.popescu-belis@heig-vd.ch

Abstract

In this paper, we present the ForwardQuestions data set, made of human-generated questions related to knowledge triples. This data set results from the conversion and merger of the existing SimpleDBPediaQA and SimpleQuestionsWikidata data sets, including the mapping of predicates from DBPedia to Wikidata, and the selection of 'forward' questions as opposed to 'backward' ones. The new data set can be used to generate novel questions given an unseen Wikidata triple, by replacing the subjects of existing questions with the new one and then selecting the best candidate questions using semantic and syntactic criteria. Evaluation results indicate that the question generation method using ForwardQuestions improves the quality of questions by about 20% with respect to a baseline not using ranking criteria.

Keywords: Question generation, linked data, knowledge triples, semantic mapping.

1. Introduction

Question generation from linked data is a promising approach for producing large corpora of questions and answers. A primary use of these corpora is for training and evaluating question answering systems (Duan et al., 2017), while other uses are for education (Pham et al., 2018), tutoring (Su et al., 2019), or entertainment. Automatic question generation can be based on texts or on large repositories of linked data. In the latter case, an initial set of human-generated questions is often necessary to generate new ones, but such data sets are strongly related to specific linked data formats, and are difficult to port to new repositories.

In this paper, we present the ForwardQuestions corpus of human-generated questions associated to knowledge triples from the Wikidata knowledge base. We constructed this corpus by converting and merging two partially overlapping corpora of questions, SimpleDBPediaQA and SimpleQuestionsWikidata, which were separately derived from subsets of the SimpleQuestions corpus. These three data sets are respectively based on DBpedia, Wikidata and Freebase, but the latter resource is no longer available.

Specifically, we enriched SimpleQuestionsWikidata with a substantial number of questions from SimpleDBPediaQA, by converting DBpedia predicates to Wikidata ones and keeping only the 'forward' questions, given our final goal of quiz generation.[1] The overlap between these two resources is only of 32%, showing that the resulting data set has considerable novelty. As a result, we make available,

under the Creative Commons Attribution license (BY), the ForwardQuestions corpus of 38k questions related to 94 different Wikidata predicates.[2]

Furthermore, we show how ForwardQuestions can be used to generate new questions from previously unseen triples, by replacing the subjects of existing questions with new ones, and then ranking candidate questions on semantic and syntactic criteria. The questions can be used, for instance, in a chatbot that generates quizzes on any topic indicated by a user, thanks to a strategy for selecting relevant triples from Wikidata. The evaluation results with human subjects who rate the quality of the questions show that the best questions generated by our method reach about 80% approval, of which 10 points are due to the question ranking method.

The paper is organized as follows. In Section 2, we review related work and present the SimpleQuestions, SimpleDBpediaQA and SimpleQuestionsWikidata resources. In Section 3 we explain how the latter two data sets were converted and merged into the new ForwardQuestions data set. In Section 4, we describe our template-based question generation method and the semantic and syntactic ranking strategies, used in a chatbot presented briefly in Section 5. In Section 6, we define the evaluation protocol and quantify the improvements brought by our resource and question generation method.

2. Relation to Previous Work

Question answering (QA) has been extensively researched in the past. Many methods use textual documents to find answers, while others consider knowledge bases, such as large sets of knowledge triples (*subject, predicate, object*). QA over knowledge bases requires data sets with questions and their answers, for training and evaluation. For instance, the data sets used for the QALD evaluations (Unger et al., 2016) typically include hundreds of questions, most

---

[*]Work conducted while the first author was at HEIG-VD.

[1] 'Forward' questions are those bearing on the object of a (*subject, predicate, object*) triple. They typically have smaller sets of correct answers than 'backward' questions (see 2.2 and 3.2). Note that 'subject' and 'object' refer to the entities appearing in first and third position in the triples, but depending on how the predicate is expressed in a sentence, their grammatical functions can be reversed.

[2] github.com/johannamelly/ForwardQuestions.

of which can be answered based on a single triple, while others require a combination of triples.

In the past, triple stores such as Freebase (with around 40 million entities) or DBpedia (an order of magnitude smaller) have been used to design QA systems (Bast and Haussmann, 2015). The termination of the Freebase repository raised the question of resource conversion to DBpedia, or to the more recent Wikidata triple store,[3] which is a knowledge graph derived from Wikipedia infoboxes and allows data querying with SPARQL (Malyshev et al., 2018). The main challenge remains however the generation of questions from triples, which is a costly process that has been partially automated in the past, as we briefly review hereafter.

2.1. Automatic Question Generation

Existing methods for question generation start either from textual data or from knowledge triples. Heilman and Smith (2010) defined rules for syntactic transformation of declarative sentences into questions, which were then ranked by a logistic regression model, reaching an acceptance rate of about 50% for the 20% top-ranked questions. Chali and Hasan (2015) used named entity and predicate-argument information to generate questions, but evaluated them only automatically. They used LDA to estimate topic relevance, and syntactic tree kernels for grammaticality judgments. A rule-based approach to generate questions from relative subordinate sentences extracted from Wikipedia was proposed by Khullar et al. (2018). This method generated better questions than Heilman and Smith, but relied crucially on the availability of relative pronouns and adverbs.

More recent models attempt to generate questions from sentences using deep neural networks, e.g. starting from a sentence and the intended answer word (Sun et al., 2018; Zhao et al., 2018). Currently, their accuracy on long sentences such as those from Wikipedia is sufficient for quiz generation, especially since they were only evaluated by quantitative comparisons to the SQuAD data set (Rajpurkar et al., 2016)). Recent improvements aim at predicting the question type from the answer and then add this prediction to the neural generator (Zhou et al., 2019).

Serban et al. (2016) proposed two methods for question generation from Freebase. The neural network approach used TransE multi-relational embeddings (Bordes et al., 2013) and leveraged conditional language generation models. They generated a corpus of 30 million questions based on Freebase triples, which were evaluated with the BLEU metric and partly with human judges. Their template-based baseline model scored only slightly below, but is applicable also when TransE embeddings are not available – hence, it is the starting point of our present proposal.

2.2. Human-generated Questions from Triples

The SimpleQuestions dataset (Bordes et al., 2015)[4] features 108,442 questions in English obtained through a crowdsourcing platform. Each question is accompanied by the knowledge triple from Freebase on which it is based, which

also provides its answer. For instance, one question is "What does Jimmy Neutron do?", and the triple ('Jimmy Neutron', 'fictional character occupation', 'inventor') indicates that the answer is "inventor".

An important distinction introduced by SimpleQuestions, coming from the observation of human-generated questions, is between forward and backward questions. A forward question bears on the object of a triple, while a backward one bears on its subject, and is often formulated using passive voice. For instance, from the triple ('The Dishwasher: Dead Samurai', 'publisher', 'Xbox Game Studios'), someone generated the question "What company published The Dishwasher: Dead Samurai?", which is a forward one. However, from the triple ('Rampage', 'publisher', 'Midway Games'), someone wrote the question "What game is published by Midway Games?", which is a backward one. One reason to consider this distinction is that predicates do not appear in both active and passive forms in the triple store, so questions are allowed to bear on the subject or or object of a triple.

Due to the termination of Freebase, the triples of a subset of questions from SimpleQuestions have been converted to DBpedia triples, resulting in the SimpleDBpediaQA data set (Azmy et al., 2018).[5] Two formatted questions from this data set are presented in Table 1. 'Query' is the original question formulated over a Freebase triple, whose former predicate URL is given under 'Freebase Predicate'. 'Subject' points to the URL of the concept on DBpedia. There are three subfields under 'predicate list': the DBpedia URL of the predicate, the direction of the question (forward or backward), and a constraint on the expected answer type for backward questions.

A subset of SimpleQuestions different from the one above has been converted to Wikidata triples, resulting in the SimpleQuestionsWikidata set (Diefenbach et al., 2017).[6] The resource is available as a text document, formatted as shown in Table 2. Each line has four tab-separated fields, containing the Wikidata identifier of the triple's subject, predicate, and object, and the question itself. The predicates of forward questions have Wikidata identifiers prefixed with 'P', e.g. 'P413' refers to the Wikidata property at `www.wikidata.org/wiki/Property:P413` with the English label "position played on team / speciality". Backward questions are indicated by predicates whose initial letter was changed from 'P' to 'R', as in the third example from Table 2, where 'R509' indicates the fact that the 'P509' property ("cause of death", `www.wikidata.org/wiki/Property:P509`) holds between the object and the subject and not vice-versa, and that the actual triple in Wikidata is (Q6371569, R509, Q12152), "Karl Anton Rickenbacher died of myocardial infarction."

Finally, a smaller set of about 700 questions collected from users over Wikidata triples is also available as the WDAquaCore0Wikidata set (Diefenbach et al., 2017).[7]

ID	00035
Query	what is the place of birth of sam edwards?
Subject	`http://dbpedia.org/resource/Sam_Edwards_(physicist)`
Freebase Predicate	`www.freebase.com/people/person/place_of_birth`
Predicate List	
Predicate	`http://dbpedia.org/ontology/birthPlace`
Direction	forward
Constraint	null
ID	00042
Query	which home is an example of italianate architecture?
Subject	`http://dbpedia.org/resource/Italianate_architecture`
Freebase Predicate	`www.freebase.com/architecture/architectural_style/examples`
Predicate List	
Predicate	`http://dbpedia.org/ontology/architecturalStyle`
Direction	backward
Constraint	`http://dbpedia.org/ontology/ArchitecturalStructure`

Table 1: Examples of SimpleDBpediaQA entries: a forward and a backward question.

Subject	Pred.	Object	Question
Q2747238	P413	Q5059480	what position does carlos gomez play?
Q1176417	P136	Q37073	what type of music does david ruffin play
Q12152	R509	Q6371569	which swiss conductor's cause of death is myocardial infarction?

Table 2: Examples of SimpleWikidataQA entries.

2.3. Comparison of SimpleDBpediaQA and SimpleQuestionsWikidata

From the 108,442 entries in SimpleQuestions, 43,086 were included in SimpleDBpediaQA, while 49,202 were included in SimpleQuestionsWikidata. There is therefore a potential to select more of the original questions for inclusion in ForwardQuestions.

Questions in SimpleDBpediaQA are not accompanied by the object of their triple, which means that their correct answer cannot be verified directly from the data set, unlike those from SimpleQuestionsWikidata, as it appears when comparing Table 1 with Table 2. This is not a major problem, nevertheless, because: (1) in general, the correct answer may not be unique even if the question is based on a single triple (e.g. "who are the children of Barack Obama?"), so the underlying triple store is still needed to verify the answer; (2) for our intended use, the questions from the database are only used as templates to generate new questions from new triples (see Section 4), therefore the objects of the original triples are never needed.

Qualitatively, the questions in SimpleDBpediaQA cover a smaller range of predicates than those in SimpleQuestions-Wikidata, and contain fewer questions per triple. The latter set uses Wikidata predicates, which are often more fine-grained than the DBpedia ones (for instance distinguishing 'father' and 'mother' where DBpedia has only 'parent'). Another qualitative observation is that SimpleDBpediaQA contains a somewhat larger proportion of triples that are not useful for question generation, as they correspond to various numeric identifiers of entities in 3rd party repositories.

3. The ForwardQuestions Data Set

3.1. Motivation for ForwardQuestions

DBpedia or Wikidata triples represent only small subsets of the knowledge embodied in Wikipedia, which is why it may seem that generating questions directly from Wikipedia sentences could lead to more varied questions (Heilman and Smith, 2010; Chali and Hasan, 2015). However, our pilot experiments in this direction pointed to strong limitations. For instance, we considered identifying patterns such as *verb + named entity* in sentences from Wikipedia, and then reversing them to build a question, e.g. from "World War II ended in 1945" we aimed to derive "When did World War II end?" However, several difficulties appeared: (1) the VB+NE pattern also applies to relative clauses (e.g. "Billie Joe Armstrong took two years to write American Idiot") from which questions cannot be easily generated; (2) the interrogative word is hard to predict; (3) pronouns lead to unintelligible questions; (4) answers should not be limited to named entities.

Therefore, we turned to the use of knowledge triples, following the template-based baseline proposed by Serban et al. (2016). Triples enable a straightforward generation method: transform the triple (*subject, predicate, object*) into a question bearing on the 'predicate' property of the 'subject', knowing that 'object' one of the correct answers. For instance, from ('Harry Potter', 'mother', 'Lily Potter') one can construct "Who is the mother of Harry Potter?". Note that 'subject' and 'object' do not necessarily have these grammatical functions in the sentence from which the triple was generated, as these functions depend on the form of the predicate. In the above example, the natural formulation "Lily Potter is the mother of Harry Potter" actually reverses these roles.

It appeared however that, in general, the specific wordings describing the subject, the predicate, and the expected type of answer are difficult to generate correctly. For instance, from ('Harry Potter', 'composer', 'John Williams'), the derived question "Who is the composer of Harry Potter?" is incorrectly formulated – a correct version is "Which composer wrote the music for the film Harry Potter?". This is why we use template-based generation from questions written by humans in the ForwardQuestions data set.

3.2. Construction of the Data Set

SimpleDBpediaQA and SimpleQuestionsWikidata are both subsets of SimpleQuestions. Hence, they have a certain amount of overlapping questions, but also some that are specific to each set. Therefore, merging the two subsets results in a larger one, named ForwardQuestions. Given their different formats, we decided to convert them to a new format, which preserves all the information from both data sets. This format also includes a template derived from each question, which can be used for question generation.

The main added value of the resource is the conversion of DBpedia predicates to Wikidata ones, resulting in a resource that is enriched with respect to both of its sources, although it still cannot recover all original SimpleQuestions items based on Freebase predicates, as not all of them have mappings in Wikidata.

We do not include backward questions, because they are not convenient for generating new questions. Indeed, they typically accept a much larger number of possible answers than forward ones, and may therefore appear as either too open or too easy. Indeed, asking about a property of a subject makes a good question, as subjects have a limited number of properties. However, asking which subjects have a given property is generally not a good question because the same property can potentially apply to a very large number of subjects. For instance, "In what country is Geneva?" is a good question, while "What city is in Switzerland?" is not, although both are based on ('Geneva', 'country', 'Switzerland'). Given our goal of quiz generation, we exclude backward questions, of which there are 14,632 in SimpleDBpediaQA (34%) and 12,420 in SimpleQuestions-Wikidata (25%).

We now describe the mapping process for the SimpleQuestionsWikidata entires, and discuss afterwards the differences with SimpleDBpediaQA. We process each (*subject, predicate, object, question*) line as follows. We first exclude predicate starting with an 'R' (backwards question). Then, we query the Wikidata API to find the English labels of the subject, predicate, and object, and exclude questions for which the subject or the predicate cannot be found. Next, we build a template from each question, for question generation. We identify the position of the subject in the question, and replace it with the string '<placeholder>'. As different referring expressions were sometimes used for subjects, we allow for some flexibility when matching subject labels. For instance, we replace dashes, apostrophes and non-ASCII characters with white spaces, to increase the number of matches. Still, due to misspellings, simplifications, confusion of subject or object, or insertion of external knowledge about the subject, no match can be identified

for about 4% of the questions, which are excluded.

A similar conversion was performed for SimpleDBpediaQA entries, but this required a mapping of DBpedia predicates to Wikidata ones, which we explain in the next subsection. The subjects were also mapped to their Wikidata equivalent, using requests to the APIs and matching the English labels of the entities (as stated above, objects are missing in this case).

As a result, each item appears in ForwardQuestions as follows:

- Question: full text and template based on it;
- Subject: label (English words) and Wikidata code;
- Predicate: label and Wikidata code;
- Object: if available, label and Wikidata code.

3.3. Converting DBpedia Predicates to Wikidata

Predicates from DBpedia appearing in SimpleDBpediaQA questions must be mapped to Wikidata ones before inclusion in ForwardQuestions. For instance, 'playerPosition' from DBpedia must be mapped to 'position played on team / speciality' (P413) in Wikidata. For some of the 6,236 Wikidata predicates, their equivalent in DBpedia is specified, but this happens only for 177 predicates out of the 365 ones appearing in SimpleDBpediaQA, leaving 188 predicates with no known DBpedia equivalents.

We mapped these 188 remaining predicates using two approaches. Firstly, we looked for partial matches of the DBpedia labels with those from an online list of 1,872 Wikidata predicates with labels.[8] For example, for DBPedia's 'populationTotal' predicate, we could easily find the equivalent Wikidata predicate 'population'. Secondly, for non-matched labels, we performed a manual word-based search on Wikidata and selected the closest matching predicate.

The final mapping of predicates is provided with the ForwardQuestions data set in the `mapping.json` file of the Github repository (footnote 2). Each entry includes the DBpedia name and the matching Wikidata code, e.g. ('primeMinister', 'p6'). The first 177 predicates are those with explicit DBpedia equivalents in Wikidata, while the following 188 ones are those we mapped. In fact, we mapped many more predicates than those actually appearing in the selected questions, in anticipation of future needs.

3.4. Results

To sum up, we merged the forward questions from SimpleDBpediaQA and SimpleQuestionsWikidata, discarded backwards ones, removed duplicates (32% of the SimpleDBpediaQA), converted DBpedia predicates to Wikidata ones, and generated question templates by replacing subjects with <placeholder>. The ForwardQuestions data set contains 38,480 questions, having in total 94 different predicates. The various filtering operations, especially backward question removal and subject matching, have led us to keep only about 35% of the original SimpleQuestionsWikidata entries.

The most frequent predicate in ForwardQuestions is 'genre', which appears in more than 8,000 questions. Its meaning is quite general (akin to 'type' or 'category') and it can appear in triples concerning movies, books, music albums, artists, etc.[9] The next predicates by decreasing frequency are 'place of birth', 'country of citizenship', 'sex or gender', and 'position played on team / speciality'. The full list with frequencies is provided with the data set.

4. Question Generation from Triples

The ForwardQuestions is intended to help with the generation of new questions, from knowledge triples not included in the set. We propose a method inspired from the rule-based baseline from Serban et al. (2016), with the following differences. Their data set used Freebase, but we use Wikidata as the underlying triple store: our observations show that these predicates are often more precise, and specify sufficiently the type of the expected answer. For this reason, we created for each item in ForwardQuestions a template with a generic placeholder for the subject, unlike Serban et al. (2016) who use type-specific placeholders such as <location placeholder>, which strongly reduces the number of questions available for generation. It is still an open question whether the size of ForwardQuestions allows the training of deep learning models; for the time being, we use the following template-based generation method.

We generate a sample set of questions using 20 randomly selected templates among all those having the same predicate as the given triple, by replacing the placeholder of the question with the subject of the triple.[10] We then rank the questions using semantic similarity (4.1) and a language model (4.2).

The main issue to address can be illustrated with the following example. If we use a template such as "What kind of music does <placeholder> play?", derived from ('John Duffey', 'genre', 'bluegrass music'), but we want to generate a question based on the new triple ('Claude Monet', 'genre', 'portrait'), then we obtain the question "What kind of music does Claude Monet play?", with the expected correct answer being 'portrait'. The question is incorrect because the rendering of the predicate 'genre' in the initial question is too specific and incompatible with the sense of the new triple. Alternatively, the reference to the subject in the template can also be too specific, e.g. if we use the template "What genre is the tv program <placeholder>?" with the triple above, we obtain the incorrect question "What genre is the tv program Claude Monet?"

4.1. Ranking with semantic similarity

To avoid the issues exemplified above, we use semantic similarity between the word vectors provided by the word2vec library (Mikolov et al., 2013).[11] We compare the average of the word vectors from the opening Wikipedia paragraph of the subject with the average of word vectors of the question template using cosine similarity. We also compute the similarity between the words of the template and those from the opening Wikipedia paragraph of the object, and retain the maximum of the two similarities as the semantic compatibility score of the question and the triple.

4.2. Ranking with a language model

We observed that some ungrammatical questions obtained high semantic compatibility scores. Our second goal is thus to filter them out, using the KenLM language modeling software (Heafield et al., 2013)[12] with a language model for English provided by Zamia.[13] The perplexity score of the language model for the full question provides an estimate of the well-formedness of the question, i.e. a syntactic fluency score.

Therefore, for a given triple, we combine the semantic and fluency scores, giving more weight to the first one, and select the question which has the highest average score.

5. Use of Questions for a Quiz Chatbot

The method for generating questions from arbitrary triples, using ForwardQuestions, can be used to build a quiz chatbot which prompts the user to select a topic. This topic is matched to a Wikipedia page, from which we find a reasonable number of interesting triples, from which questions can be generated as explained above. The chatbot proposes the questions one by one to the user, and compares their answers to the expected ones.[14]

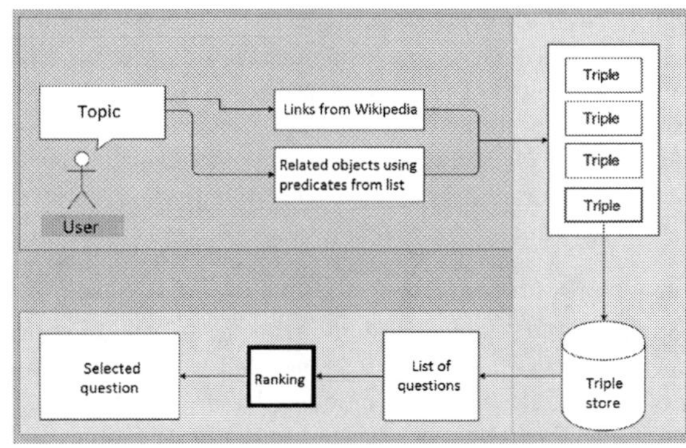

Figure 1: Overview of the quiz generation chatbot.

5.1. Selection of Triples for a Given Topic

The Wikidata entry of the topic indicated by the user may contain a large triple set, but all of them have the topic itself as the subject. This reduces the diversity of questions, as all of them will bear on some property of the subject.

---

[9]For instance, the triple ('John Duffey', 'genre', 'bluegrass music') has the associated question "What kind of music does John Duffey play?"

[10]We filter out any parentheses from the subject's description, e.g. 'The Danton (1983 film)' is reduced to 'The Danton'.

[11]As implemented in the Gensim package (radimrehurek.com/gensim/models/word2vec.html) with Google's pre-trained model. As the templates are very short, and for simplicity reasons, we did not experiment with more elaborate paragraph representation models.

[12]github.com/kpu/kenlm

[13]goofy.zamia.org/zamia-speech/lm/, large model

[14]In other words, there are no follow-up questions, unlike Su et al.'s (2019) system, based on an ontology with RDF triples restricted to the dialogue domain.

For instance, if the topic is 'Queen', the British rock band (Q15862), then all questions from triples on their Wikidata page will have 'Queen' as the subject: "When was Queen founded?", "What country is Queen from?", "What is the music genre of Queen?", etc.

To increase diversity, we select additional triples from entities that are related to the main one, as follows. First, we select a list of Wikidata predicates that tend to connect the subject to meaningful objects, such as 'has part' (P527). Using the Wikidata entries of these objects, we select additional triples. For instance, from ('Queen', 'has part', 'Freddie Mercury') we infer that 'Freddie Mercury' is a related entity, and find the triple ('Freddie Mercury', 'religion', 'Zoroastrianism') which allows us to build the question: "What was Freddie Mercury's religion?" for the topic 'Queen'. We identified about 50 such predicates that allow the extension of the topic.

However, some notions such as 'Rock Music' or 'Cooking' have few properties on their Wikidata pages, which is why we also use a second strategy, relying on the Wikipedia page of the subject. We use the "See also" or "Related topics" section to retrieve related subjects, but these sections are not always present and contain only a small list of subjects, of variable relevance. Therefore, we consider all hyperlinks from the page to other Wikipedia entries, and select the 20 first random subjects whose Wikidata entries contain at least 25 triples (so that each related subject has sufficient substance).

In addition, we merge the objects of triples that have the same subject and predicate, to obtain the list of all possible correct answers. For instance, from ('Barack Obama', 'child', 'Malia Obama') and ('Barack Obama', 'child', 'Sasha Obama'), we obtain a single triple for question generation, with a list of two acceptable answers.

Finally, for any topic selected by the user, we randomly select 10 subjects found with the first method, and 20 found with the second one, with the aim of obtaining about 100 knowledge triples from which questions are generated.

5.2. Implementation of a Chatbot Prototype

We implemented a chatbot demo with the following components. Actions on Google[15] is the front-end proposed by Google to create apps for its Google Home smart speaker. Dialogflow[16], which is connected to Actions, enables the design of simple dialogue models. The backend, running on one of our servers, is coded in Python with the Flask web development framework. As we found that our question generation is too slow to run in real time (taking several minutes on a mid-range computer, especially due to querying Wikipedia pages), we generated questions offline for several subjects ("Olympic Games", "Politics of the United States", "Rock music", "Super Mario Bros.", "Switzerland", "The Legend of Zelda", and "World War II"). The chatbot proposes to the user three randomly selected topics, among which one must be chosen. Sample questions (Q) and their correct answers (A) for "World War II" are:

- Q: Which country was involved in the Eastern Front?
  A: Nazi Germany, Soviet Union, ...

- Q: Who was one of the major figures in the Attack on Pearl Harbor?
  A: Husband Edward Kimmel, Mitsuo Fuchida, ...

- Q: Who was the developer for A6M Zero?
  A: Mitsubishi Heavy Industries

- Q: What was the cause of death for Adolf Hitler?
  A: shot to the head, suicide by shooting

6. Evaluation of the Questions

The following evaluation protocol is targeted at the quality of the questions and their correct answer(s), and not at the usability of the chatbot, which depends also on the dialogue model and the speech recognition system.[17] For each triple and question, we asked human judges to rate the following quality aspects:

1. **Triple**

   - *Importance of predicate and object.* How interesting are the predicate and the object? For instance, for the triple ("North America", "located in time zone", {"Hawaii-Aleutian Time Zone", ...}), the predicate and its value do not appear to be interesting.

2. **Question**

   (a) *Specification of the subject.* For instance, in the question "Who was responsible for the music in the film Super Mario Bros.?", the specification of the subject is incorrect given that Super Mario Bros. is a video game, not a film.

   (b) *Specification of the object.* For instance, in "Which city in Scotland did J. R. R. Tolkien come from?", the specification of the expect answer (the triple's object) is wrong because Tolkien is from Birmingham, which is not in Scotland.

   (c) *Formulation of the question.* Is the question understandable and well-formed in English? This includes spelling mistakes. For instance, "Who was the published the game Harry Potter?" is poorly formulated.

   (d) *Correctness of the expected answer..* For instance, for "Who was the film Harry Potter and the Deathly Hallows based on the story by?", the expected answer is 'Steve Kloves' (author of the screenplay), but one may estimate that 'J. K. Rowling' should be the correct answer, as she is the author of the original book.

3. **Overall:** is this a good item for a quiz?

We asked four persons not familiar with the project to perform the following comparison. Given a knowledge triple, we show them the best question found by our method and the worst one (also according to our method) from a random

---

[15]console.actions.google.com
[16]dialogflow.com

[17]The complete chatbot could be evaluated with the recent set of 17 metrics made available by Csáky et al. (2019).

subset of 20 questions generated for the triple. The human must rate each of the questions, without knowing their origin, on a five-point scale for each criterion. The goal is thus to measure the improvement brought by our method, with respect to a rather poor question, but still much stronger than the worst of all questions. For a set of 105 triples and 210 questions, we obtained 472 ratings.

Criterion	Score	
	Best question	**Poor question**
Predicate + object	4.12	
Subject specification	4.51	3.51
Object specification	4.02	3.55
Question formulation	4.19	4.25
Answer correctness	3.80	3.40
Overall quality	3.35	2.84

Table 3: Average scores of the best question and of a random poor question on a five-point scale.

The results are presented in Table 3. On all but one dimension, the best question shows clear improvement with respect to the poor one. The best questions score below poor ones regarding "formulation", but both scores are in fact rather high. With an overall quality of 3.35 out of 5, the questions are satisfactory, but there is also potential for progress.

The largest improvement brought by our method (1 point out of 5) is for the specification of the subject, which is excellent for the best questions. The specification of the object (expected answer) is also improved. This was indeed one of our main goals, given that user-generated questions often include specifiers which become incorrect when the subject is replaced with another one. The improvement of the expected answer is quite similar to the one for the specification of the object, as these two elements are closely related. Finally, the relevance of the predicate + object is quite high, showing that the triple selection method is effective.

7. Conclusion

In this paper, we presented the ForwardQuestion data set, which we make available under the same CC-BY licence. The data set results from the conversion and combination of the SimpleDBpediaQA and SimpleQuestionsWikidata datasets, in particular by mapping predicates from Freebase to Wikidata. The 38,480 questions of the data set are accompanied by templates where the subject is replaced by a placeholder, in preparation for question generation that can be used in a quiz chatbot. The difficulties of triple conversion and predicate mapping strongly point to the need for interoperable semantic annotation in the realm of knowledge-based question generation.

In future work on quiz generation, we aim to improve the relevance of the triples selected for a topic, as well as the diversity of the questions. While the size of the data set remains modest for use with deep learning generation methods, the triples could be used in conjunction with a pre-trained language model such as GPT-2 (Radford et al., 2019) or CTRL (Keskar et al., 2019), to serve as adaptation data for neural question generation conditioned on the triples.

Acknowledgments

We thank the University of Applied Sciences of Western Switzerland (HES-SO) for the PLACAT grant that partly supported this work (AGP n. 82681), as well as the evaluators for the time they devoted to rating the questions submitted to them.

8. Bibliographical References

Azmy, M., Shi, P., Lin, J., and Ilyas, I. (2018). Farewell Freebase: Migrating the SimpleQuestions dataset to DBpedia. In *Proceedings of the 27th International Conference on Computational Linguistics*, pages 2093–2103, Santa Fe, New Mexico, USA. Association for Computational Linguistics.

Bast, H. and Haussmann, E. (2015). More accurate question answering on freebase. In *Proceedings of the Conference of Knowledge Management (CIKM'15)*, pages 1431–1440, Melbourne, Australia.

Bordes, A., Usunier, N., Garcia-Duran, A., Weston, J., and Yakhnenko, O. (2013). Translating embeddings for modeling multi-relational data. In *Advances in Neural Information Processing Systems (NeurIPS)*, pages 2787–2795.

Bordes, A., Usunier, N., Chopra, S., and Weston, J. (2015). Large-scale simple question answering with memory networks. *CoRR*, abs/1506.02075.

Chali, Y. and Hasan, S. A. (2015). Towards topic-to-question generation. *Computational Linguistics*, 41(1):1–20.

Csáky, R., Purgai, P., and Recski, G. (2019). Improving neural conversational models with entropy-based data filtering. In *Proceedings of the 57th Annual Meeting of the Association for Computational Linguistics*, pages 5650–5669, Florence, Italy. Association for Computational Linguistics.

Diefenbach, D., Tanon, T. P., Singh, K. D., and Maret, P. (2017). Question answering benchmarks for Wikidata. In *Proceedings of the ISWC 2017 Posters & Demonstrations and Industry Tracks co-located with 16th International Semantic Web Conference*, Vienna, Austria.

Duan, N., Tang, D., Chen, P., and Zhou, M. (2017). Question generation for question answering. In *Proceedings of the 2017 Conference on Empirical Methods in Natural Language Processing*, pages 866–874, Copenhagen, Denmark. Association for Computational Linguistics.

Heafield, K., Pouzyrevsky, I., Clark, J. H., and Koehn, P. (2013). Scalable modified Kneser-Ney language model estimation. In *Proceedings of the 51st Annual Meeting of the Association for Computational Linguistics (ACL 2013)*, pages 690–696, Sofia, Bulgaria.

Heilman, M. and Smith, N. A. (2010). Good question! Statistical ranking for question generation. In *Human Language Technologies: The 2010 Annual Conference of the North American Chapter of the Association for Computational Linguistics*, pages 609–617, Los Angeles, CA, USA, June. Association for Computational Linguistics.

Keskar, N. S., McCann, B., Varshney, L. R., Xiong, C., and Socher, R. (2019). CTRL: a conditional transformer language model for controllable generation. *arXiv cs.CL*, 1909.05858.

Khullar, P., Rachna, K., Hase, M., and Shrivastava, M. (2018). Automatic question generation using relative pronouns and adverbs. In *Proceedings of ACL 2018, Student Research Workshop*, pages 153–158, Melbourne, Australia. Association for Computational Linguistics.

Malyshev, S., Krötzsch, M., González, L., Gonsior, J., and Bielefeldt, A. (2018). Getting the most out of Wikidata: Semantic technology usage in Wikipedia's knowledge graph. In *Proceedings of the 17th International Semantic Web Conference (ISWC 2018), LNCS volume 11137*, pages 376–394, Monterey, CA, USA.

Mikolov, T., Sutskever, I., Chen, K., Corrado, G. S., and Dean, J. (2013). Distributed representations of words and phrases and their compositionality. In *Advances in Neural Information Processing Systems (NIPS)*, pages 3111–3119.

Pham, X. L., Pham, T., Nguyen, Q. M., Nguyen, T. H., and Cao, T. T. H. (2018). Chatbot as an intelligent personal assistant for mobile language learning. In *Proceedings of the 2018 2nd International Conference on Education and E-Learning (ICEEL 2018)*, page 16–21, Bali, Indonesia. Association for Computing Machinery.

Radford, A., Wu, J., Child, R., Luan, D., Amodei, D., and Sutskever, I. (2019). Language models are unsupervised multitask learners. *OpenAI Blog*, 1(8).

Rajpurkar, P., Zhang, J., Lopyrev, K., and Liang, P. (2016). SQuAD: 100,000+ questions for machine comprehension of text. In *Proceedings of the 2016 Conference on Empirical Methods in Natural Language Processing*, pages 2383–2392, Austin, Texas. Association for Computational Linguistics.

Serban, I. V., García-Durán, A., Gulcehre, C., Ahn, S., Chandar, S., Courville, A., and Bengio, Y. (2016). Generating factoid questions with recurrent neural networks: The 30M factoid question-answer corpus. In *Proceedings of the 54th Annual Meeting of the Association for Computational Linguistics (Volume 1: Long Papers)*, pages 588–598, Berlin, Germany. Association for Computational Linguistics.

Su, M.-H., Wu, C.-H., and Chang, Y. (2019). Follow-up question generation using neural tensor network-based domain ontology population in an interview coaching system. In *Proceedings of INTERSPEECH*, pages 4185–4189, Graz, Austria.

Sun, X., Liu, J., Lyu, Y., He, W., Ma, Y., and Wang, S. (2018). Answer-focused and position-aware neural question generation. In *Proceedings of the 2018 Conference on Empirical Methods in Natural Language Processing*, pages 3930–3939, Brussels, Belgium. Association for Computational Linguistics.

Unger, C., Ngomo, A.-C. N., and Cabrio, E. (2016). Sixth open challenge on question answering over linked data (QALD-6). In *Semantic Web Challenges, CCIS 641*, pages 171–177, Berlin. Springer-Verlag.

Zhao, Y., Ni, X., Ding, Y., and Ke, Q. (2018). Paragraph-level neural question generation with maxout pointer and gated self-attention networks. In *Proceedings of the 2018 Conference on Empirical Methods in Natural Language Processing*, pages 3901–3910, Brussels, Belgium. Association for Computational Linguistics.

Zhou, W., Zhang, M., and Wu, Y. (2019). Question-type driven question generation. In *Proceedings of the 2019 Conference on Empirical Methods in Natural Language Processing and the 9th International Joint Conference on Natural Language Processing (EMNLP-IJCNLP)*, pages 6032–6037, Hong Kong, China. Association for Computational Linguistics.

Proceedings of the 16th Joint ACL-ISO Workshop Interoperable Semantic Annotation (ISA-16), pages 67–74
Language Resources and Evaluation Conference (LREC 2020), Marseille, 11–16 May 2020
© European Language Resources Association (ELRA), licensed under CC-BY-NC

The Annotation of Thematic Structure and Alternations face to the Semantic Variation of Action Verbs.
Current Trends in the IMAGACT Ontology

Massimo Moneglia, Rossella Varvara
University of Florence
DILEF Department
massimo.moneglia@unifi.it, rossella.varvara@unifi.it

Abstract

We present some issues in the development of the semantic annotation of IMAGACT, a multimodal and multilingual ontology of actions. The resource is structured on action concepts that are meant to be cognitive entities and to which a linguistic caption is attached. For each of these concepts, we annotate the minimal thematic structure of the caption and the possible argument alternations allowed. We present some insights on this process with regard to the notion of thematic structure and the relationship between action concepts and linguistic expressions. From the empirical evidence provided by the annotation process, we discuss the very nature of thematic structure, arguing that it is neither a property of the verb itself nor a property of action concepts. We further show what is the relation between thematic structure and 1- the semantic variation of action verbs; 2- the lexical variation of action concepts.

Keywords: thematic structure, semantic roles, action verbs, action concepts

1. Introduction

In the last decades, great attention has been devoted to the development of computational verb lexicons in the field of natural language processing. Verbs are indeed the core of the sentence to which the other elements relate. VerbNet is a well-known outcome of this kind of effort, which has provided a comprehensive account of possible syntactic frames and argument structures associated with verbs (Kipper-Schuler, 2005). More recently, Uresova et al. (2018) started the implementation of a bilingual verb lexicon based on synonym relations. General information about verb lemmas can be found also in other lexical resources, such as FrameNet (Fillmore et al., 2004), PropBank (Palmer et al., 2005) among many others.

The IMAGACT ontology of actions[1] (Moneglia et al., 2012b; Panunzi et al., 2014) inserts itself in this trend, offering a multilingual repository of action verbs. The ontology consists of fine-grained categorization of action concepts, each represented by prototypical visual scenes in the form of short recorded videos or 3D animations. IMAGACT defines the meaning of an action verb through a set of scenes in the ontology, rather than towards dictionary definition or propositional representations within decompositional approaches (Dowty, 1979; Rappaport Hovav and Levin, 2012). Each action concept can be referred to one or more verbs (within and across languages). Moreover, action verbs are frequently general and refer to a set of action concepts. The visual representations convey information in a language-independent environment, modeling concepts without the bias coming from a monolingual approach.

In this paper, we present some insights on the semantic annotation of the IMAGACT ontology. For each action concept, we annotate the thematic structure (henceforth TS) and argument alternations for each of its linguistic captions. The resulting annotation can be inspected also from the ac-

tion verb point of view, looking at its possible thematic configurations throughout the different concepts it can refer to. Starting from the empirical evidence provided by the annotation process, we reflect on the very nature of thematic structure, arguing that it is neither a property of the verb itself nor a property of the action concept. Moreover, we highlight what we can learn about the semantic variation of action verbs and the lexical variation of concepts from the annotation of TSs. It is possible indeed to inspect not only all the possible TSs for a given verb but also the TSs associated with a specific action concept. We believe that this is an additional value of the ontology and we show how it helps in understanding the relationship between the conceptualization of events and their linguistic encoding.

2. The IMAGACT ontology of actions

The IMAGACT multilingual Ontology of Actions contains 1010 scenes that represent the action concepts most commonly referred to in everyday language. Each scene is conceived as a prototypical instance (Rosch, 1983) of an action concept and constitutes the basic entity of reference of the action ontology. The scenes represented have been derived from occurrences of action verbs[2] in two large spoken resources of English and Italian (Moneglia et al., 2012a). After this initial phase, the linguistic annotation for many other languages has been obtained through competence-based judgments by native speakers (Brown et al., 2014; Pan et al., 2018; Moneglia et al., 2018).

The database evolves continuously: at present, it contains around 8700 verbs from 15 languages[3].

---

[2]Only in their basic, physical meaning, so excluding all metaphorical and phraseological uses. We refer the reader to Frontini et al. (2012; Moneglia et al. (2012a) for a description of the infrastructure and the annotation procedure; to Gagliardi (2013; Gagliardi (2014) for a summary of inter-annotator agreement values for this procedure.

[3]Besides English and Italian, the list of fully mapped language

---

[1]http://www.imagact.it/

IMAGACT can be queried in multiple ways. First, an action verb lemma can be searched to obtain the list of action concepts it refers to. This describes the semantic variation of a verb. Second, two verbs from the same language or from two different languages can be compared (fig 2), looking at the scenes that both can refer to (the column in the center in fig 2) and at those they separately describe. Third, a single action concept can be selected to look at the different verbs with whom it is associated in one or two languages. In fig 1, for example, the scene representing the action of pressing a button is shown together with its linked verbs in English (on the left) and Italian (on the right). Lastly, actions can be searched among 9 classes, based on the informative focus of the action:

- Perspective centered on the Actor:
    - Actions referring to facial expression
    - Actions referring to the body
    - Movement in space

- Perspective centered on the Actor-Theme relation:
    - Modifications of the object
    - Deterioration of the object
    - Forces on the object

- Perspective centered on the Theme-Destination relation:
    - Change of location of the object
    - Setting relations among objects
    - Actions in inter-subjective space

3. Minimal Thematic Structure Annotation

Computational lexicons frequently provide information about the thematic structure and syntactic frame of verbs (see e.g. VerbNet (Kipper-Schuler, 2005), FrameNet (Fillmore et al., 2004) and PropBank (Palmer et al., 2005)). In these resources, the different entries of a verb are associated with their possible thematic structures and possible alternations are listed. Particularly, VerbNet has been built around the syntactic frames of verbs, following the identification of verb classes done by Levin (1993). This kind of annotation has shown to be useful for the development of statistical approaches for Semantic Role Labeling (Gildea and Jurafsky, 2002) and numerous NLP applications (e.g. information extraction (Surdeanu et al., 2003), summarization (Melli et al., 2006), and machine translation (Boas, 2002)).

Usually, for a given verb, semantic roles are annotated, in order to specify the semantic relationship between the predicate and its arguments. In the IMAGACT ontology, we annotate the caption associated with a specific action concept in its minimal form. By minimal thematic structure, we refer to the simplest structure that is sufficient to interpret a verb as an instance of a specific action concept. The caption should indeed disambiguate the verb in referring to the specific scene represented.

---

comprehends Arab, Chinese, Danish, German, Hindi, Japanese, Polish, Portuguese, Serbian, Spanish, Greek, French and Urdu.

The annotation interface allows us to select each argument in a caption and to assign a thematic role to it. An example of the result of this procedure is shown in fig. 3.

The set of semantic roles, based on those used in VerbNet (Kipper-Schuler, 2005), comprehends 13 roles, which are described as follows:

- Theme (TH): the subject/object that is undergoing to the event/action/motion denoted by the verb, both for a participant that change location and for a participant that change state (it comprehends both "theme" and "patient" roles);

- Agent (AG): an animate subject that intentionally performs the action denoted by the verb;

- Causer (CA): a "non-intentional agent", such as machines and natural forces;

- Experiencer (EX): an animate subject that actively receives sensory or emotional input;

- Actor (AC): a participant that simultaneously play the roles of both Agent/Causer/Experiencer and Theme;

- Instrumental (IN): the medium used by an agent to act;

- Source (SO): the starting point of the motion or the origin of the action (it comprehends both "source" and "origin" roles);

- Destination (DE): the endpoint of the motion or the entity that benefits from the action (e.g. a change of possession; it comprehends "goal", "destination", "direction", "beneficiary" and "recipient" roles);

- Location (LO): the place where the event/action/motion denoted by the verb occurs; also used for the path of the motion (it comprehends "location" and "path" roles);

- Time (TI): the time at which the event/action/motion occurs;

- Measure (ME): an expression of extension, range or degree along a dimension (length, weight, duration, cost, etc.)

- Unspecified reference (UN): an object of reference involved in the event/action/motion denoted by the verb, not identifiable in any other of the thematic roles proposed in the tag-set.

- Coagent (CO): a participant who performs the action denoted by the verb together with the main agent

Given this setting, we obtain a representation of the different thematic structures (based on different verbs) that may describe the action concept. Moreover, similarly to other resources, we can look at the different thematic structure shown by a single verb (with reference to the different action concepts it may refer to).

In what follows, we report an overview of these two kinds of inspections of the TS annotation, showing what it is possible to observe once the annotation is completed. With examples from the English and Italian languages, we inspect

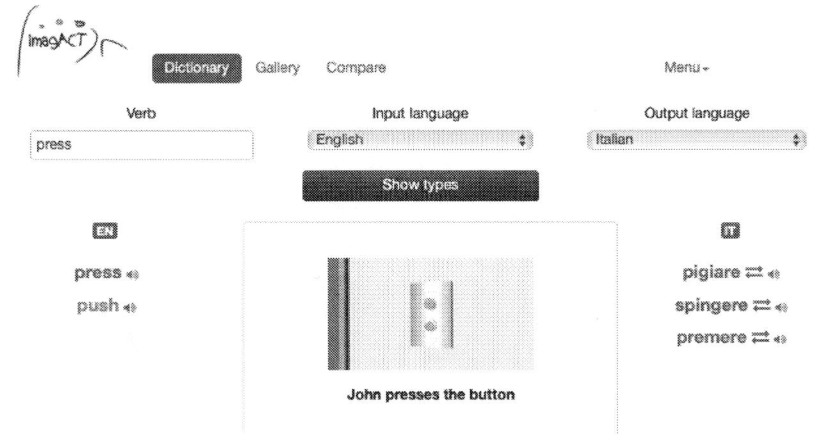

Figure 1: An example of action concept in IMAGACT.

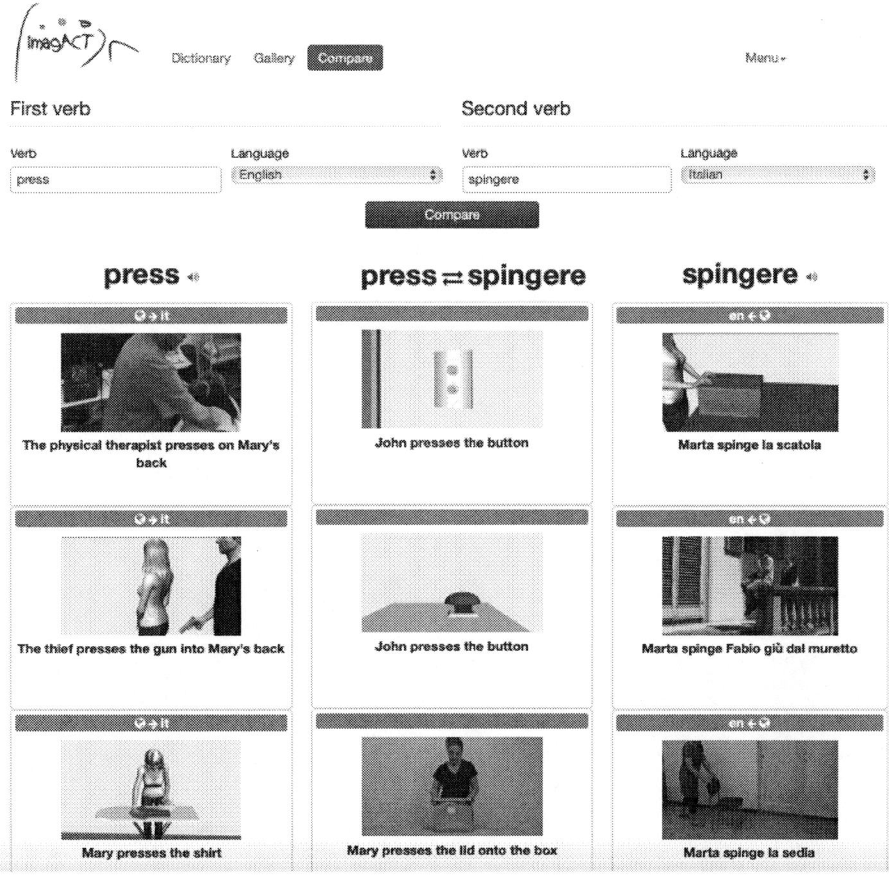

Figure 2: An example of verbs comparison in IMAGACT.

the semantic variation of some specific verbs and, also, the linguistic variation of a specific action concept.

3.1. Thematic structure and the semantic variation of verbs

The innovative methodology assumed by the IMAGACT ontology allows us to represent the meaning of an action verb through its referential properties, rather than by an

Figure 3: A screenshot of the thematic structure annotation interface.

intensional definition. We can thus analyze the semantic variation of a verb through the prototypical action concepts it has been associated to, rather than by a list of senses. Furthermore, the annotation of captions TSs brings us an inventory of the possible syntactic frames the verb occurs with.

From the annotation process of the IMAGACT verbs inventory, we observe that different possibilities occur:

- verbs may present only one TS;

- verbs may show different TS.

The first case is shown by so-called activity verbs, such as *to drink*, which present only one TS through their variation. In this case, this fact is linked to the low range of meanings associated with the verb. *To drink*, indeed, can be interpreted as having only one meaning. Its minimal TS will be always AG-V (since the theme is not necessary to correctly identify the action concept), no matter the kind of agents involved:

(1)   John drinks.

(2)   The cat drinks.

(3)   The horse drinks.

However, not only activity verbs can present only one TS. The verb *to close*, for example, shows a significant variation in the IMAGACT ontology (7 action types, four of them represented in fig. 4), but all types present the same TS (AG-V-TH).

Figure 4: Semantic variation of *to close*.

As an example of a verb with multiple TSs, consider the verb *to press*. It shows ten different action types in IMA-GACT and it is possible to observe how concepts group based on their TS. Two action types (represented in table 1

and 2) share the Agent - Verb- Theme - Destination structure. In both cases, the Destination is necessary to represent the action concept, which cannot be identified otherwise. Both concepts concern the change of shape of the Theme, whose form is modified by the event. In this case, sharing the same TS is linked to a cognitive similarity of the action concept.

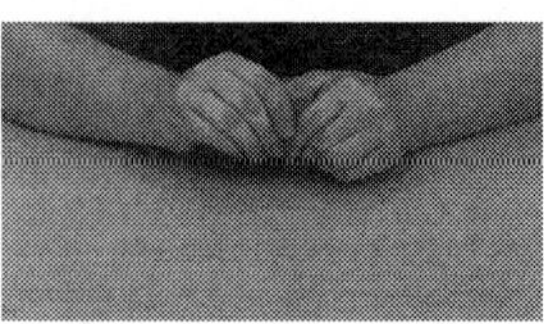

Table 1: *To press*, type *a*

Table 2: *To press*, type *b*

A different set of concepts in the variation of *to press* shows the structure AG- V- TH, without the need for further arguments to explicitly disambiguate the action concept. These are represented in tables 3, 4, 5. They differ from concepts in tables 1 and 2 since they do not cause a change of shape of the theme, and this is mirrored by a difference in TS. However, despite the common TS, they present some cognitive features that clearly differentiate them. The action concept in table 3 implies an animate theme, contrary to actions in tables 4 and 5. These two latter concepts, moreover, differ from each other for the type of pressure, either in the form of a single impulse (table 4) or as a continuous scalar pressure (table 5).

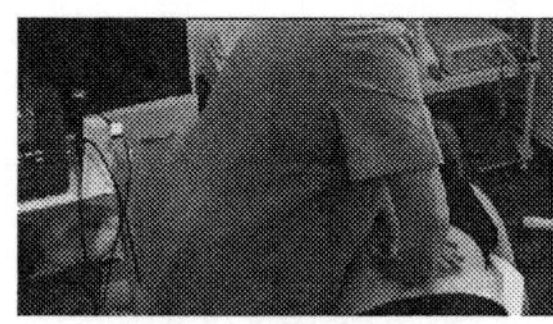

Table 3: *To press*, type *c*

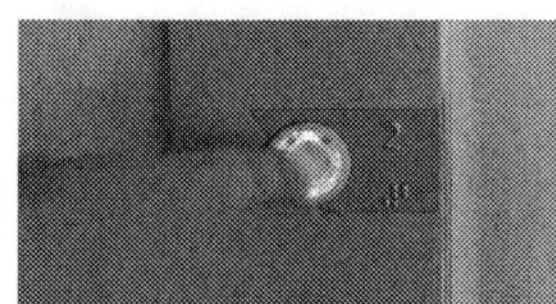

Table 4: *To press*, type *d*

These latter three action concepts are associated also by the different argument alternations they allow, contrary to the scenes in tables 1 and 2. Their thematic structures can be modified so that the arguments have different syntactic re-

Table 5: *To press*, type *e*

lations with the verb. Specifically, they allow a conative alternation (Levin, 1993) and what we call theme-instrument alternation. The first one can be defined as "a transitivity alternation in which the objects of the verb in the transitive variant turns up in the intransitive conative variant as the object of the preposition in a prepositional phrase headed by the preposition at (sometimes on with certain verb of ingesting and the push/pull verbs)" (Levin, 1993, p.42).

- Type 3: The doctor presses the shoulder → The doctor presses on the shoulder

- Type 4: John presses the button → John presses on the button

- Type 8: John presses the pedal → John presses on the pedal

This alternation is not allowed for the action concepts in table 1 and 2, as the next sentences show:

- Type 1: *John presses at/on the scraps into a block.

- Type 2: *John presses at/on the fabric into a ball.

The alternation between the Theme and the Instrument is not listed in Levin (1993). In this case, the Instrument from sentence b (which can be seen as the result of a conative alternation) becomes the Theme in sentence c.

(4)   a.   The doctor presses the shoulder with his hand
      b.   The doctor presses on the shoulder with his hand
      c.   The doctor presses his hand on the shoulder

This alternation can be considered as a particular case of a *locative alternation*. In terms of Levin, the noun *shoulder* would represent the location argument, whereas *hand* would be considered the *locatum*. Also, in this case, the *theme-instrument alternation* does not apply to all types of the variation of *to press* but rather characterizes specific types.

(5)   John presses the button → John presses the button with his finger → John presses his finger on the button

(6)   *John presses the pedal → John presses the pedal with his foot → John presses the foot on the pedal

(7)   *John presses the hand on the scraps

(8)   *John presses the hand on the fabric

From the examples above, we have already seen from only 5 different action concepts that every concept is cognitively different for at least a specific property of the event. However, only some differences of features are mirrored by a

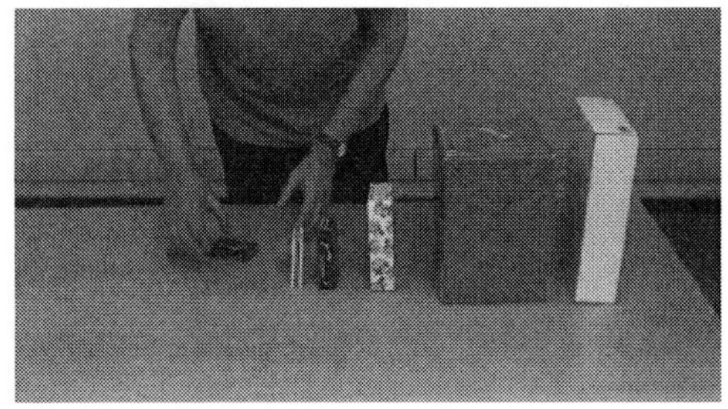

Figure 5: Frame from the scene "Maria puts the objects in order".

different linguistic encoding. Each language divides the cognitive space of actions in different ways, prioritizing some features instead of others. Moreover, we have seen that TS is not a property of the verb itself, but rather a property of the verb within the action concept.

In the next section, we will observe the relation between TS and specific action concepts.

3.2. Thematic Structure and the lexical variation of action concepts

The annotation of TS in IMAGACT brings us to an overview of TS for single action concepts, rather than only for the semantic variation of a verb. From the annotation done so far, we notice first, that the main trend among action concepts is to show the same TS among different verbs. This is mainly because we consider the minimal TS, i.e. the simplest structure that can disambiguate the linguistic caption, and it frequently contains the agent, the verb and the theme only.

However, a variety of different cases has been found in which multiple TSs can be observed among the various verbs associated with a specific action concept. These cases are frequently due to specific semantic features of one verb or, rather, to the different focus the verb brings. In what follows, we describe these cases observed during the annotation process:

1. verbs that lexicalize an argument (usually the manner, the theme or the destination) expressed by other verbs.

2. verbs that present the same arguments but with different thematic roles.

As an example of the cases in 1, consider the scene in fig. 5.

In Italian, in addition to the verb *mettere* ('to put'), this action concept can be described also with verbs like *disporre* ('to arrange'), *sistemare* ('to set'), but also with *ordinare* ('to put in order'). Consider the following sentences, which can all describe the scene under consideration.

(9)   Maria mette gli oggetti in fila.
      (AG–V–TH–MANNER)
      'Maria puts the objects in line.'

(10)   Maria dispone gli oggetti in fila.
      (AG-V-TH-MANNER)
      'Maria places the objects in line.'

(11)   Maria sistema gli oggetti in fila.
         (AG-V-TH-MANNER)
         'Maria arranges the objects in line.'

(12)   Maria   ordina gli oggetti.
         (AG-V-TH)
         'Maria puts in order the objects.'

The sentence in (12) differs from the others because it does not express the manner in its minimal TS. In fact, the verb *ordinare* (contrary to its English translation 'to put in order') incorporates in its semantics how the action is performed, without the need to express it separately (in what Talmy (2000) calls a *satellite*). It lexicalizes the manner component, similarly to what well-known *manner of motion* verbs do (e.g. *to run*). However, other components of meaning (in addition to the manner) can be lexicalized in a verb, and thus TSs associated with an action concept will show these differences. The theme may be incorporated as well: the theme *colore* ('paint') from sentence (13) is lexicalized into the verb in (14), thus resulting in different TSs for those captions of the same action concept.

(13)   Maria mette il colore sul foglio.
         (AG-V-TH-DEST)
         'Maria puts paint on the paper.'

(14)   Maria colora il foglio.
         (AG-V-TH)
         'Maria paints the paper.'

The same can be observed for various verbs. The verb *salare* ('to salt') encodes the theme expressed by *mettere* ('to put') in sentence (15), and the verbs *tappare* ('to plug', ex. (18)) the theme expressed in (17). *Chiudere* ('to close', ex. (19)) can refer to the same scene, but it does not encode the argument *tappo* (which could be expressed as Instrument, e.g. ex. (20).

(15)   Maria mette il sale sulle acciughe.
         (AG-V-TH-DEST)
         'Maria puts salt on the anchovies.'

(16)   Maria sala le acciughe.
         (AG-V-TH)
         'Maria salts the anchovies.'

(17)   Maria mette il tappo nel buco.
         (AG-V-TH-DEST)
         'Maria puts a cap in the hole.'

(18)   Maria tappa il buco.
         (AG-V-TH)
         'Maria plugs the hole.'

(19)   Maria chiude il buco.
         (AG-V-TH)
         'Maria seals the hole.'

(20)   Maria chiude il buco con un tappo.
         (AG-V-TH-INSTR)
         'Maria seals the hole with a cap.'

Similarly, the destination may be not necessarily expressed: *mettere* requires it in its minimal TS, whereas *piantare* ('to plant') already expresses it:

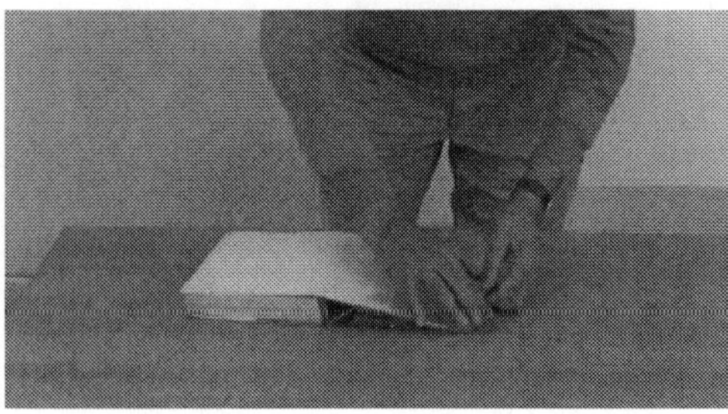

Figure 6: Frame from the scene "Maria puts the plastic on the book".

(21)   Maria mette il palo nel terreno.
         (AG-V-TH-DEST)
         'Maria puts the pole into the ground.'

(22)   Maria pianta il palo.
         (AG-V-TH)
         'Maria plants the pole in the ground.'

Note that it is possible to express an additional destination with *piantare* (ex. (23), even if in this case it is not the minimal TS that is considered), but the same is not possible with *mettere* ((24)): in this case, the sentence would not refer unambiguously to the same action concept as in (23), but it could be interpreted as denoting another action, such as those of putting the pole horizontally on the ground.

(23)   Maria pianta il palo nel suo giardino.
         (AG-V-TH-DEST)
         'Maria plants the pole in her garden.'

(24)   ≠ Maria mette il palo nel suo giardino.
         (AG-V-TH-DEST)
         ≠ 'Maria puts the pole in her garden.'

All these differences considered may be attributed to a more general distinction among general verbs and more specific ones, but also to the different focus the verbs bring. *Mettere* focuses on the process of the event ((24)), whereas *piantare* on the goal/result of the action.

Let's consider now some examples from the second case, i.e. action concepts that can be described by verbs that encode the same arguments but with different roles. Consider the scene represented in fig.6 and by the next two sentences:

(25)   Maria mette la copertina al libro.
         (AG-V-TH-DEST)
         'Maria puts the plastic on the book'.'

(26)   Maria riveste il libro con la copertina.
         (AG-V-TH-INSTR)
         'Maria covers the book with plastic.'

The noun *libro*, which is encoded as destination in the sentence (25), becomes the theme in sentence (26) where the predicate is *rivestire* ('to cover'). On the contrary, the noun *copertina* is encoded as theme in (25), and as instrument in (26).

A similar case is given by the verb *mettere* ('to put') in contrast with the verb *caricare* ('to load'). The latter is well-known for its possibility to show the locative alternation (Levin, 1993), as for its English translation:

(27)   Maria carica le assi con i pacchi.
       (AG-V-TH-INSTR)
       'Maria loads the shelfs with boxes.'

(28)   Maria carica i pacchi sulle assi.
       (AG-V-TH-DEST)
       'Maria loads the boxes on the shelfs.

The verb *mettere*, instead, can refer to this scene only with one argument configuration:

(29)   Maria mette i pacchi sulle assi.
       (AG-V-TH-DEST)
       'Maria puts the boxes on the shelfs.'

(30)   *Maria mette le assi con i pacchi.
       (AG-V-TH-INSTR)
       '*Maria puts the shelfs with boxes.'

Again, the different TSs bring a different focus on the action. If we represent the noun *pacchi* as theme ((28) and (29)) we are focusing on the processual part of the event in which the boxes are been moved. If we represent the noun *shelves* as theme, instead, the result of the action is in focus, i.e. the shelves becoming loaded. The different TSs differ for the informative focus they realize.

In this section, we have shown that if TS is not a property of the verb, it is not even a necessary property of an AT. Indeed, verbs that can be equivalently applied to one type may record different alternative structures.

The cognitive representation of an action scene consists of multiple elements (a theme, a recipient, a destination, an instrument), but the linguistic expression (by means of one verb or the other) frequently forces us to focus on some of these elements. The construal of the scene by the linguistic expression can vary in reason of which aspect we want to put in focus.

4. Conclusion

In this paper, we have seen what analyses are enabled by the annotation of Thematic Structure in the IMAGACT ontology. By looking at the TS variation across verbs and action concepts, it has been shown that TS is not a property of the verb, but neither a property of the action concept. It is a lexical property of the verb with reference to its action concept.

Moreover, it has been highlighted how in some cases the same TS can mirror cognitive similarities among concepts and, on the other side, how different TSs referring to the same concept can vary for the informative focus they realize.

5. Bibliographical References

Boas, H. C. (2002). Bilingual framenet dictionaries for machine translation. In *Proceedings of LREC*.

Brown, S. W., Gagliardi, G., and Moneglia, M. (2014). Imagact4all. mapping spanish varieties onto a corpus-based ontology of action. *CHIMERA: Journal of Romance Corpora and Linguistic Studies*, (1):91–135.

Dowty, D. (1979). *Word Meaning and Montague Grammar*. Reidel Publishing Co, Dordrecht.

Fillmore, C. J., Ruppenhofer, J., and Baker, C. F. (2004). Framenet and representing the link between semantic and syntactic relations. *Frontiers in linguistics*, 1:19–59.

Frontini, F., De Felice, I., Khan, F., Russo, I., Monachini, M., Gagliardi, G., and Panunzi, A. (2012). Verb interpretation for basic action types: annotation, ontology induction and creation of prototypical scenes. In *Proceedings of the 3rd Workshop on Cognitive Aspects of the Lexicon*, pages 69–80.

Gagliardi, G. (2013). *Validazione dell'ontologia dell'azione IMAGACT per lo studio e la diagnosi del mild cognitive impairment (MCI)*. Ph.D. thesis, University of Florence.

Gagliardi, G. (2014). Rappresentazione dei concetti azionali attraverso prototipi e accordo nella categorizzazione dei verbi generali: una validazione statistica. *Proceedings of the First Italian Conference on Computational Linguistics CLiC-it 2014 and the Fourth International Workshop EVALITA 2014*, pages 180–185.

Gildea, D. and Jurafsky, D. (2002). Automatic labeling of semantic roles. *Computational linguistics*, 28(3):245–288.

Kipper-Schuler, K. (2005). *VerbNet: A broad-coverage, comprehensive verb lexicon*. Ph.D. thesis, University of Pennsylvania.

Levin, B. (1993). *English verb classes and alternations: A preliminary investigation*. University of Chicago press.

Melli, G., Wang, Y., Liu, Y., Kashani, M. M., Shi, Z., Gu, B., Sarkar, A., and Popowich, F. (2006). Description of squash, the sfu question answering summary handler for the duc-2005 summarization task. *Proceedings of the HLT/EMNLP Document Understanding Workshop (DUC)*.

Moneglia, M., Gagliardi, G., Panunzi, A., Frontini, F., Russo, I., and Monachini, M. (2012a). Imagact: Deriving an action ontology from spoken corpora. In *Proceedings of the Eight Joint ACL - ISO Workshop on Interoperable Semantic Annotation (ISA-8). Pisa, October 3-5, 2012*, pages 42–47.

Moneglia, M., Monachini, M., Calabrese, O., Panunzi, A., Frontini, F., Gagliardi, G., and Russo, I. (2012b). The imagact cross-linguistic ontology of action. a new infrastructure for natural language disambiguation. In Nicoletta Calzolari, editor, *Proceedings of the Eight International Conference on Language Resources and Evaluation*, pages 948–955. European Language Resources Association (ELRA).

Moneglia, M., Panunzi, A., and Gregori, L. (2018). Taking events in hindi. a case study from the annotation of indian languages in imagact. In *Proceedings of the LREC 2018 Workshop WILDRE4– 4th Workshop on Indian Language Data: Resources and Evaluation*, pages 46–51. LREC.

Palmer, M., Gildea, D., and Kingsbury, P. (2005). The proposition bank: An annotated corpus of semantic roles. *Computational linguistics*, 31(1):71–106.

Pan, Y., Moneglia, M., Panunzi, A., and Gregori, L. (2018).

Imagact4all. una ontologia per immagini dell'azione per l'apprendimento del lessico verbale di base delle lingue seconde. In Anna De Meo et al., editors, *Usare le lingue seconde*, pages 120–150. Officinaventuno.

Panunzi, A., De Felice, I., Gregori, L., Jacoviello, S., Monachini, M., Moneglia, M., and Quochi, V. (2014). Translating action verbs using a dictionary of images: the imagact ontology. In *Proceedings of the XVI EURALEX International Congress: The User in Focus. Bolzano: EURAC research*, pages 1163–1170.

Rappaport Hovav, M. and Levin, B. (2012). Building verb meanings. In Miriam Butt et al., editors, *The projection of arguments: Lexical and compositional factors*, pages 97–134. CSLI Publications, Stanford, CA.

Rosch, E. (1983). Prototype classification and logical classification: The two systems. *New trends in conceptual representation: Challenges to Piaget's theory*, pages 73–86.

Surdeanu, M., Harabagiu, S., Williams, J., and Aarseth, P. (2003). Using predicate-argument structures for information extraction. In *Proceedings of the 41st Annual Meeting of the Association for Computational Linguistics*.

Talmy, L. (2000). *Toward a cognitive semantics*, volume 1-2. MIT press.

Uresova, Z., Fucíková, E., Hajicová, E., and Hajic, J. (2018). Creating a Verb Synonym Lexicon Based on a Parallel Corpus. In *Proceedings of the Eleventh International Conference on Language Resources and Evaluation (LREC 2018)*.

Proceedings of the 16th Joint ACL-ISO Workshop Interoperable Semantic Annotation (ISA-16), pages 75–87
Language Resources and Evaluation Conference (LREC 2020), Marseille, 11–16 May 2020
© European Language Resources Association (ELRA), licensed under CC-BY-NC

Adapting the ISO 24617-2 Dialogue Act Annotation Scheme for Modelling Medical Consultations

Volha Petukhova[1] and Harry Bunt[2]
[1]Spoken Language Systems Group, Saarland University, Germany
[2]Department of Cognitive Science and Artificial Intelligence, Tilburg University, The Netherlands
`v.petukhova}@lsv.uni-saarland.de; harry.bunt@uvt.nl`

Abstract

Effective, professional and socially competent dialogue of health care providers with their patients is essential to best practice in medicine. To identify, categorize and quantify salient features of patient-provider communication, to model interactive processes in medical encounters and to design digital interactive medical services, two important instruments have been developed: (1) medical interaction analysis systems with the Roter Interaction Analysis System (RIAS) as the most widely used by medical practitioners and (2) dialogue act annotation schemes with ISO 24617-2 as a multidimensional taxonomy of interoperable semantic concepts widely used for corpus annotation and dialogue systems design. Neither instrument fits all purposes. In this paper, we perform a systematic comparative analysis of the categories defined in the RIAS and ISO taxonomies. Overcoming the deficiencies and gaps that were found, we propose a number of extensions to the ISO annotation scheme, making it a powerful analytical and modelling instrument for the analysis, modelling and assessment of medical communication.

Keywords: dialogue act, semantic annotations, medical interaction analysis

1. Introduction

The current call for cost-effective, accessible and user-friendly health care services, together with recent advances in interactive technologies, has triggered an enormous interest in digital medical applications. Many such services are provided online, e.g. ordering medicines, making doctor appointments, accessing medical records (Turgiss et al., 2011). Self-service healthcare is actively promoted. Interactive health screening kiosks are deployed where people can measure their vision, blood pressure, weight and body mass index, receive an overall health assessment, and access a database of local doctors (Bluth, 2009). Health care providers are sometimes replaced by virtual conversational agents (DeVault et al., 2014).

Of chief importance is that the quality of technology-enhanced and technology-mediated services is not significantly lower than conventional in person patient-provider encounters, but adopt a user-centred approach to achieve high effectiveness, relevance and quality. For successful designs and innovations, attention needs to be paid not only to technical possibilities but also very much to the social interactive environment in which these innovations may be placed. Consequently, it is important to understand how well a technical solution fits in with the activities and needs of the users in a proposed setting. Systematic and comprehensive interaction analysis and dialogue modelling methods are often used for obtaining a satisfactory degree of understanding of human interactive behaviour for the subsequent specification of mechanisms of human dialogue that need to be incorporated into a system. A multi-disciplinary analysis of user behavioural, physiological and functional data is required, with processes and results that are understandable by medical and non-medical experts, for staying close to the reality of doctors and patients, and for developing products that are well accepted by their users. The data analysis often involves annotation with dialogue act information. Annotation schemes have been constructed that are useful both for empirically-based studies of interactive and task-related phenomena, and for data-driven design of interactive systems.

A number of studies have proposed the use of a dialogue act taxonomy tailored to the medical domain (Sandvik et al., 2002; Miller and Nelson, 2005; Chang et al., 2013; Bolioli and others, 2019). Most of them are based on the RIAS scheme (Chang et al., 2013; Miller and Nelson, 2005; Bolioli and others, 2019), which has proved efficient for the analysis of various kinds of medical encounters[1], but which cannot be directly used for building a dialogue system or its components. The widely used domain-independent ISO 24617-2 dialogue act taxonomy, on the other hand, needs some adaptation to the medical domain, but is well suited for computational modelling and for dialogue system design. This study tests the assumption that the two schemes are in this sense complementary, and when combined together in a sensible way provide a unified model that supports the quantitative and qualitative analysis of observed behaviour in natural interactive medical settings, while also being useful for quality assessment of interactive and task-related performance of medical professionals, including technology-enhanced and technology-mediated interactions. Moreover, the combined taxonomy can facilitate user-based interactive data collection (real or simulated), as well as the design of conversational medical applications.

The paper is structured as follows. Section 2 specifies the use cases and discusses the related work performed in the analysis and modelling of medical encounters. Section 3 introduces the RIAS and ISO 24617-2 taxonomies. Section 4 presents annotation experiments performed to assess the compatibility of concepts defined in both taxonomies. We specify the corpus data and discuss the obtained results. Section 5 defines a mapping between the RIAS and ISO 24617-2 taxonomies, and proposes extensions to ISO

---

[1]For an overview see (Pires and Cavaco, 2014).

24617-2 in order to make it powerful and accurate, as required for the use cases of analysing and modelling medical interactions. Finally, Section 6 summarizes our findings and outlines directions for future research and development.

2. Use Cases

Dialogue occurs in almost all kinds of patient-provider encounters. It forms a foundation for diagnosis, examination, treatment and therapeutic management. Recording and automatic processing of patient-provider dialogues is desirable in many contexts. Large volumes of patient-related dialogue data can be useful for informed decision making by caregivers. Speech, language and interactive multimodal data has been used to detect dementia and related disorders (Chapman et al., 1998; Cuetos et al., 2007; Mirheidari et al., 2016), depressions and post-traumatic stress disorders (DeVault et al., 2013; Stepanov et al., 2018; Dham et al., 2017). Analysed dialogue data can enhance communication with patients by understanding their concerns and needs. Dialogue data also forms the source for design and training dialogue systems, personalized recommendations and interventions. We consider three important use cases: (1) medical interaction analysis; (2) quality assessment of technology-enhanced or technology-mediated interactions; and (3) dialogue system design.

2.1. Medical interaction analysis

An average physician conducts more than 200,000 consultations in his/her professional career (Silverman et al., 2016). The success of medical consultations relies heavily on how doctors respond to their patients' communicative actions (Langewitz et al., 2002; Conigliaro, 2001; Patel Kuehl, 2011). The principle characteristics of medical communication have been the subject of many studies. Asymmetries are observed where medical staff have the right to initiate and control the interaction and patients have limited initiative rights and responsive tasks, even though the patient has a foreground role in the interaction. Doctors provide and request information, give instructions, i.e. prohibiting or issuing commands, and patients respond 'submissively' to doctors' questions and rarely ask their own (Roter and Hall, 2006). Research on the effects of institutional frameworks on medical communication has been carried out using pragmalinguistic and discourse analyses (Bührig, 1996; Atkinson, 1999). With the current shift to a patient's autonomy in defining and following their medical treatments, interaction analysis can help healthcare providers to assess the degree of patient participation in medical encounters (Street Jr and Millay, 2001).

The success of interactive processes often depends not only on the medical competence of the doctor, but also on his/her linguistic, social and cultural competences (Suchman et al., 1997; Lindemann, 2015). Doctors can exercise several attitudes, e.g. active listening or empathetic silence, and use the emotional context of reassurance, support, and understanding (Kaplan et al., 1989; Lazare et al., 1995). Numerous studies have identified challenges related to cultural differences in language use in doctor-patient interactions (Schyve, 2007; Brach and Fraserirector, 2000; Collins et

al., 2002). Studies on social factors affecting the outcome of medical consultations often focus on politeness and cooperativeness (Robins and Wolf, 1988; Adams, 2013). A considerable body of research has been carried out, with quantitative and qualitative studies reporting results on the number and types of questions asked by doctors and patients, on the use of indirect speech acts and social obligation acts, on the number of times a doctor interrupts a patient and vice versa, on the quantity of speech production repairs, etc., see e.g. (Aronsson and Sätterlund-Larsson, 1987; Ong et al., 1995; Kindler et al., 2005; Roter and Larson, 2002). Interaction analysis is useful to study how effectively caregivers talk to patients, how active patients are when they talk to their caregivers, and how the communicative behaviour of caregivers and that of their patients are related.

2.2. Quality assessment of technology-enhanced medical encounters

A growing body of research results demonstrates that the incorporation of health technologies can make health care more effective and efficient by electronically connecting clinicians to clinicians, patients to clinicians, and even patients to other patients (Clark et al., 2007; Kulshreshtha et al., 2010; Caiata-Zufferey et al., 2010; Weiss, 2004).

With many online and mobile applications now being developed, the effect of telemedicine and other digital health intervention systems on the quality of health provision is of particular concern. Many professionals argue the case for strict regulations, even discussing so-called 'Digital service prescription' of certified services (Murray et al., 2016). To assess the quality of these applications, a variety of evaluation frameworks has been proposed (Field and others, 1996; Grigsby et al., 1995). Although the majority of the research findings favour telemedicine, respondents have reported both positive (cost-effectiveness and accessibility) and negative results (e.g. relating to non-verbal behaviour and lack of touch) (Miller, 2001).

So far not a great deal of research has been devoted to the analysis of communication in technology-enhanced or -mediated consultations. While some attention has been paid to general communicative efficacy, the focus was more broadly on overall performance and satisfaction with the general (including technical) attributes of telemedicine and e-health (Bell, 2018). The impact of technology use on patient's and provider's task-related ('data-gathering' and 'education and counselling') behaviour and socio-emotional aspects ('building a relation' and 'activating and partnership building') is still understudied. Detailed interaction analysis is a useful instrument in the design of a successful technology-enhanced application. It enables the systematic identification, categorization, and quantification of salient features of doctor-patient communication, and when linked with a wide range of outcomes, including patient and provider satisfaction, adherence to treatment, health and clinical status, recall and understanding, and psychological well-being can serve the development of valid and efficient measurement/assessment systems.

Socio-emotional exchange	Task-focused exchange		Global affect ratings
personal remarks, social conversation	transition words		anger/irritation
laughs, tells jokes	gives orientation		anxiety/nervousness
shows (dis-)approval - direct	paraphrase/checks for understanding		depression/sadness
gives compliment - general	bid for repetition		emotional distress/upset
shows agreement or understanding	asks for understanding		dominance/ assertiveness
back-channel responses	asks for opinion		interest/ attentiveness
empathy	asks (open-/close-ended) questions	medical condition,	friendliness/warmth
shows concern/worry	gives information	therapeutic regimen,	responsiveness/engagement
reassures, encourages/shows optimism	counsels/directs behaviour	lifestyle,	sympathetic/empathetic
legitimizes		psychological feelings,	hurried/rushed
partnership		other	respectfulness
shows criticism	requests	services	
asks for reassurance		or medication	

Table 1: Taxonomy of the RIAS actions.

2.3. Dialogue system design

Multimodal dialogue (combinations of spoken and typed language, videos, pictures, facial expressions, haptic and other gestures) is not only the most natural and social form of interaction which is increasingly becoming the most attractive human-machine interface, but is proven to have positive effects in the treatment of certain cognitive impairments (Woods et al., 2012; Hughes et al., 2013), and in health self-management, (Luperfoy, 2004; Reid et al., 2018) patient education (Brixey et al., 2017; Wolf et al., 2019), health behaviour change (Petukhova et al., 2019), and mental and emotional well-being (Fitzpatrick et al., 2017; Inkster et al., 2018; DeVault et al., 2014).

The vast majority of existing dialogue systems make use of dialogue acts[2] as core semantic units to describe and model what is happening in dialogue. Dialogue data annotated with dialogue act information is used to train machine-learning algorithms for the automatic recognition and prediction of dialogue acts in a human-machine dialogue system. The dialogue act taxonomies used for these purposes vary from a simple list of mutually exclusive tags, modelling closed limited domains, to complex hierarchical multidimensional open-domain taxonomies, see (Petukhova, 2011) for an overview.

Currently, a steadily growing interest can be observed in data-driven modelling of dialogue phenomena and dialogue system design. Malchanau et al. (2018) proposed the Continuous Dialogue Corpus Creation (D3C) methodology, where a corpus is used as a shared repository for analysis and modelling of interactive dialogue behaviour, and for implementation, integration and evaluation of dialogue system components. The ISO 24617-2 standard data model is used to facilitate these purposes.

3. Semantic analysis: taxonomy of medical communicative actions

3.1. The Roter Interaction Analysis System

Interaction analysis has been employed in a wide variety of health care settings. The Roter Interaction Analysis System (RIAS) (Roter and Larson, 2002) is the most widely used analysis and evaluation system in medical communication. It was been designed to systematically study and assess medical dialogues in a variety of medical fields, including nursing, adult care, emergency medicine, pediatric

primary care, oncology, etc. RIAS has also been used for training health care providers in communication skills.

RIAS views patient-provider communication as having at least three core functions in parallel: (1) to determine and monitor a medical problem; (2) to develop, maintain, or conclude a therapeutic relationship; and (3) to carry out patient education and implementation of treatment plans, see the 'three functions model' (Lazare et al., 1995). Thus, medical dialogue involves in the first place a **task-related** exchange, consisting of *question-asking* and *information-providing* actions in order to gather data, and *counselling* actions produced by a medical professional to educate a patient and direct/influence his future behaviour, motivating him to adhere to a treatment. Actions related to discussion (negotiation) and implementation of a treatment plan are not defined in RIAS. These actions have the purpose to determine areas/issues of differences (conflicts) between patient and provider, and negotiate to resolve them; communicate the diagnostic significance of the problem; negotiate and recommend appropriate diagnostic procedures and treatment; negotiate and recommend appropriate preventive measures and lifestyle changes; and enhance the coping ability by understanding and dealing with the social and psychological consequences of the disease and the treatment (Tuckett et al., 1985). Negotiation relevant actions such as offer, promise and acceptance/rejection of counselling acts, as well as modal operators for expressing importance, likelihood, desirability, possibility, necessity and ability are important in shared decision making for health behaviour change (Petukhova et al., 2019). In RIAS, task-focused actions also involve *activation strategies* that facilitate the expressions of partner's expectations, preferences and perspectives, such as asking for an opinion, understanding, paraphrasing and interpretation, and are important for a meaningful participation in treatment and decision making (Roter, 2000).

A second type of communicative actions is concerned with **therapeutic relation management**. This category comprises actions in order to (1) define the nature of the relationship; (2) communicate professional expertise; (3) communicate interest, respect, support and empathy; (4) recognize and resolve various relational barriers to patient-provider communication; and (5) elicit the patient's perspective (Lazare et al., 1995). Functions of type (5) are included in RIAS as task-focused actions as discussed above; functions of type (3) and (4) are defined in RIAS as *socio-emotional exchange* and are concerned mostly with **social and interpersonal relations management**. They comprise

---

expressions of worry and concern, optimism and reassurance, empathy and partnership building (social talk, jokes). Functions for (1) and (2) are partially covered in RIAS by the *give orientation* category.

Another important aspect concerns **affective** behaviour performed in order to *build an emotional relation* with the patient through the development of rapport and responsiveness to patient's emotions. The affective aspect includes expressions of and reactions to anger, anxiety, distress, sadness, dominance, etc.

Table 1 gives an overview of the RIAS analysis categories.

3.2. ISO 24617-2 dialogue act annotation scheme

ISO 24617-2 (ISO, 2012) is not just a theoretically grounded and empirically tested inventory of dialogue acts with fine-grained distinctions, it presents a semantic framework for the systematic analysis and computational modelling of multimodal behaviour of dialogue participants. It takes a multidimensional view on dialogue in the sense that participation in a dialogue is viewed as performing several activities in parallel, such as pursuing the dialogue task or activity, providing and eliciting feedback, and taking turns. These activities in various 'dimensions' are called *dialogue acts* and are formally interpreted as update operations on the information states of the dialogue participants. Dialogue acts have two main components: a *semantic content* corresponds to what the utterance is about, e.g. objects, events, etc.; and a *communicative function*, which specifies how an addressee updates his information state with the semantic content when he understands the corresponding aspect of the meaning of a dialogue utterance. A communicative function captures beliefs and intentions of the speaker.

The ISO 24617-2 taxonomy distinguishes 9 dimensions, addressing information about: the domain or task (*Task*), feedback on communicative behaviour of the speaker (*Auto-feedback*) or other interlocutors (*Allo-feedback*), managing difficulties in the speaker's contributions (*Own-Communication Management*) or those of other interlocutors (*Partner Communication Management*), the speaker's need for time to continue the dialogue (*Time Management*), about who should have the next turn (*Turn Management*), the way the speaker is planning to structure the dialogue (*Dialogue Structuring*), and the information motivated by social conventions (*Social Obligations Management*). An updated version of the standard (Bunt et al., 2020) includes additionally the *Contact Management* dimension, adopted from the DIT^{++3} annotation scheme, for acts that serve to establish and manage contact and attention. Moreover, the *Task Management* dimension, known from the DAMSL annotation scheme, is defined as a possible extension, for dealing with discussion or explanation of a certain task or activity that is pursued through the dialogue (as opposed to performing that task/activity).

For each dimension, at most one communicative function can be assigned, which can occur either in this dimension alone (the function is *dimension specific*) or occur in all dimensions (the function is *general purpose*). For example, an utterance with the dimension-specific function Self

---

³https://dit.uvt.nl/

Correction exclusively addresses the *Own Communication Management* dimension. Utterances with a *general purpose* function, such as Inform, can address any dimension (such as e.g. *Task* or *Discourse Structuring*).

The tagset contains 30 dimension-specific functions and 26 general-purpose functions, see Appendix A. When a unit addresses several dimensions simultaneously, multiple tags are assigned. To perform this systematically and accurately, ISO 24617-2 offers flexible segmentation strategies for identifying meaningful dialogue units in multiple dimensions, called 'functional segments', defined as the functionally relevant minimal stretches of communicative behaviour.

Speaker intentions may be complex and may be expressed with a particular attitude or emotion. Nuances concerning certainty, conditionality, or sentiment are captured by means of *qualifiers*. Moreover, dialogue acts are not produced in isolation, but various relations exists between them: functional dependence, feedback dependence and rhetorical relations, see (Bunt et al., 2018) for an updated view.

ISO 24617-2 includes the specification of the XML-based Dialogue Act Markup Language (DiAML) for the representation of dialogue act annotations (Bunt et al., 2012).

4. Applying the ISO 24617-2 standard to annotate medical dialogues

This section reports the results of small-scale annotation experiments, preformed with the aim to assess the applicability of the ISO 24617-2 dialogue act annotation standard to medical interactions and RIAS and ISO compatibility.

4.1. Corpus data

Unfortunately, publicly available dialogue corpora featuring real doctor-patient interactions are rare, primarily for ethical reasons concerning participants' privacy and data security. The corpus considered in this study is the **Distress Analysis Interview Corpus** (DAIC, Gratch et al., 2014), which contains clinical interviews to assist the detection of psychological disorders like anxiety, depression and post-traumatic stress disorder. The part of the corpus publicly released contains interviews collected in the Wizard-of-Oz setting (DAIC-WOZ corpus) where a virtual agent - Ellie - was controlled by humans playing the role of an interviewer who simulates standard protocols for identifying people at risk for post-traumatic stress disorder (PTSD) and depression based on the PTSD Checklist - Civilian Version (Blanchard et al., 1996). Wizards interact with humans who were (pre-)assessed by a professional therapist being either distressed or not-distressed. The DAIC corpus is a multimodal collection of semi-structured clinical interviews starting with neutral questions designed to build rapport and make the participant comfortable, progressing to more specific questions about symptoms and events related to depression and PTSD, and ending with a 'cool-down' phase to ensure that participants do not leave the interview in a distressed state of mind. The corpus contains audio, video, and depth sensor (Microsoft Kinect) recordings of 189 dialogues, and is used in a variety of studies, e.g. in the

Dimension	Functional segments (in %)		
	ALL	from those	
		Interviewer	Interviewee
Task/Activity	62.8	29.1	70.9
Auto Feedback	18.5	76.0	24.0
Allo Feedback	1.9	91.9	8.1
Discourse Structuring	1.1	100.0	0.0
Own Communication Man.	1.9	0.0	100.0
Social Obligations Man.	5.2	76.5	23.5
Turn Management	14.5	0.0	100.0
Time Management	9.4	0.0	100.0

Table 2: Distribution of functional segments across dimensions produced by the interviewer and an interviewee, in terms of relative frequency (in %).

analysis of verbal and non-verbal indicators of psychological distress (DeVault et al., 2013), in automatic depression and PTSD detection from multimodal behaviour (Stepanov et al., 2018; Dham et al., 2017), in the analysis of patient's (disclosure) behaviour when interacting with a virtual therapist, as well as in comparison to human-human interaction using the (unreleased) face-to-face dialogues of the DAIC dataset (Lucas et al., 2014) and the development of a virtual interviewer (DeVault et al., 2014).

To some extent, the DAIC-WOZ data covers all three use cases defined in Section 2. The dialogues are based on a real scenario, involving humans who are patients and humans who simulate medical interviewer behaviour in a role-playing setting. Previous research showed that open and closed role plays are effective for eliciting authentic interactive behaviour and for examining the impact of various factors on the participants' interactive behaviour (Kasper, 2000; Bardovi-Harlig and Hartford, 2005; Al-Gahtani and Roever, 2012). The role-playing method is commonly used in interactive dialogue data collection efforts (Brône and Oben, 2015), and underpins high-fidelity simulations of clinical cases and medical communication training (Kaplonyi et al., 2017; Ker and Bradley, 2013; McGaghie et al., 2010). The DAIC-WOZ dialogues feature technology-enhanced application in the domain of telemedicine, and form the basis for a dialogue system development - the SimSei Kiosk (DeVault et al., 2014).

4.2. Annotations

From the DAIC-WOZ corpus, 11 randomly selected dialogues were manually re-segmented and annotated with ISO 24617-2 dialogue acts and independently with RIAS categories. The selected dataset comprises 2,819 functional segments. The annotations were compared and mapped. If RIAS categories were more specific and captured the utterance meaning more accurately, or if they were not defined in the ISO taxonomy, they were proposed as elements for a future plug-in for as defined in (Bunt, 2019).

Annotations were performed using the ANVIL tool[4], which allows segmentation and annotation in multiple tiers so that for each participant all ISO dimensions and RIAS categories can be specified. Two randomly selected dialogues were annotated by two trained annotators who were not medical experts and were novice users of the RIAS scheme. Inter-coder agreement was measured in terms of Cohen's

---

[4] www.anvil-software.de

kappa for each tagset resulting in moderate agreement for RIAS (kappa of 0.52) and for ISO (kappa of 0.58) on average. Annotators disagreed the most when classifying social and feedback acts from both schemes, and the ISO sentiment qualifiers and the RIAS categories for global affect.

4.3. Results

The analysis shows that the majority of the functional segments is assigned to the **Task** dimension where the Interviewee produced twice as many task-related acts as the Interviewer. The Interviewer is thus successful in achieving the goal to encourage the Interviewee to talk and disclose information and feelings. From the task-related acts about 27% are *questions*, mostly asked by the Interviewer. Following RIAS, questions where annotated as *closed-* (58.8%) and *open-question* (41.2%). It may be noticed here that the inter-annotator agreement assigning these two categories was rather low, measured as 0.47 in terms of kappa, which may be explained by the fact that the RIAS definitions are not very precise, leaving room for subjective interpretation, see (Sandvik et al., 2002; Roter and Larson, 2002) and our discussion in Section 5.

Information-providing acts constitute about 69% of all functional segments and are produced mainly by an Interviewee. The fact that there are almost twice as many information-providing than information-seeking acts can be explained by the fact that the Interviewees' answers were very elaborate. Directives account for about 4% of the observed dialogue acts, mostly in the form of Interviewer *requests* to provide more information or to give examples. These directive dialogue acts cannot be directly mapped to RIAS *counselling* acts since the latter mostly concern medical actions to be undertaken by the patient, described in the semantic content. We mapped them to requests, however, applied to a broader range of semantic content categories than originally specified in RIAS.

As for the semantic content of task-related acts, this concerns discussion of social and demographic conditions including relationships with partners, family and friends plus living conditions and employment details (48.3%), feelings and emotions (27.4%), life style issues such as diets, habits, holidays and exercise/sporting activities (12.4%). and medical conditions which include own and family medical history, illnesses and hospitalizations, recent/current symptoms; and tests and references to diagnostic and prognostic issues (11.4%).

The second large category of dialogue acts is formed by those that report about the speaker's and addressee's processing achievements. This category comprises positive and negative **Auto-** and **Allo-Feedback** acts, and is rather heterogeneous when taking *sentiment qualifiers* into account. While on a binary classification (positive vs negative) almost perfect inter-annotator agreement was achieved (kappa of 0.83), the assignment of qualifiers posed a problem. ISO does not provide a fixed set of sentiment qualifiers. The W3C recommendation EmotionML does not provide a single repository of emotion descriptors, and the available alternative emotion vocabularies it provides are rather general. We used the RIAS categories for 'socio-emotional exchange' and 'global affect'. Our analysis

RIAS category	Segments (in %)	
	Interviewer	Interviewee
task-focused exchange	16.3	83.3
- Open-ended questions	6.2	0.0
- Closed-ended questions	7.8	0.4
- Gives information	0.3	66.3
- Requests	2.5	0.0
- Transition words	0.0	14.5
- Gives orientation	0.4	0.0
- Bid for repetition	0.0	0.4
- Checks for understanding	0.0	1.2
socio-emotional exchange	66.0	34.0
- Show approval	37.1	0.0
- Asks approval	2.6	10.2
- Back-channel responses	12.9	0.0
- Show understanding	17.1	0.0
- Laughs	2.9	0.0
- Personal remarks, social talk	14.3	0.0
- Gives compliment	2.9	0.0
global affect	76.2	23.8
- engagement/responsiveness	4.8	4.8
- interest/attentiveness	9.5	0.0
- anger/irritation	0.0	19.0
- friendliness/warmth	52.4	4.8
- respectfulness	4.7	0.0

Table 3: Distribution of interviewer and interviewee communication categories according to the Roter Interaction Analysis System (RIAS), in terms of relative frequency (in %).

shows that some RIAS socio-emotional acts address participants' processing of own or partner(-s) previous communicative behaviour, such as *back-channel responses*, others are performed for a slightly different purpose (although having that meaning as well), namely to establish and maintain a respectful interpersonal relationship between interlocutors, aiming at a form of partnership and trust for triggering self-disclosure acts and making participants comfortable. We therefore propose to add an additional dimension for social activities management called **Interpersonal Relation Management**. These acts are different from *Social Obligations Management* acts since they are not motivated by social conventions and norms. For example, the utterance 'I'm sorry' in the analysed medical dialogues is not produced with the purpose to apologize for mistakes, dispreferred reactions, misunderstandings or any other infelicitous behaviour, but to express empathy and compassion with the situation the addressee (mostly the patient) is experiencing.

Global affect categories are annotated as ISO sentiment qualifiers. Since the terminology related to emotion, mood, attitude, and sentiment can be rather confusing, we suggest to adopt 'affect' as a general term which denotes a concept used in psychology to describe the experiencing of feeling or emotion, and 'affective states' that are psychophysiological constructs which connect mental and physical processes (Hogg and Abrams, 2007). For ISO 24617-2 plug-ins for affective state qualifiers in medical discourse see the next section.

Table 2 shows the distribution of annotated dialogue acts across ISO dimensions, indicating also the percentage of identified functional segments per dimension produced by different speakers, i.e. by Interviewer and an Interviewee. It is interesting to observe that certain behaviour is performed exclusively by Interviewer, like for the purpose to structure the discourse. This is not surprising, since medical care providers are those who as experts have the power to make decisions concerning what will be discussed. Other dialogue acts, on the other hand, are produced exclusively by an Interviewee like Own Communication, Turn and Time Management acts. This is however assumed to be an artefact of this corpus. In real patient-doctor interaction, it is highly likely that doctors exhibit such behaviour as well since it is very human to stall for time, edit one's own speech, and regulate turn allocations. Virtual conversational agents can improve if they generate these types of dialogue acts as well. What types, where and how frequently, should be estimated when analysed real face-to-face interactions.

Table 3 summarizes the results of annotation performed with the RIAS scheme.

5. RIAS inspired plug-ins for ISO 24617-2

The latest revised version of the ISO 24617-2 dialogue act annotation standard[5] defines **ten** core dimension. RIAS clusters medical actions into **three** categories as discussed above. Even if not explicitly defined, a systematic mapping of RIAS acts to ISO 24617-2 dialogue acts shows that the majority of ISO dimensions is addressed in RIAS and shows a one-to-one correspondence. Other RIAS acts are domain- or use-case dependent, are not defined in ISO but represent a useful extension of the latter in the form of plug-ins. The ISO scheme makes several extensions possible provided they meet certain requirements and formal constraints specified in (Bunt et al., 2018; Bunt, 2019) and summarized in DIT++ Release 5.2[6]. Figure 1 provides an overview of the resulting high-level categorization, where ISO dimensions are highlighted in grey boxes and the extensions obtained from the mapping to RIAS are marked in red.

A top-level distinction is made between communicative actions advancing the underlying **task** and *managing the task*, such as instructions, questions, and answers, and actions that *control the dialogue* (see Bunt, 1994). Dialogue control acts are concerned with cognitive processing (*feedback*) of previously produced behaviour, *interaction management* and *social activities management*.

5.1. Task-focused actions

Medical interactions may be motivated by various purposes, however, the majority of them involve question-answering parts, e.g. for medical history taking, to collect complaints, and to survey problems. For medical professionals, mastering interviewing skills is very important for mature decision-making and action-taking.

RIAS differentiates between more directed focussed questions (*closed-ended*) and more open questions (*open-ended*) that allow greater respondent discretion and a more

---

[5]A proposed second edition is submitted to ISO for circulation and reviewing by ISO member bodies and their experts in September 2019.

[6]`https://dit.uvt.nl/#Release5.2`

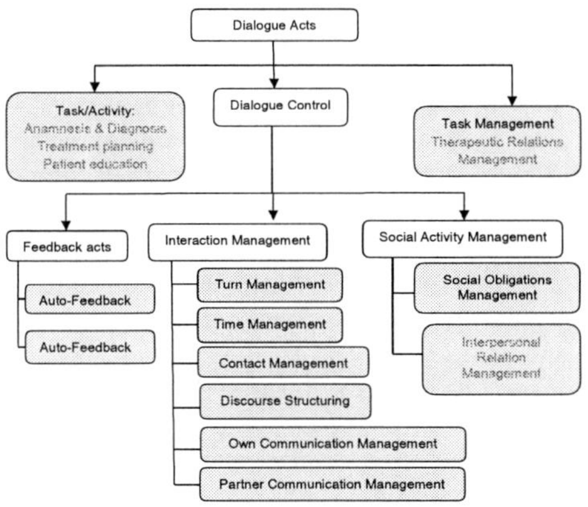

Figure 1: ISO 24617-2 modified to fit medical interaction use cases based on mapping to the RIAS categories. Dimensions are given in grey boxes; optional dimensions in dotted grey boxes; and the modifications obtained from RIAS are marked red.

detailed response. In our annotation experiments, annotation of question forms was found to be complicated but important, as Roter and Larson (2002) also noted. For instance, it has been observed that it is good to start a medical interview with an open-ended question which convey an interest in listening (Patel Kuehl, 2011), whereas an early pursuit of closed questioning may prevent doctors from discovering all the issues and even lead to an incorrect diagnosis (Silverman et al., 2016). RIAS suggests that closed-ended questions produce focused and curtailed responses, while open inquiries and exploratory, investigative or unspecific probing is indicative for the open nature of open-ended questions. Questions where the speaker wants to obtain the truth of a proposition or where the speaker wants to know some or all of the elements of a certain set, thus requiring a specific answer, are closed-ended questions. An open-ended question, as its name suggests, does not seek a specific answer at all, see also (Dhillon et al., 2004).

To elaborate on the response framing power of questions, it has been observed that minor changes in question wording can have a major impact on responses (Schwarz and Oyserman, 2001), and can easily and inadvertently direct the patient away from self-disclosure (Beckman and Frankel, 1984). Linguistic and psychological studies revealed that questions may shape answers (Kellermann, 2007), e.g. suggesting ones and excluding others by open, focused choice, leading, confirmatory questions (De Dreu and Van Kleef, 2004); by carrying assumptions (Zillmann, 1972); and inviting (dis-)agreement, openness or evasion, and threat or comfort (Schuman and Presser, 1996). The ISO 24617-2:2012 set of question types can be further extended to model these differences.

Medical encounters also involve counselling, where doctors *direct* behaviour of their patients expressing their wish that the patient performs or avoids a certain action, possibly dependent on a condition. Different types of directives carry different strengths of the speaker's assumptions about the ability and willingness of the addressee to perform an action (Bunt, 2011).

As noticed above, *commissives* acts are not covered by RIAS, although they play an important role in medical negotiations. For adequate modelling, we need to take into account that negotiators may perform several types of dialogue acts expressing various levels of commitment, but also qualified ('modalised') actions expressing participants' attitudes and preferences, and negotiation strategies (Petukhova et al., 2016; Petukhova et al., 2017; Petukhova et al., 2019).

5.2. Task Management

There is still an ongoing discussion whether Task Management should be included as a separate dimension in ISO 24617-2, as is the case in the DAMSL multidimensional annotation scheme to define acts that discuss the problem solving process or experimental scenario ((Allen and Core, 1997). To model DBOX games (Petukhova et al., 2014) and Metalogue multi-issue bargaining and debate dialogues (Petukhova et al., 2016; Petukhova et al., 2018), Task Management acts were introduced as an ISO 24617-2 extension to address aspects related to game, debate or negotiation processes, phases and procedures. In dialogues in institutional settings, as in a court room or doctor-patient dialogues, task management acts may occur rather frequently, since there is often a clear power relation between the participants. We leave this set largely unspecified for the time being, however, we propose two communicative functions to illustrate this dimension: (1) *Give Orientation* for statements and directives related to an examination or clinical visits, e.g. 'The signal is faint, please speak louder'; and (2) *Discuss Expertise* related to participant roles and areas of expertise, e.g. 'I am your cardiologist'. Other communicative functions can be defined specifically to scenario and/or therapeutic regime management and other arrangements.

5.3. Feedback

In medical interactions, it is important for the doctor not only to signal active listening but also to show a genuine interest and understanding of the patient's behaviour by repeating the information revealed, rephrasing the previously asked questions or provided instructions, confirming or checking for understanding, consistency and validation of the information revealed. Doctors also need to encourage patients to ask questions, express their attitudes, preferences, concerns, fears and opinions. In RIAS, these acts are defined as *activation* strategies.

5.4. Interaction Management

Concerning the Interaction Management functions, only **Turn Management** together with **Time Management** and **Discourse Structuring** are defined in RIAS. However, our annotation experiments indicate that medical interaction analysis will benefit from inclusion of **Contact Management** acts, in particular when applying to telemedicine; of **Own Communication Management** acts when analysing specific patient speech production behaviour; and of specifying **Partner Communication Management** acts to analyse the abilities of participants to detect difficulties and errors in a partner's communicative behaviour.

5.5. Social Activity Management

5.5.1. Social Obligations Management

Participating in a dialogue is a social activity, where one is supposed to do certain things and not to do other things, and to act in accordance with the norms and conventions for social behaviour. A dialogue participant has besides functional also ethical tasks and obligations, and performs social obligation management acts to fulfil these. Social Obligations Management acts are not just 'social', they also improve the transparency of the dialogue. For example, people greet each other also for establishing their presence, and say good-bye also to close the conversation. Such acts, defined in ISO 24617-2, are not covered by RIAS.

5.5.2. Interpersonal Relation Management

A goal in any medical encounter is to establish and maintain a kind of partnership between doctor and patient. Utterances produced for this purpose are not so much meant to exchange information or influence each other's behaviour, but to establish a certain bond between the dialogue participants. Successful partnership building actions promote better cooperation. Here, statements are important that convey the doctor's alliance with the patient in terms of health and support, decision-making, or the development of a therapeutic plan. Patients are often anxious about their medical condition, express concerns or worry, and seek reassurance or special attention. RIAS is particularly explicit concerning these acts, which can be clustered in a separate ISO dimension - **Interpersonal Relation Management** addressing information about the process of patient-provider relationship building, which is important to improve patient satisfaction and health outcomes (Lucas et al., 2014). This is a reason to incorporate types of relational (but also emotional see below) communicative behaviour into the analysis and further modelling.

5.6. Affect

Doctors must be aware of the patient's feelings, motivations, insecurities, engagement and reasons for whether they want to do certain things or not. In ISO 24617-2 this information can be annotated using sentiment qualifiers for which the standard does not specify any specific set of tags. In the revised 2nd edition of the ISO scheme, it is recommended to look to EmotionML (Burkhardt and Schröder, 2008) for specifications of possible sets of emotion and attitude values, and for more sophisticated annotation of the affective aspects of dialogue behaviour. RIAS defines a set of *global affects* that can be used in an ISO 24617-2 plug-in for the specification of participants' attitudes (such as responsiveness, attentiveness, friendliness) and local affective states relating to dialogue acts (such as anger, irritation).

5.7. Semantic Content

ISO 24617-2 focuses on the functional meaning of dialogue acts and does not annotate the semantic content. In the 2nd edition of ISO24617-2, plug-ins are introduced for extending annotations of the functional meaning of dialogue acts with information about their semantic content. it is shown that the degree of detail in which the semantic content of a dialogue act is appropriately represented depends on the application domain (Bunt, 2019). For some domains a simple representation as a list of attribute-value pairs may be adequate. For others a representation in terms of events with their participants, time and place may be more appropriate, and again for more advanced applications it may be necessary to take general aspects of natural language utterance meaning into account, including quantification and modification phenomena.

RIAS supports a high-level specification of the semantic content of medical actions. Task-focused actions are about *medical conditions, therapeutic regime, lifestyle, psychological feelings, services, medication* and *other* content. Miller and Nelson (2005) define a semantic content category related to *technology* used in medical dialogue. An alternative medical interaction analysis system, Medical Interaction Process System (MIPS) (Ford et al., 2000), defines additional semantic content categories, such as *tests, side-effects, drugs, social/demographic circumstances* and *administrative/practical details*.

The table in Appendix A gives an overview of ISO 24617-2 dimensions (in bold) and communicative functions (black), and proposed extensions for medical interaction analysis and modelling in terms of dimensions, communicative functions, sentiment qualifiers and high-level semantic content (in red).

6. Conclusions and Future Efforts

In this paper we proposed a number of extensions to the standard dialogue act annotation scheme, ISO 24617-2, to make it a powerful analytical and modelling instrument for medical interactive data analysis and design of digital services/applications. We started from the assumption that the ISO 24617-2 dialogue act taxonomy and the de-facto standard system for medical interactions analysis, RIAS, would have complementary strengths and weaknesses. Derived from social-exchange theories related to interpersonal influence, problem-solving and empowerment, RIAS has been proven to be useful in in-depth studies of communication dynamics and its relationship to outcomes of patient-provider encounters. Taking the complexities of natural human dialogue into account, ISO 24617-2 adopts a multidimensional view on communication, which has been recognized to be empirically well motivated and to allow accurate modelling of theoretical distinctions. The multidimensional nature of the ISO taxonomy also enables various extensions and offers the opportunity to tailor it to specific applications and domains.

We considered a number of use cases related to medical interaction analysis, quality assessment and dialogue system design. We presented significant findings of communication research performed in face-to-face, technology-enhanced and technology-mediated interaction between healthcare providers and their patients. In addition, we performed a mapping between the ISO and RIAS schemes. Dialogues from the DAIC-WOZ corpus were annotated according to each of them, and the correspondences between assigned tags were analysed. In this way, systematic differences and correspondences between schemes, and their strengths and weaknesses became apparent.

The research reported here has some practical limitations. First of all, the corpus used in this study comprises dialogues in the mental healthcare domain. In such interactions, rapport and trust building is essential for patient's self-disclosure. In other types of medical dialogue, different doctor and patient actions, their sequences and distributions may be observed. However, since the RIAS scheme has been applied for many medical domains and is commonly acknowledged as a generic medical scheme, we do not expect that important aspects (dimensions) are missing in our analysis. Nevertheless, other schemes will be explored which are specific to a particular type of interaction, e.g. the ISBAR scheme for medical handover communication analysis, see e.g. (Spooner et al., 2018), OPTION5 and OPTION12 for shared decision making (Elwyn et al., 2003), or specific to an element of communicative behaviour such as emotions, e.g. the Verona Coding Definition of Emotional Sequences (VR-CoDES) (Del Piccolo et al., 2011).

Not all the labels defined in the two schemes are present in our annotations since the available corpus we used was not large and not very specific. Another limitation is that we could not find multiple annotators equally experienced with both schemes to apply them reliably. Nevertheless, meaningful extensions for medical dialogues were identified that can be converted to plug-ins for the general ISO scheme and can be applied in the future on larger datasets. The plug-ins need to be tested for their usability and coverage in manual and automatic annotation.

Future efforts will be also directed towards larger collections of simulated and real patient-provider dialogue data, with the perspective to enrich task-focused, relationship-building and effective verbal and non-verbal communication strategies for multimodal dialogue systems in healthcare settings and medical training applications.

7. Bibliographical References

Adams, R. L. (2013). *Politeness strategies in decision-making between GPs and patients*. Ph.D. thesis, University of Birmingham.

Al-Gahtani, S. and Roever, C. (2012). Role-playing l2 requests: Head acts and sequential organization. *Applied Linguistics*, 33(1):42–65.

Allen, J. and Core, M. (1997). Draft of damsl: Dialog act markup in several layers. Available at http://www.cs.rochester.edu/research/cisd/resources/damsl/.

Aronsson, K. and Sätterlund-Larsson, U. (1987). Politeness strategies and doctor-patient communication. on the social choreography of collaborative thinking. *Journal of Language and Social Psychology*, 6(1):1–27.

Atkinson, P. (1999). Medical discourse, evidentiality and the construction of professional responsibility. *Talk, work and institutional order: Discourse in medical, mediation and management settings*, 1.

Bardovi-Harlig, K. and Hartford, B. S. (2005). *Interlanguage pragmatics: Exploring institutional talk*. Routledge.

Beckman, H. B. and Frankel, R. M. (1984). The effect of physician behavior on the collection of data. *Annals of Internal medicine*, 101(5):692–696.

Bell, T. (2018). Can telemedicine be both cost efficient and high quality. *US News and World Report*.

Blanchard, E. B., Jones-Alexander, J., Buckley, T. C., and Forneris, C. A. (1996). Psychometric properties of the ptsd checklist (pcl). *Behaviour research and therapy*, 34(8):669–673.

Bluth, C. P. (2009). Community based managed health kiosk system for soliciting medical testing and health study participants, September 24. US Patent App. 12/407,677.

Bolioli, A. et al. (2019). How do physiotherapists and patients talk? developing and annotating rimotivazione dialogue corpus. In *Proceedings of the Sixth Italian Conference on Computational Linguistics*, Bari, Italy.

Brach, C. and Fraserirector, I. (2000). Can cultural competency reduce racial and ethnic health disparities? a review and conceptual model. *Medical Care Research and Review*, 57(1_suppl):181–217.

Brixey, J., Hoegen, R., Lan, W., Rusow, J., Singla, K., Yin, X., Artstein, R., and Leuski, A. (2017). Shihbot: A facebook chatbot for sexual health information on hiv/aids. In *Proceedings of the 18th annual SIGdial meeting on discourse and dialogue*, pages 370–373.

Brône, G. and Oben, B. (2015). Insight interaction: a multimodal and multifocal dialogue corpus. *Language resources and evaluation*, 49(1):195–214.

Bührig, K. (1996). *Reformulierende Handlungen: Zur Analyse sprachlicher Adaptierungsprozesse in institutioneller Kommunikation*, volume 23. Gunter Narr Verlag.

Bunt, H., Alexandersson, J., Choe, J.-W., Fang, A. C., Hasida, K., Petukhova, V., Popescu-Belis, A., and Traum, D. R. (2012). ISO 24617-2: A semantically-based standard for dialogue annotation. In *LREC*, pages 430–437. Citeseer.

Bunt, H., Gilmartin, E., Keizer, S., Pelachaud, C., Petukhova, V., Prévot, L., and Theune, M. (2018). Downward compatible revision of dialogue annotation. In *Proceedings 14th Joint ACL-ISO Workshop on Interoperable Semantic Annotation*, pages 21–34.

Bunt, H., Petukhova, V., Gilmartin, E., Pelachaud, C., Fang, A., Keizer, S., and Prévot, L. (2020). The ISO Standard for Ddialogue Act Aannotation, Ssecond Eedition. In *Proceedings 12th International Conference on Language Resources and Evaluation (LREC(2020)*, Paris. ELRA.

Bunt, H. (2011). The semantics of dialogue acts. In *Proceedings of the Ninth International Conference on Computational Semantics*, pages 1–13. Association for Computational Linguistics.

Bunt, H. (2019). Plug-ins for content annotation of dialogue acts. In *Workshop on Interoperable Semantic Annotation (ISA-15)*, page 33.

Burkhardt, F. and Schröder, M. (2008). Emotion markup language: Requirements with priorities. *W3C Incubator Group report*.

Caiata-Zufferey, M., Abraham, A., Sommerhalder, K., and Schulz, P. J. (2010). Online health information seeking in the context of the medical consultation in switzerland. *Qualitative health research*, 20(8):1050–1061.

Chang, C. L., Park, B. K., and Kim, S. S. (2013). Conversational analysis of medical discourse in rehabilitation: A study in korea. *The journal of spinal cord medicine*, 36(1):24–30.

Chapman, S. B., Highley, A. P., and Thompson, J. L. (1998). Discourse in fluent aphasia and alzheimer's disease: Linguistic and pragmatic considerations. *Journal of Neurolinguistics*, 11(1-2):55–78.

Clark, R. A., Inglis, S. C., McAlister, F. A., Cleland, J. G., and Stewart, S. (2007). Telemonitoring or structured telephone support programmes for patients with chronic heart failure: systematic review and meta-analysis. *Bmj*, 334(7600):942.

Collins, K. S., Hughes, D. L., Doty, M. M., Ives, B. L., Edwards, J. N., and Tenney, K. (2002). *Diverse communities, common concerns: assessing health care quality for minority Americans*. Commonwealth Fund New York.

Conigliaro, R. L. (2001). Communicating with today's patient: Essentials to save time, decrease risk, and increase patient compliance. *Jama: The Journal of the American Medical Association*, 286(6):725.

Cuetos, F., Arango-Lasprilla, J. C., Uribe, C., Valencia, C., and Lopera, F. (2007). Linguistic changes in verbal expression: a preclinical marker of alzheimer's disease. *Journal of the International Neuropsychological Society*, 13(3):433–439.

De Dreu, C. K. and Van Kleef, G. A. (2004). The influence of power on the information search, impression formation, and demands in negotiation. *Journal of Experimental Social Psychology*, 40(3):303–319.

Del Piccolo, L., De Haes, H., Heaven, C., Jansen, J., Verheul, W., Bensing, J., Bergvik, S., Deveugele, M., Eide, H., Fletcher, I., et al. (2011). Development of the verona coding definitions of emotional sequences to code health providers' responses (vr-codes-p) to patient cues and concerns. *Patient education and counseling*, 82(2):149–155.

DeVault, D., Georgila, K., Artstein, R., Morbini, F., Traum, D., Scherer, S., Morency, L.-P., et al. (2013). Verbal indicators of psychological distress in interactive dialogue with a virtual human. In *Proceedings of the SIGDIAL 2013 Conference*, pages 193–202.

DeVault, D., Artstein, R., Benn, G., Dey, T., Fast, E., Gainer, A., Georgila, K., Gratch, J., Hartholt, A., Lhommet, M., et al. (2014). Simsensei kiosk: A virtual human interviewer for healthcare decision support. In *Proceedings of the 2014 international conference on Autonomous agents and multi-agent systems*, pages 1061–1068. International Foundation for Autonomous Agents and Multiagent Systems.

Dham, S., Sharma, A., and Dhall, A. (2017). Depression scale recognition from audio, visual and text analysis. *arXiv preprint arXiv:1709.05865*.

Dhillon, R., Bhagat, S., Carvey, H., and Shriberg, E. (2004). Meeting recorder project: Dialog act labeling guide. Technical report, INTERNATIONAL COMPUTER SCIENCE INST BERKELEY CA.

Elwyn, G., Edwards, A., Wensing, M., Hood, K., Atwell, C., and Grol, R. (2003). Shared decision making: developing the option scale for measuring patient involvement. *BMJ Quality & Safety*, 12(2):93–99.

Field, M. J. et al. (1996). *Telemedicine: A guide to assessing telecommunications for health care*. National Academies Press.

Fitzpatrick, K. K., Darcy, A., and Vierhile, M. (2017). Delivering cognitive behavior therapy to young adults with symptoms of depression and anxiety using a fully automated conversational agent (woebot): a randomized controlled trial. *JMIR mental health*, 4(2):e19.

Ford, S., Hall, A., Ratcliffe, D., and Fallowfield, L. (2000). The medical interaction process system (mips): an instrument for analysing interviews of oncologists and patients with cancer. *Social Science & Medicine*, 50(4):553–566.

Grigsby, J., Schlenker, R. E., Kaehny, M. M., Shaughnessy, P. W., and Sandberg, E. J. (1995). Analytic framework for evaluation of telemedicine. *Telemedicine Journal*, 1(1):31–39.

Hogg, M. A. and Abrams, D. (2007). Social cognition and attitudes.

Hughes, T., Flatt, J., Fu, B., Chang, C.-C., and Ganguli, M. (2013). Engagement in social activities and progression from mild to severe cognitive impairment: the myhat study. *International psychogeriatrics*, 25(04):587–595.

Inkster, B., Sarda, S., and Subramanian, V. (2018). An empathy-driven, conversational artificial intelligence agent (wysa) for digital mental well-being: real-world data evaluation mixed-methods study. *JMIR mHealth and uHealth*, 6(11):e12106.

ISO. (2012). *Language resource management – Semantic annotation framework – Part 2: Dialogue acts. ISO 24617-2*. ISO Central Secretariat, Geneva.

Kaplan, S. H., Greenfield, S., and Ware Jr, J. E. (1989). Assessing the effects of physician-patient interactions on the outcomes of chronic disease. *Medical care*, pages S110–S127.

Kaplonyi, J., Bowles, K.-A., Nestel, D., Kiegaldie, D., Maloney, S., Haines, T., and Williams, C. (2017). Understanding the impact of simulated patients on health care learners' communication skills: a systematic review. *Medical education*, 51(12):1209–1219.

Kasper, G. (2000). Data collection in pragmatics research. *Culturally speaking: Managing rapport through talk across cultures*, 316341.

Kellermann, K. (2007). Persuasive question asking: how question wording influences answers. In *Annual Meeting of the State Bar Association of California, Anaheim, CA*.

Ker, J. and Bradley, P. (2013). Simulation in medical education. *Understanding medical education: Evidence, theory and practice*, pages 175–192.

Kindler, C., Szirt, L., Sommer, D., Häusler, R., and Langewitz, W. (2005). A quantitative analysis of anaesthetist–patient communication during the pre-operative visit. *Anaesthesia*, 60(1):53–59.

Kulshreshtha, A., Kvedar, J. C., Goyal, A., Halpern, E. F., and Watson, A. J. (2010). Use of remote monitoring to improve outcomes in patients with heart failure: a pilot trial. *International journal of telemedicine and applications*, 2010:3.

Langewitz, W., Conen, D., Nübling, M., and Weber, H. (2002). Communication matters–deficits in hospital care from the patients' perspective. *Psychotherapie, Psychosomatik, medizinische Psychologie*, 52(8):348–354.

Lazare, A., Putnam, S. M., and Lipkin, M. (1995). Three functions of the medical interview. In *The medical interview*, pages 3–19. Springer.

Lindemann, K. (2015). Emotionen in medizinischer kommunikation. *Handbuch Sprache in der Medizin*, 11:154.

Lucas, G. M., Gratch, J., King, A., and Morency, L.-P. (2014). It's only a computer: Virtual humans increase willingness to disclose. *Computers in Human Behavior*, 37:94–100.

Luperfoy, S. (2004). Retrofitting synthetic dialog agents to game characters for lifestyle risk training. In *AAAI Fall Symposium on Dialogue Systems for Health Communication*.

Malchanau, A., Petukhova, V., and Bunt, H. (2018). Towards continuous dialogue corpus creation: Writing to corpus and generating from it. In *Proceedings of the 11th International Conference on Language Resources and Evaluation(LREC 2018)*, Myiazaki, Japan.

McGaghie, W. C., Issenberg, S. B., Petrusa, E. R., and Scalese, R. J. (2010). A critical review of simulation-based medical education research: 2003–2009. *Medical education*, 44(1):50–63.

Miller, E. A. and Nelson, E.-L. (2005). Modifying the roter interaction analysis system to study provider–patient communication in telemedicine: promises, pitfalls, insights, and recommendations. *Telemedicine Journal & e-Health*, 11(1):44–55.

Miller, E. A. (2001). Telemedicine and doctor-patient communication: an analytical survey of the literature. *Journal of telemedicine and telecare*, 7(1):1–17.

Mirheidari, B., Blackburn, D., Reuber, M., Walker, T., and Christensen, H. (2016). Diagnosing people with dementia using automatic conversation analysis. In *Proceedings of interspeech*, pages 1220–1224. ISCA.

Murray, E., Hekler, E. B., Andersson, G., Collins, L. M., Doherty, A., Hollis, C., Rivera, D. E., West, R., and Wyatt, J. C. (2016). Evaluating digital health interventions: key questions and approaches.

Ong, L. M., De Haes, J. C., Hoos, A. M., and Lammes, F. B. (1995). Doctor-patient communication: a review of the literature. *Social science & medicine*, 40(7):903–918.

Patel Kuehl, S. (2011). Communication tools for the modern doctor bag. physician patient communication part 1: beginning of a medical interview. *Journal of community hospital internal medicine perspectives*, 1(3):8428.

Petukhova, V., Gropp, M., Klakow, D., Schmidt, A., Eigner, G., Topf, M., Srb, S., Motlicek, P., Potard, B., Dines, J., et al. (2014). The DBOX corpus collection of spoken human-human and human-machine dialogues. In *Proceedings of the Ninth International Conference on Language Resources and Evaluation (LREC 14)*. European Language Resources Association (ELRA).

Petukhova, V., Stevens, C. A., de Weerd, H., Taatgen, N., Cnossen, F., and Malchanau, A. (2016). Modelling multi-issue bargaining dialogues: Data collection, annotation design and corpus. In *LREC*.

Petukhova, V., Bunt, H., and Malchanau, A. (2017). Computing negotiation update semantics in multi-issue bargaining dialogues. In *Proceedings of the SemDial 2017 (SaarDial) Workshop on the Semantics and Pragmatics of Dialogue*, Saarbrücken, Germany.

Petukhova, V., Malchanau, A., Oualil, Y., Klakow, D., Luz, S., Haider, F., Campbell, N., Koryzis, D., Spiliotopoulos, D., Albert, P., Linz, N., and Alexandersson, J. (2018). The metalogue debate trainee corpus: Data collection and annotations. In *Proceedings of the 11th International Conference on Language Resources and Evaluation*. Paris: ELRA.

Petukhova, V., Sharifullaeva, F., and Klakow, D. (2019). Modelling shared decision making in medical negotiations: Interactive training with cognitive agents. In *International Conference on Principles and Practice of Multi-Agent Systems*, pages 251–270. Springer.

Petukhova, V. (2011). *Multidimensional Dialogue Modelling. PhD dissertation*. Tilburg University, The Netherlands.

Pires, C. M. and Cavaco, A. M. (2014). Communication between health professionals and patients: review of studies using the rias (roter interaction analysis system) method. *Revista da Associação Médica Brasileira*, 60(2):156–172.

Reid, M., Walsh, C., Raubenheimer, J., Bradshaw, T., Pienaar, M., Hassan, C., Nyoni, C., and Le Roux, M. (2018). Development of a health dialogue model for patients with diabetes: A complex intervention in a low-/middle income country. *International journal of Africa nursing sciences*, 8:122–131.

Robins, L. S. and Wolf, F. M. (1988). *Confrontation and politeness strategies in physician-patient interactions*. Elsevier.

Roter, D. and Hall, J. A. (2006). *Doctors talking with patients/patients talking with doctors: improving communication in medical visits*. Greenwood Publishing Group.

Roter, D. and Larson, S. (2002). The roter interaction analysis system (rias): utility and flexibility for analysis of medical interactions. *Patient education and counseling*, 46(4):243–251.

Roter, D. (2000). The medical visit context of treatment decision-making and the therapeutic relationship. *Health Expectations*, 3(1):17–25.

Sandvik, M., Eide, H., Lind, M., Graugaard, P. K., Torper, J., and Finset, A. (2002). Analyzing medical dialogues: strength and weakness of roter's interaction analysis system (rias). *Patient education and counseling*, 46(4):235–241.

Schuman, H. and Presser, S. (1996). *Questions and answers in attitude surveys: Experiments on question form, wording, and context*. Sage.

Schwarz, N. and Oyserman, D. (2001). Asking questions about behavior: Cognition, communication, and questionnaire construction. *The American Journal of Evaluation*, 22(2):127–160.

Schyve, P. M. (2007). Language differences as a barrier to quality and safety in health care: the joint commission perspective. *Journal of general internal medicine*, 22(2):360–361.

Silverman, J., Kurtz, S., and Draper, J. (2016). *Skills for communicating with patients*. CRC Press.

Spooner, A. J., Aitken, L. M., Corley, A., and Chaboyer, W. (2018). Developing a minimum dataset for nursing team leader handover in the intensive care unit: A focus group study. *Australian Critical Care*, 31(1):47–52.

Stepanov, E. A., Lathuiliere, S., Chowdhury, S. A., Ghosh, A., Vieriu, R.-L., Sebe, N., and Riccardi, G. (2018). Depression severity estimation from multiple modalities. In *2018 IEEE 20th International Conference on e-Health Networking, Applications and Services (Healthcom)*, pages 1–6. IEEE.

Street Jr, R. L. and Millay, B. (2001). Analyzing patient participation in medical encounters. *Health communication*, 13(1):61–73.

Suchman, A. L., Markakis, K., Beckman, H. B., and Frankel, R. (1997). A model of empathic communication in the medical interview. *Jama*, 277(8):678–682.

Tuckett, D., Boulton, M., Olson, C., and Williams, A. (1985). *Meetings Between Experts. An Approach to Sharing Ideas in Medical Consultations*. London: Tavistock.

Turgiss, J. L., Boylan, R. M., and Harrison, G. R. (2011). Interactive, internet supported health and fitness management system, September 27. US Patent 8,027,822.

Weiss, N. (2004). E-mail consultation: clinical, financial, legal, and ethical implications. *Surgical neurology*, 61(5):455–459.

Wolf, M., Petukhova, V., and Klakow, D. (2019). Term-based extraction of medical information: Pre-operative patient education use case. In *Proceedings of the International Conference on Recent Advances in Natural Language Procesing (RANLP 2019)*, Varna, Bulgaria.

Woods, B., Aguirre, E., Spector, A., and Orrell, M. (2012). Cognitive stimulation to improve cognitive functioning in people with dementia. *Cochrane Database Syst Rev*, 2(2).

Zillmann, D. (1972). Rhetorical elicitation of agreement in persuasion. *Journal of personality and social psychology*, 21(2):159.

8. Language Resource References

Gratch et al. 2014 The distress analysis interview corpus of human and computer interviews. In Proceedings of LREC 2014, pages 3123–3128

Appendix A ISO 24617-2:2012 dimensions and communicative functions in extended with RIAS acts, semantic content and sentiment qualifiers

General-Purpose Communicative Functions	Semantic Content	Dimension-Specific Communicative Functions		Sentiment Qualifiers
		Function	Dimension	
Open-ended Question	medical conditions	Give orientation	**Task Management**	anger/irritation
- Open-ended Set-Question	- symptoms	Discuss Expertise		anxiety/nervousness
- Open-ended Propositional Question	- diagnosis	AutoPositive	**Auto-Feedback**	depression/sadness
Close-ended Question	- prognosis	AutoNegative		emotional distress/upset
- Close-ended Set-Question	- history	AlloPositive	**Allo-Feedback**	dominance/assertiveness
- Close-ended Propositional Question	therapeutic regimen	AlloNegative		interest/attentiveness
- - Check-Question	- tests	FeedbackElicitation		friendliness/warmth
- Choice-Question	- medication	- Elicit Understanding		responsiveness/engagement
Inform	- treatment	- Elicit Opinion		sympathetic/empathetic
- Agreement	psychological feeling	Stalling	**Time Management**	hurried/rushed
- Disagreement	- dreams	Pausing		respectfulness
- - Correction	- memories	Turn Take	**Turn Management**	
- Answer	- thoughts	Turn Grab		
- - Confirm	- images	Turn Accept		
- - Disconfirm	lifestyle	Turn Keep		
Request	- habits	Turn Give		
- Instruct	- diet	Turn Release		
- Counsel	- hobby	Self-Error	**Own Communication Man.**	
Address Offer	- occupation	- Retraction		
- Accept Offer	- sport	- - Self-Correction		
- Decline Offer	soc./demographic circumstances	Completion	**Partner Communication Man.**	
Suggest	- family	Correct Misspeaking		
Address Suggestion	- partners	Interaction Structuring	**Discourse Structuring**	
- Accept Suggestion	- friends	- Opening		
- Decline Suggestion	- living conditions	Init-Greeting	**Social Obligations Man.**	
Offer	- education	Return Greeting		
- Promise	- employment	Init-Self-Introduction		
Address Request	administrative details	Return Self-Introduction		
- Accept Request	- GP contact	Apology		
- Decline Request	- appointments	Accept Apology		
	- med.forms	Thanking		
	- other arrangements	Accept Thanking		
	services	Init-Goodbye		
	- collection medication	Return Goodbye		
	- transport	Compliment	**Interpersonal Relation Man.**	
	- calling up	Empathy		
	- home visits	Concern/worry		
	- shopping	Reassurance		
	- cleaning	Legitimize		
	other	Criticism		
		Compassion		
		Self-disclosure		
		Jokes		
		Small talk		

Table 4: ISO 24617-2 dimensions (in bold) and communicative functions (black), and proposed RIAS extensions for medical interaction analysis and modelling in terms of dimensions, communicative functions, sentiment qualifiers and high-level semantic content (in red).

Proceedings of the 16th Joint ACL-ISO Workshop Interoperable Semantic Annotation (ISA-16), pages 88–93
Language Resources and Evaluation Conference (LREC 2020), Marseille, 11–16 May 2020
© European Language Resources Association (ELRA), licensed under CC-BY-NC

Detection and Annotation of Events in Kannada

Suhan Prabhu, Ujwal Narayan, Alok Debnath, Sumukh S, Manish Shrivastava
Language Technologies Research Center
International Institute of Information Technology
Hyderabad, India
{suhan.prabhuk, ujwal.narayan, alok.debnath, sumukh.s}@research.iiit.ac.in
m.shrivastava@iiit.ac.in

Abstract

In this paper, we provide the basic guidelines towards the detection and linguistic analysis of events in Kannada. Kannada is a morphologically rich, resource poor Dravidian language spoken in southern India. As most information retrieval and extraction tasks are resource intensive, very little work has been done on Kannada NLP, with almost no efforts in discourse analysis and dataset creation for representing events or other semantic annotations in the text. In this paper, we linguistically analyze what constitutes an event in this language, the challenges faced with discourse level annotation and representation due to the rich derivational morphology of the language that allows free word order, numerous multi-word expressions, adverbial participle constructions and constraints on subject-verb relations. Therefore, this paper is one of the first attempts at a large scale discourse level annotation for Kannada, which can be used for semantic annotation and corpus development for other tasks in the language.

Keywords: Corpus Annotation, Kannada Event Analysis, Event Detection

1. Introduction

Event detection and analysis is a rapidly evolving field of Natural Language Processing (NLP) and Information Retrieval and Extraction, as it allows us to generalize temporal data in terms of actual time and relative to other occurrences and events. Providing temporal and sequential information can enrich text and its representations which can be used for multiple downstream NLP tasks such as question answering, automatic summarization and inference, in an interpretable and linguistically informed manner. However, automatic event analysis, like many discourse analysis and representation tasks, requires extensive manually annotated training data.

Kannada is a resource poor, morphologically rich Dravidian language with about 45 million speakers[1], mostly located in southern India. Work in Kannada NLP has been limited to the development of tools for syntactic and morphological analysis, almost no work has been done in semantic tasks in this language (Mallamma and Hanumanthappa, 2014), due to few experts, lack of training data and the morphological and semantic characteristics of the language. This paper is one of the first attempts to introduce a semantic analysis and enrichment task at a semantic level into Kannada, i.e. semantic level event detection and analysis.

In this paper, we aim to understand the various parts of speech, syntactic structures, and associated semantic patterns that allow the identification and representation of events in Kannada. We also present the challenges associated with identifying events in Kannada due to morphosyntactic constraints such as multi-word expressions, ubiquity of verbal, adverbial and adjectival participles, analytic verb negation, and absence of copula (Kittel, 1993). We follow a derivation from the TimeML event definition, which has been modified to adapt the zero-copula and participial constructions, so as to make it less ambiguous for annotators.

Finally, we present a dataset of 3,500 annotated sentences, along with a detailed analysis of the dataset including some basic dataset statistics. We annotate events on the Kannada Dependency Treebank (Rao et al., 2014), which consisted of approximately 4,800 event mentions. We show that our guidelines are succinct to a Kannada annotator by our high inter-annotator agreement, along with a distribution over various syntactic structures and a linguistically motivated explanation for challenges in some constructions that have been elaborated in Section 5. The corpus has been made freely available[2].

2. Related Work

In this section, we introduce some of the work done in event detection in low resource and morphologically rich languages, with a focus on TimeML event extraction, or event representation in Indian languages. TimeML was introduced by Pustejovsky et al. (2003) as a mechanism of recognizing, annotating, classifying and representing events in text for the purpose of question answering. TimeML has been used in event detection across languages such as Italian (Caselli et al., 2011), French (Bittar et al., 2011), Romanian (Forăscu and Tufiş, 2012), and Spanish (Saurı, 2010). Of course, corpora annotated with TimeML events have often been done alongside the detection of other temporal information such as time expressions, temporal links and other notions.

For languages which have syntactic structures that vary significantly from English, event detection is used as an introductory task and the definition of an event is modified to be true to the syntactic structure of the language. Examples of this include event detection in Turkish (Seker and Diri, 2010), Hindi (Goud et al., 2019), Hungarian (Subecz, 2019) and Swedish (Berglund, 2004).

Much of the work done in event detection in Indian languages is based on events in social media. Rao and Devi

---

[1] https://www.ethnologue.com/language/kan

[2] https://drive.google.com/drive/folders/ 11ZXpP4mQcDcM91SKHiSNEtWi_mAkXku7

(2018) has provided a forum dedicated to social media event extraction for Indian languages. Deep learning methods have also been used for a few Indian languages such as Hindi, Tamil and Malayalam (Kuila and Sarkar, 2017). However, these events are based on the ACE definition and analysis of events, which does not consider all event predicates (Ahn, 2006), and views event analysis solely as a task in semantic prediction, without the explicit demarcation and analysis of the surrounding syntax (Ji and Grishman, 2008).

3. Kannada Grammar and Event Representation

In this section, we explore the facets of Kannada grammar that facilitate the representation of events. We begin by considering the notion of a TimeML event. According to Pustejovsky et al. (2003) and Saurí et al. (2006), TimeML defines an event as *a cover term for situations that happen or occur*, as well as *predicates in which something obtains or holds true*. Adopting Goud et al. (2019)'s definition, we consider an event mention as the textual span expected to provide complete information about an event, such as tense, aspect, modality and negation. We also consider the event nugget to be the semantically meaningful unit that expresses the event in a sentence (Mitamura et al., 2015). Kannada is a free word order, morphologically rich language. However, by convention, verbs usually occur at the end of the sentence. Passive voice is rare. The subject often occurs in nominative case, the object in dative. There are a few primary notions of Kannada syntax which are crucial to event annotation. These include:

- **Kannada is a zero-copula language** (Schiffman, 1979). Copular constructions in Kannada occur without an overt verb (Bhat, 1981). In copular sentences, tense is represented by a modification of the predicate. These predicates are used for copular clauses. As the state is represented by a morphaffixed form of a simple nominal predicate, we do not consider these events at the moment.

  1. *nanna   hesaru   ujwal*
     my   name   Ujwal
     My name is Ujwal

- **Every sentence has only one finite or conjugated verb** (Schiffman, 1979). Therefore, sentences with coordinating and subordinating verbs are modified into adjectival and adverbial participle constructions as non-finite verb forms. The tense and aspect information is morphaffixed onto the verb. These adverbial or adjectival participles provide the semantic connotation of an occurrence which describes another action or occurrence, so we annotate these participles in our event mention.

  2. *Oorige   bandidda   Arjun,*
     town to   come had   Arjun

     jaatrege   hodanu
     festival to   go
     Arjun, who had come to town, went to the festival.

Since Kannada has only one verb per sentence, relative clauses are converted into adjectival constructions, which *describe* the verb in the relative clause as a description of the subject of the main verb. Therefore, the sentence "Arjun came to town and went to the festival" can not be translated into Kannada directly. There is no possible mechanism to represent this sentence, other than the inclusion of an adverbial clause to the coordinating verb that occurs semantically prior to the main verb (i.e. is meant to take place before the main verb). This implies a general notion of sequentiality between the main verb and the adjectival construction.

- **Kannada employs tenseless negative forms** (Lindblom, 2014). Negative forms are analytically represented by a single functional negative term. While there are no semantically negative words in Kannada, a single functional negative form is morphaffixed onto the finite verb, or the non-finite adjectival or adverbial participle. Therefore, negations are considered a part of the event mention.

  3. *Sumukh   ootakke   baralilla*
     Sumukh   dinner for   didn't come
     Sumukh did not come for dinner

- **Tense, aspect and modality of Kannada verbs** are represented morphologically (Shastri, 2011). Tense and aspect markers are morphaffixed onto both finite and non-finite forms. Therefore, adverbial and adjectival participles have tense, aspect and modality. Therefore, this information is inherently a part of the event mention.

  4. *Ram   tale   tirugi   biddanu*
     Ram   head   spin   fell
     Ram, after getting dizzy, fell down

4. Annotation Guidelines

In this section, we provide comprehensive guidelines for the annotation of events in Kannada. Inspired by TimeML, we present these guidelines categorized by the POS of the event nugget. These parts of speech include nouns, finite verbs, non-finite verb constructions such as infinitives, as well as adjectival and adverbial participle constructions.

The TimeML definition of event was used for event annotation in Kannada, following a slight modification based on the changes adopted by Goud et al. (2019). These changes were associated with the analysis and representation of copular constructions as states. Given the morphology of Kannada and the notion of an event nugget being restricted to a lexical or supra-lexical span, we do not annotate copula as events as of now, as Kannada is a zero-copula language, and the representation of such constructions is based on predicate inflections.

In the subsections that follow, we describe the guidelines for annotating events by parts of speech and provide an example for each type. The event of that category is represented in bold in the Kannada transliteration of the sentence.

4.1. Nouns

Nouns can also be events, albeit they occur much more rarely than verbs. Nominal events are abstract nouns which pertain to a temporal phenomenon (i.e. possess a semantically inherent notion of finiteness), such as *yuddha* (war), *kshaama* (famine), *cunaavanegalu* (elections) etc.
For example:

Bharat	*bandina*	*bagge*
India	Strike	about

5.

mantrigallu	*yaccharike*	*needidaru*
minister	warning	give

The minister issued a warning about an all India strike.

4.2. Verbs

Verbs are often morphologically marked due to the relaxed constraints on word order, and therefore events can occur at any place in the sentence and can be identified by identifying the main verb. (Veerappan et al., 2011).

4.2.1. Finite Verbs

Finite verbs are considered events as they represent an action that alters that state of the world, possess tense and aspect information, which provides it an inherent notion of temporality.

rajeyannu	*tagedikollalu*	*ramanu*
holiday	take	Ram

6.

arji	*sallisidanu*
application	submit

Ram submitted an application to take a vacation

4.2.2. Non-finite verb forms

Kannada syntax enforces the rule of one finite verb per sentence, all other verb forms are participles (adjectival or adverbial), infinitives and subjunctives. Kannada does not have a gerund verb form.

Adjectival Participle Construction   In adjectival participle constructions, the verb is converted into an adjective, so as to describe the noun participating in the main verb by its previous actions. The semantics of the adjectival participle enforces a notion of sequentiality with respect to the main verb, and also represents a notion of finiteness of the action. Furthermore, the adjectival participle is inflected with tense, aspect and modality. Therefore, these constructions are annotated as events.
For example:

7.

avalu	*malagalu*	*manege*	*hodalu*
she is	to bed	home	gone

She slept after going home.

Adverbial Participle Construction   Similar to adjectival constructions, the adverbial participle form is used to represent those verbs performed by or associated to the noun in dative (or accusative) case. Here, there is no direct sequentiality applied or associated with the main verb and the adverbial participle.
For example:

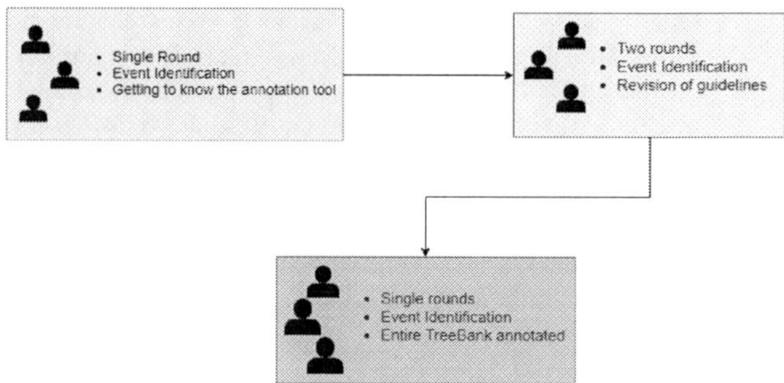

Figure 1: Annotation Procedure

8.

oodtiruva	*jinkeyannu*	*betegaaranu*	*hodedanu*
running	deer	hunter	hit

The hunter shot the running deer.

Infinitives   Infinitive verbs in Kannada occurs with the characteristic inflective ending of *'lu'* These infinivitve forms of the verb are also marked as events.
For example:

9.

naanu	*iiga*	*aata*	*aadalu*	*hoguttene*
I'm	now	game	play	go

I'm going to play games now.

Subjunctives   The subjunctive is a rare type of verb that expresses something that is desired or imagined. Subjunctives are used to indicate events that are not certain to happen, and hence subjunctive verbs are also annotated as events. Subjunctives can be morphologically inflected for tense, aspect and modality.
For example:

10.

ninage	*olleyadagali*	*yendu*	*naanu*	*bayasutene*
You	be good	that	I	wish

I wish you good.

5.   Dataset Preparation and Challenges

In this section, we describe the annotation procedure used to create the Kannada Event Annotated Dataset, and some of the linguistic challenges associated with this task.

5.1.   Annotation Procedure

In order to identify events in our corpus, we iteratively annotated the dataset in four rounds. There were three annotators, undergraduate and graduate students annotating this corpus. Each annotator is a native speaker of Kannada and between the ages 20 and 25. We used the BRAT tool for annotating event spans. (Stenetorp et al., 2012).

For the first three rounds of annotation, the sentences were shuffled and each annotator was asked to annotate half the dataset for events, based on a version of the guidelines provided. After each round of annotation, the inter-annotator agreement was calculated based on the *complete overlap*. Two annotations are said to be in complete overlap if both annotations have the same span of text annotated as an event. Partial overlap is not considered for the inter-annotator agreement score.

The first round was dedicated to the annotators getting used to the tool in general, while the second and third rounds was intended to modify the guidelines for event annotation. In the final round of annotation, the dataset was shuffled and the entire Kannada Dependency Treebank was annotated for events by each annotator. As before, annotations were compared and the inter-annotator agreement was computed for *complete overlap*. The final annotations in the dataset presented with this paper consist of that annotation which was agreed upon by the annotators after computing the scores by majority agreement.

5.2. Challenges in Event Annotation

We describe here, in detail, some of the major linguistic challenges faced during annotating events in Kannada. We consider this description to be crucial due to the properties shared by Kannada and other Dravidian languages. We believe that a thorough analysis of these challenges will make the annotation of events in other Dravidian languages easier.

Copular constructions   As mentioned in Section 3., Kannada is a zero-copula language. This means that the tense information for existential terms is carried by the predicate of the sentence. However, the semantic equivalent of the verb "to be" is not represented lexically in sentences. This raises the question that for a sentence such as:

11.
   karu   *kempu*   *bannadallide*
   car   red   colour
The car is red in color.

is "having colour" the event trigger? In this paper, we do not consider this an event nugget, because neither is the event trigger a lexical marker, nor is it consistent with the definition of event nugget for the other syntactic categories of events. Note that in the past tense, the standard copular construction is represented as an adjectival phrase with tense information. Therefore:

12.
   karu   *kempu*   *baNaDaagittu*
   car   red   coloured
The car was red in color.

Explicator Compound Verbs   An explicator compound verb (ECV) is a sequence of two verbs, where the main verb of a sentence is followed by a delexicalized verb in the construction (Abbi and Gopalakrishnan, 1991). South Asian languages show an affinity to ECV constructions for semantic emphasis as well as verbalization of nominal predicates (Kachru and Pandharipande, 1980). An example of such a construction includes:

13.
   Ramanu   *ravananannu*   **kondu**   **hakidanu**
   Ram   Ravana   kill   laid
Ram decimated Ravana.

In this sentence, we see that the compound verb *kondu hakidanu* is a single semantic unit which represents the event of "killing". The second word *hakinadu* (literally, "laid to rest") loses its lexical meaning in order to act as an emphasis marker for the main verb *kondu* (literally, "to kill").

Conjunct Verbs   Conjunct verbs in Kannada are a combination of a noun or adjective with a verb, such that the verb is delexicalized and serves as a verbalizer to provide a single semantic notion of an occurence or action. The verbalizer is often inflected with the tense, aspect and modality, while the noun contains the semantics of the event. Therefore, while the verb is included in the event span, the noun accounts for the event nugget. For example:

14.
   naanu   *raamige*   **bharavase**   **niDiddene**
   I   Ram to   trust   request
I promised Ram.

We see here that the phrase *bharavase niDiddene* is an idiomatic phrase (literally "to request trust") which forms a noun and verb compound which has a single semantic connotation, i.e. "to promise". Therefore it is a compound verb.

6.   Generalizing Dataset Development

In this section, we present the procedure and analysis of the development of guidelines for event detection from a holistic, language independent perspective. While the paper thus far depicts the detection and annotation of events, the development of guidelines for event representation, and the associated challenges specifically for Kannada, we would like to emphasize that events are a real-world constructs which are being given a representation in a given language. Therefore, there are some task-specific but language agnostic steps that can be taken for annotating and representing events in morphologically rich languages in general.

As presented above, an understanding of the linguistic philosophy behind event representation is critical to understand how a language's syntax allows for the linking of participants to an action or occurrence. Furthermore, event analysis depends on the morphological or syntactic components associated with marking time, duration, telicity, durativity as well as case relations (Pustejovsky, 1991).

Therefore, the first step in the generalized understanding of events in a morphologically rich language is the isolation of inflections that provide tense, aspect and modality information. The heterogeneity of the markers provides the various possible inflections (and irregular constructions if any) in which an event can take place. While in most language tense and aspect are fairly rigorous (Giorgi and Pianesi, 1997), the modality of verbs and verbal predicates need to be analyzed on a granular level.

Morante and Sporleder (2012) presents a thorough study into annotation and corpus linguistics into the role of modality and negation as extra-propositional aspects. Indeed, in event annotation, both negation and modality play a role in the complete description of an event. However, languages vary in their representation of modal verbs and negative polarity, and therefore, development of guidelines for these event features becomes a language specific problem. Indeed, while the guidelines developed and challenges faced in Section 4. are to be seen, if development in event detection takes place in Telugu, Tamil and other Dravidian languages, it should be noted that modality and polarity are represented differently in each of these languages. Therefore, it is one of the major challenges in event representation.

Data Type	Total Number
Tokens	37020
Sentences	3583

Table 1: Corpus Statistics

Event type	Total Number of Events
Single Word Events	3114
Multi Word Events	1686

Table 2: Event Type Statistics

7. Corpus Statistics

In this section, we explain the corpus, and some basic statistics associated with it, including the dataset size, the number of events, and their category-wise distribution. Finally, we consider the computation of the inter-annotator agreement and show that the dataset is in fact quite reliable, as it shows a high Fliess' Kappa Score of 0.91 in the final round of annotation.

We annotated the Kannada Dependency Treebank (Rao et al., 2014)[3] for event mentions. The Dependency Treebank corpus consists of 37,020 tokens, from distinct domains such as tourism, general and conversational.

As presented in Table 1 the dataset is divided into 3,583 sentences. The dataset has been annotated with 4,800 events, out of which 3,114 events consist of a single word in the event span, while 1,686 events have a multiword event span as seen in Table 2. There are 686 sentences which do not have any events as they are entirely copular in nature. This implies that sentences with multiple events are not uncommon in general.

In all the rounds of annotation mentioned in section 5., inter-annotator agreement was computed using the Fleiss' Kappa metric for multiple annotators (Fleiss, 1971), where the categories for annotation are 1 for complete match and 0 otherwise. Fleiss Kappa score is computed as follows:

$$\kappa = \frac{\bar{P} - \bar{P}_e}{1 - \bar{P}_e} \qquad (1)$$

where $P - P_e$ is the actual degree of agreement achieved and $1 - P_e$ is the degree of agreement above chance. Given N tokens to be annotated and n annotators, with k categories to annotate the data. We first calculate the proportion of annotations in the j category as:

$$p_j = \frac{1}{Nn} \sum_{i=1}^{N} n_{ij} , \quad 1 = \sum_{j=1}^{k} p_j \qquad (2)$$

We then calculate P_i, the degree of agreement with the ith annotator as:

[3]https://tdil-dc.in/index.php?option=com_
download&task=showresourceDetails&toolid=
1979&lang=en

$$P_i = \frac{1}{n(n-1)} \sum_{j=1}^{k} n_{ij}(n_{ij} - 1) \qquad (3)$$

$$= \frac{1}{n(n-1)} \left[\left(\sum_{j=1}^{k} n_{ij}^2 \right) - n \right] \qquad (4)$$

Finally we calculate $\bar{P}$ and $\bar{P}_e$ as:

$$\bar{P} = \frac{1}{N} \sum_{i=1}^{N} P_i \qquad (5)$$

$$\bar{P}_e = \sum_{j=1}^{k} p_j^2 \qquad (6)$$

The inter-annotator agreement in the final round of annotations is 0.91, after four rounds of annotation. We noted that the inter-annotator agreement increased across the stages.

8. Conclusion

In this paper, we present a comprehensive set of guidelines for the annotation of events in Kannada, based on TimeML guidelines of event detection. Using these guidelines, we annotate the Kannada Dependency Treebank with event nuggets. This dataset is the first attempt to perform semantic annotation tasks in Kannada, which is a low-resource language. We introduce some basic features of Kannada grammar associated with representing event information, as well as some of the challenges in detecting events in this language.

In the future, this dataset can be expanded both in size and in annotations to include other facets of the TimeML annotation schema, and provide further insight into the automated detection of events and other temporal information. Given the nature of the guidelines, challenges and the description of the corpus annotation procedure, we hope that the development of event annotated corpora for other Dravidian languages becomes easier.

9. Bibliographical References

Abbi, A. and Gopalakrishnan, D. (1991). Semantics of explicator compound verbs in south asian languages. *Language Sciences*, 13(2):161–180.

Ahn, D. (2006). The stages of event extraction. In *Proceedings of the Workshop on Annotating and Reasoning about Time and Events*, pages 1–8.

Berglund, A. (2004). Extracting temporal information and ordering events for swedish. *Master's thesis report*.

Bhat, V. (1981). The copula in kannada. *Papers in Linguistics.(Festschrift for RC Hiremath), Sharat Prakashan, Mysore*.

Bittar, A., Amsili, P., Denis, P., and Danlos, L. (2011). French timebank: an iso-timeml annotated reference corpus. In *Proceedings of the 49th Annual Meeting of the Association for Computational Linguistics: Human Language Technologies: short papers-Volume 2*, pages 130–134. Association for Computational Linguistics.

Caselli, T., Lenzi, V. B., Sprugnoli, R., Pianta, E., and Prodanof, I. (2011). Annotating events, temporal expressions and relations in italian: the it-timeml experience for the ita-timebank. In *Proceedings of the 5th Linguistic Annotation Workshop*, pages 143–151. Association for Computational Linguistics.

Fleiss, J. L. (1971). Measuring nominal scale agreement among many raters. *Psychological bulletin*, 76(5):378.

Forăscu, C. and Tufiş, D. (2012). Romanian timebank: An annotated parallel corpus for temporal information. In *Proceedings of the Eighth International Conference on Language Resources and Evaluation (LREC'12)*, pages 3762–3766.

Giorgi, A. and Pianesi, F. (1997). *Tense and aspect: From semantics to morphosyntax*. Oxford University Press on Demand.

Goud, J. S., Goel, P., Debnath, A., Prabhu, S., and Shrivastava, M. (2019). A semantico-syntactic approach to event-mention detection and extraction in hindi. In *Workshop on Interoperable Semantic Annotation (ISA-15)*, page 63.

Ji, H. and Grishman, R. (2008). Refining event extraction through cross-document inference. In *Proceedings of ACL-08: Hlt*, pages 254–262.

Kachru, Y. and Pandharipande, R. (1980). Towards a typology of compound verbs in south asian languages. *Studies in the Linguistic Sciences*, 10(1):113–124.

Kittel, F. (1993). *A Grammar of the Kannada Language: Comprising the Three Dialects of the Language (ancient, Medieval and Modern)*. Asian Educational Services.

Kuila, A. and Sarkar, S. (2017). An event extraction system via neural networks. In *FIRE (Working Notes)*, pages 136–139.

Lindblom, C. (2014). Negation in dravidian languages: A descriptive typological study on verbal and non-verbal negation in simple declarative sentences.

Mallamma, V. R. and Hanumanthappa, M. (2014). Semantical and syntactical analysis of nlp. *International Journal of Computer Science and Information Technologies*, 5(3):3236–3238.

Mitamura, T., Yamakawa, Y., Holm, S., Song, Z., Bies, A., Kulick, S., and Strassel, S. (2015). Event nugget annotation: Processes and issues. In *Proceedings of the The 3rd Workshop on EVENTS: Definition, Detection, Coreference, and Representation*, pages 66–76.

Morante, R. and Sporleder, C. (2012). Modality and negation: An introduction to the special issue. *Computational linguistics*, 38(2):223–260.

Pustejovsky, J., Castano, J. M., Ingria, R., Sauri, R., Gaizauskas, R. J., Setzer, A., Katz, G., and Radev, D. R. (2003). Timeml: Robust specification of event and temporal expressions in text. *New directions in question answering*, 3:28–34.

Pustejovsky, J. (1991). The syntax of event structure. *cognition*, 41(1-3):47–81.

Rao, P. R. and Devi, S. L. (2018). Eventxtract-il: Event extraction from newswires and social media text in indian languages@ fire 2018-an overview. In *FIRE (Working Notes)*, pages 282–290.

Rao, A. B., Murali Krishna, S., and Nayak, A. (2014). Developing a dependency treebank for kannada. *International Journal of Engineering Sciences and Research*, 15:5–7.

Saurí, R., Littman, J., Knippen, B., Gaizauskas, R., Setzer, A., and Pustejovsky, J. (2006). Timeml annotation guidelines. *Version*, 1(1):31.

Saurı, R. (2010). Annotating temporal relations in catalan and spanish timeml annotation guidelines. Technical report, Technical Report BM 2010-04, Barcelona Media.

Schiffman, H. (1979). A reference grammar of spoken kannada.

Seker, S. E. and Diri, B. (2010). Timeml and turkish temporal logic. In *IC-AI*, volume 10, pages 881–887.

Shastri, G. (2011). Kannada morphological analyser and generator using trie. *IJCSNS*, 11(1):112.

Stenetorp, P., Pyysalo, S., Topić, G., Ohta, T., Ananiadou, S., and Tsujii, J. (2012). Brat: a web-based tool for nlp-assisted text annotation. In *Proceedings of the Demonstrations at the 13th Conference of the European Chapter of the Association for Computational Linguistics*, pages 102–107. Association for Computational Linguistics.

Subecz, Z. (2019). Event detection and classification in hungarian natural texts. *European Scientific Journal July*.

Veerappan, R., Antony, P., Saravanan, S., and Soman, K. (2011). A rule based kannada morphological analyzer and generator using finite state transducer. *International Journal of Computer Applications*, 27(10):45–52.

Proceedings of the 16th Joint ACL-ISO Workshop Interoperable Semantic Annotation (ISA-16), pages 94–101
Language Resources and Evaluation Conference (LREC 2020), Marseille, 11–16 May 2020
© European Language Resources Association (ELRA), licensed under CC-BY-NC

Towards the Ontologization of the Outsider Art Domain: Position Paper

John Roberto, Brian Davis
School of Computing, DCU, ADAPT Centre
Glasnevin, Dublin 9, Ireland
{john.roberto, brian.davis}@adaptcentre.ie

Abstract
The purpose of this paper is to present a prospective and interdisciplinary research project seeking to ontologize knowledge of the domain of Outsider Art, that is, the art created outside the boundaries of official culture. The goal is to combine ontology engineering methodologies to develop a knowledge base which i) examines the relation between social exclusion and cultural productions, ii) standardizes the terminology of Outsider Art and iii) enables semantic interoperability between cultural metadata relevant to Outsider Art. The Outsider Art ontology will integrate some existing ontologies and terminologies, such as the CIDOC - Conceptual Reference Model (CRM), the Art & Architecture Thesaurus and the Getty Union List of Artist Names, among other resources. Natural Language Processing and Machine Learning techniques will be fundamental instruments for knowledge acquisition and elicitation. NLP techniques will be used to annotate bibliographies of relevant outsider artists and descriptions of outsider artworks with linguistic information. Machine Learning techniques will be leveraged to acquire knowledge from linguistic features embedded in both types of texts.

Keywords: ontology engineering, cultural heritage, outsider art

1. Introduction

Culture, creativity and inclusive society are widely represented in the innovation agenda for cultural heritage in Europe (European Commission, 2018). Since 2014, almost €5 billion was invested in cultural and cultural heritage projects under the European Regional Development Fund (Europa Nostra, 2018). Between 2014 and 2019, €495 million was invested in Horizon 2020 in cultural heritage R&I (Zygierewicz, 2019). Despite this large investment, some socio-cultural groups are still not sufficiently integrated in cultural heritage experiences, as is the case of outsider artists.

"Outsiders" are highly innovative artists that have been aesthetically and socially marginalized because of their status as psychiatric patients, homeless, recluses, disabled persons, migrants and ethnic minorities. As a consequence, Outsider Art (Cardinal, 1972) is a nebulous domain and a deeply problematic notion. The concept remains the subject of highly diverse debates as to its meaning and scope (Philby, 2011). Today a plethora of sometimes misleading terms are used to describe it: art brut, art of madmen, art singulier, autistic art, (contemporary) folk art, (faux) naïve art, fresh invention, grass-roots art, intuitive art, marginal art, mediumistic art, neuve invention, non-traditional folk art, primitive art, primitivism, pseudo-naïve art, psychopathologic art, psychotic art, raw art, self-taught art, vernacular art and visionary art. Indeed, there are those who believe that Ousider Art is a tenable concept and those who question the authenticity of the concept. For example, Marcus Davies (2007) states that the use of the term is here to stay and James Elkins (2006) says that the term is an oxymoron and, consequently, there is no such thing as Outsider Art. This evidence leads us to conclude that there is a need to perform an explicit terminological standardization of the Outsider Art domain.

We propose an inherently interdisciplinary research project that explores the links between art and society by applying Natural Language Processing (NLP) and Machine Learning (ML) techniques. Specifically, we aim to represent part of the existing knowledge about so-called Outsider Art in a machine-readable format (ontology) that allows us to deduce implicit knowledge from the existing literature on Outsider Art. The Ontology will be suitable for discovering implicit facts, relations, and contradictions by using reasoning engines. In this sense, the ontology will help to provide a better understanding of the relation between social exclusion and artistic innovation by assigning meaning to huge amounts of textual data. Our main research objectives are:

- To examine the relation between social exclusion and cultural productions by applying an interdisciplinary approach that brings together technology, art and language.
- To standardize the terminology of Outsider Art by formally conceptualizing the domain using a combination of traditional ontology engineering and corpus based techniques, in particular NLP methods for (semi)automatic ontology learning and population (Maynard, Bontcheva and Augenstein, 2016).
- To enable semantic interoperability between heterogeneous metadata by coding textual information in a machine processable format with the goal of facilitating the development of emerging technologies for European smart museums, such as virtual assistants, recommenders, dynamic tourist guides and interactive exhibits.

2. Methodology, Tools and Resources

The Outsider Art ontology will be built using Ontology Engineering methodologies. There are well-established methodologies to support the process of ontology development and maintenance: e.g. An & Park's (2018) methodology, POEM (Ali and Khusro, 2016), Bautista-Zambrana's methodology (Bautista-Zambrana, 2015), NeOn (Suarez-Figueroa et al., 2012) and DiDOn (Keet, 2012).

As can be seen in Figure 1, ontology authors vary significantly in their approach to developing their respective ontologies. The Figure 1 below shows 28 methodologies and 15 activities that are frequently used in the development of ontologies. The light-shaded green

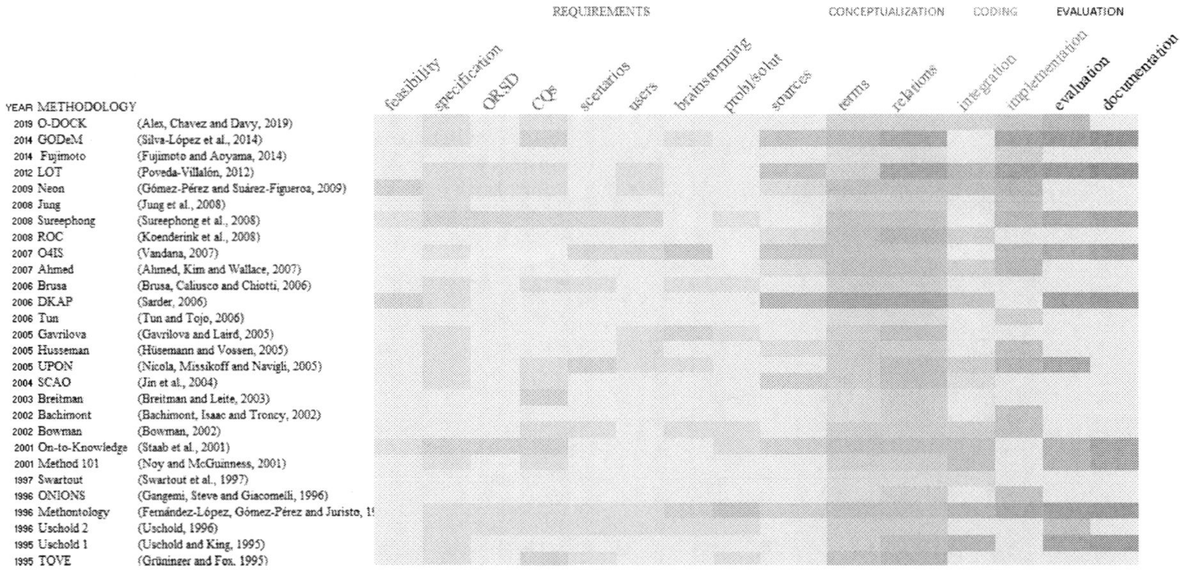

Figure 1: Ontology Engineering: methodologies and activities.

boxes are the activities that occur in the early stage of the ontologization process, while the dark shaded green boxes represent the later activities. Those activities can be arranged in four processes: requirements, conceptualization, coding and evaluation. For example, the O-DOCK methodology (Alex, Chavez and Davy, 2019) contains: 1) a very early stage for requirement analysis based on competency questions (CQs) followed by 2) a stage for the extraction of terms and relevant relationship definition (conceptualization), 3) the translation of concepts and relations into a computer-readable language, including the integration of existing ontologies (coding) and 4) a final stage for error detection (evaluation).

Our approach for Outsider Art ontology development will consider the most prevalent stages of the most outstanding methodologies for ontology engineering, as detailed below.

2.1 Specification: Requirements and Sources

The specification is a process that will be used for identifying, among other things, the purpose, scope, feasibility, intended users and requirements of the Outsider Art ontology. Taking into account existing specification techniques, we have chosen to employ competency questions (CQs), the analysis of domain specific text corpora and an online form to capture the ontology specifications. This information will be included in the so-called Ontology Requirements Specification Document (ORSD).

Competency questions is a list of questions that the Ontology of the Outsider Art should respond to correctly. Two examples of competency question are: *"What diseases/disabilities do the outsider artists suffer from?"* and *"What themes do the outsider artists paint?"* From such competency questions, a number of seed concepts will be drawn up: e.g. "bipolar disorder", "Alzheimers", "multiple sclerosis", "autism", "alcoholism", "flowers", "birds", "violence" and "sex".

In order to build an ontology for terminological purposes, it will be necessary to collect a large text corpus. In this respect, the quality of the corpus will be one of the parameters to be taken into account when we devise the Outsider Art ontology. This is particularly important for ontology learning from texts since NLP techniques depend on corpus quality. For this reason, the source text that we will use for Outsider Art ontology learning should be well-balanced and representative, i.e., a body of scientific books, papers, magazines and web pages. We will focus on two types of texts or discursive genres: bibliographies of relevant outsider artists (see Table 1 (a)) and descriptions of outsider artworks (see Table 1 (b)).

Table 1. Two types of texts in the field of Outsider Art.

(a)	Wölfli was born in Bern, Switzerland. He was abused both physically and sexually as a child, and was orphaned at the age of 10. He thereafter grew up in a series of state-run foster homes. He worked as a Verdingbub (indentured child labourer) and briefly joined the army... (Wikipedia).
(b)	André Masson, *Labyrinth*, 1938. Influenced by Freud, Masson's work represents an attempt to gain access to unconscious thought through automatic techniques. Starting with a web of rapidly formed lines... (Rhodes, 2000, p. 117) (see Figure 2).

Additionally, in order to collect ontology requirements, an online survey will be distributed among specialists in Outsider Art at different institutions across the world, e.g. Museu d'Art Brut[1] (Barcelona), Collection de l'Art Brut[2] (Switzerland), Outsider Art Fair[3] (Paris), Raw Vision Magazine[4], etc.

Figure 2: André Masson, *Labyrinth*, 1938.

2.2 Conceptualization: NLP & ML Techniques

The conceptualization stage consists of representing knowledge about the Outsider Art in a semi-formal format (i.e. in an artificial and formally defined language) using NLP and ML techniques.

The Outsider Art corpus will be normalized and annotated using linguistic pre-processing techniques (Maynard, Bontcheva and Augenstein, 2016) such as sentence splitting, tokenisation, part-of-speech (POS) tagger, chunk parsing, name entity recognition and classification (NERC) and co-reference resolution. There are many tools available for NLP in many platforms: Natural Language Toolkit[5], Stanford CoreNLP[6], Freeling[7], Ixa Pipes[8], and OpenNLP[9]. Last but not least, the General Architecture for Text Engineering (GATE) (Cunningham, et al., 2002) is a popular NLP toolkit with support for ontology based IE and ontology learning.

The supervised learning techniques will be employed to make use of the latent features embedded in the bibliographies of relevant outsider artists (see Table 1 (a)) and descriptions of outsider artworks (see Table 1 (b)) to acquire knowledge with very limited human intervention. For example, the identification of terms that are relevant to the Outsider Art domain will be done by using

distributional knowledge (Doing-Harris, Livnat and Meystre, 2015) and contextual knowledge (Hoxha, Jiang and Weng, 2016) derived from the syntactic and semantic annotation of texts. Semantic Similarity between labelled words or phrases (Liu, Li and Deng, 2017) will be applied to find additional mentions of an ontology class such as the painter's "subject matter" based on lexico-syntactic information described in Table 2.

Table 2. Information format for the class *subject matter*.

NP (as Subject)	VP (as verb)	COMPLEMENT (as object)
His work	Ranges	from idyllic scenes...
Dellschau's work	Shows	the influence of...
Hampton	Described	his work as a monument to Jesus...
The subjects of his work	Included	waterfront landscapes,...

2.3 Coding: the Web Ontology Language

Another of the key decisions to take in the Outsider Art ontology development process is the selection of the appropriate ontology language for modelling, encoding and querying the target domain. The Resource Description Framework or RDF (Schreiber and Raimond, 2014) is a language for representing binary relations between two resources on the Web. The two resources (subject and object) and the relation (predicate) form a triple: e.g. Picasso → was-born-in → Spain. The Web Ontology Language or OWL (Hitzler et al., 2012) is a language for making ontological statements whose syntax and formal semantics are derived from description logics. A number of query languages have been developed to extract information from RDF and OWL, including SPARQL (Pérez, Arenas and Gutierrez, 2006) for RDF and SQWRL (O'Connor and Das, 2009) for OWL.

2.4 Evaluation approaches

The Outsider Art ontology will be evaluated by comparing the learned ontology with the content of a text corpus (corpus-based approach) (Rospocher et al., 2012) and by measuring how efficient the ontology is for the automatic classification of text documents (task-based approach) (Pittet and Barthélémy, 2015).

Additionally, a semi-automatic approach will be applied using the CQchecker (Bezerra and Freitas, 2017; Bezerra, Freitas, and Santana da Silva, 2013), an algorithm that verifies whether the ontology answers CQs at the terminological level. The CQchecker splits a CQ expressed in natural language into tokens and tries to find the concepts and relations from the ontology described in OWL DL[10] that the CQ referred to.

3. Source Integration Method

It is a fact that most ontologies for Cultural Heritage are interdisciplinary artefacts since they describe objective manifestations of the human mind, including customs,

---

[1] https://www.museuartbrut.com/fons-dart.html

[2] https://www.artbrut.ch/

[3] https://www.outsiderartfair.com/

[4] https://rawvision.com/

[5] https://www.nltk.org/

[6] https://stanfordnlp.github.io/CoreNLP/

[7] http://nlp.lsi.upc.edu/freeling/node/1

[8] http://ixa2.si.ehu.es/ixa-pipes/

[9] https://opennlp.apache.org/

---

[10] OWL DL is a rich ontology language that supports high expressiveness and decidable reasoning.

practices, places, objects, artistic expressions and values. For that reason, building ontologies from scratch is often not a viable alternative as recent works proves.

For example, the Conservation Reasoning ontology (CORE) (Moraitou and Kavakli, 2018) extends our information about artworks from the CIDOC CRM ontology by adding knowledge about materials, chemical properties, polymers and measurement techniques based on the empirical analysis of resources such as vocabularies, thesaurus, wikis and other ontologies. In Moraitou, Aliprantis and Caridakis (2018), the CORE ontology is merged with the Semantic Sensor Network ontology (SSN) in order to create a new ontology that expresses preventive conservation guidelines and rules based on sensor data about the artworks' environmental conditions. Similarly, the Heritage Building ontology (HB) (Tibaut et al., 2018), which represents knowledge about problematic issues with historical buildings, was created by integrating related domain ontologies (e.g. building materials and structures) and non-directly related domain ontologies (e.g. time, locations and persons). The Built Cultural Heritage ontology (BCH) (Zalamea, Van Orshoven, and Steenberghen, 2018) for the preventive conservation of architectural heritage was refined by merging Geneva CityGML and Mondis ontologies. Thus, the Mondis ontology provides classes for "Risk" and "Vulnerability" and the Geneva CityGML ontology provides classes to represent buildings, geographic areas and cities.

As shown in Table 3, the existing literature on Outsider Art describes both aesthetic entities (e.g. "Jean Dubuffet", "Hayward Gallery", "fantastical botanical images") and social/medical issues (e.g. "dental technician", "military officer", "depression", "mental pain") surrounding this form of art, in addition to non-specialized knowledge (e.g. "London", "1948").

Table 3. Different entities within the Outsider Art domain (some of them are highlighted in **bold**).

As a young girl, Anna Zemánková (Czech, 1908-1986), enjoyed drawing, yet gave up the hobby to pursue a career as a **dental technician**. She married a **military officer** and in **1948**, she moved to **Prague**, where she devoted all of her time to raising her family. Later in life, she struggled with **depression**, but found an outlet for her **mental pain** in art. At the crack of dawn, she would paint in a trance-like state, therapeutically creating **fantastical botanical images** from her imagination. Her series of surreal flowers was executed in paint, as well as in crocheted tissue paper. Her work is included by **Jean Dubuffet** in the Collection de l'Art Brut and was presented at the **1979** exhibition of Outsider art at the **Hayward Gallery** in **London**.

Thus, in order to categorise aesthetical objects, we can integrate several external resources including:

- The Conceptual Reference Model (CIDOC CRM) (Le Boeuf et al., 2019) is an extensible ontology that provides definitions and a formal structure for describing the concepts and relationships used in cultural heritage documentation.

- The Europeana Data Model (EDM) (Europeana, 2017) is an ontology-based framework that is suitable for the description of cultural objects.
- The Art & Architecture Thesaurus (Alexiev et al., 2017) is a thesaurus containing generic terms, dates, relationships, sources, and notes for work types, roles, materials, styles, cultures, techniques, and other concepts related to art.
- The Cultural Objects Name Authority (CONA) (Harpring, 2019) compiles titles/names and other metadata for works of art.
- The Getty Iconography Authority (AI) (Harpring, 2019b) is a thesaurus that covers topics relevant to art.
- The Getty Thesaurus of Geographic Names (TGN) (Harpring, 2019c) focuses on places relevant to art.
- The Getty Union List of Artist Names (ULAN) (Harpring, 2019d) is a structured vocabulary, including names and biographies of the people involved in the creation and study of art (see Figure 3).

There are a number of existing ontologies and terminologies that we can use to categorize social and medical concepts in the Outsider Art ontology:

- The UNESCO Thesaurus (UNESCO, 2019) is a controlled and structured list of terms in the fields of education, culture, natural sciences, social and human sciences, communication and information.
- The Human Disease Ontology (Schriml et al., 2018) provides the biomedical community with consistent, reusable and sustainable descriptions of human disease terms.

Figure 3: Example of search term in the ULAN (Harpring, 2019d).

On the other hand, the description of general knowledge, such as time and location, can be handled using specific and generic tools. Time Ontology (W3C 2017) and CRMgeo (Hiebel, Doerr and Eide, 2016) are examples of specific tools. The Time Ontology provides vocabulary for expressing information about relations between instants and intervals, durations and temporal position, including date-time information. CRMgeo is a geospatial ontology for cultural heritage documentation which has been integrated with GeoSPARQL vocabulary to categorize spatio-temporal classes and properties such as "Prague" or "London". Generic semantic resources include the Dbpedia and Schema.org. Dbpedia (Auer, 2007) is a knowledge base that stores structured data extracted from Wikipedia (3.64 million items organised in

320 classes and 1,650 different properties). Schema.org is a shared vocabulary to structure metadata models for around 614 different types of content, such as Creative works, Event and Place.

4. Current state of the research

Purpose, scope, feasibility, intended users and other general requirements of the Outsider Art ontology have been identified. We are currently working on collecting and labelling the Outsider Art corpus. In order to guarantee the quality of the data, we are compiling a short but highly normalized version of the corpus by hand. In addition to syntactic information, this corpus will be enriched with semantic information by using the resources described in Section 3. For example, by mapping the concept "Jean Dubuffet" in the corpus in ULAN vocabulary (RDF version), we are able to discover that: *(i)* the full name of this outsider artist was "Jean Philippe Arthur Dubuffet", *(ii)* "Louis-Léon Forget" was his pseudonym and *(iii)* he had a professional relationship with the painter Asger Jorn (see Table 4).

Table 4. Snippet of the ULAN vocabulary in RDF version.

<bibo:locator>(**Jean Philippe Arthur Dubuffet**; born 31 July 1901; died 12 May 1985; French painter and sculptor)</bibo:locator>
<bibo:locator>t.p. (**Louis-Léon Forget**) p. 8 (pseudonym of Jean Dubuffet, Forget is the name of his grand-mother)</bibo:locator>
<dc:description>Dubuffet, Jean (500019113) 'collaborated with' **Jorn, Asger** (500007669);</dc:description>

This enriched version of the corpus will be used to train a machine learning model for automatically classifying new texts about Outsider Art. That is because it has been proved that training corpora in conjunction with deep learning methods outperforms classical techniques for feature extraction and the classification of text, particularly on imbalanced datasets (Chen, McKeever and Delany, 2018).

5. Conclusions

We aim to develop the first ontology of Outsider Art. This is an innovative research project that focuses on three axes that have a significant impact on social diversity[11], the standardization of knowledge and the semantic interoperability of cultural data.

On the technical level, the Outsider Art ontology will contribute to the deployment of digital technologies for virtual and smart museums (e.g. concept/ aspect based opinion mining and opinionated semantic search tools, virtual assistants, dynamic tourist guides, interactive exhibits and chatbots) by standardizing data and knowledge about Outsider Art. In fact, the cultural sector is characterized by a complex data integration problem for which a solution is being sought through the development of metadata standards. Ontologies have found fertile ground in the cultural heritage domain due to the need to preserve, conserve, curate, and disseminate physical and digital objects.

The final ontology will be distributed online in a findable, accessible, interoperable and reusable format based on W3C standards: OWL, RDF and SQWRL. The Outsider Art ontology will be integrated into the Europeana Data Model and be mapped to Schema.org

6. Acknowledgements

This research has been supported by the Irish Research Council (Grant GOIPD/2019/463). This work has also received funding from the ADAPT Centre for Digital Content Technology which is funded under the SFI Research Centres Programme (Grant 13/RC/2106).

7. Bibliographical References

Ahmed, S., Kim, S., and Wallace, K. M. (2007). A methodology for creating ontologies for engineering design. *Journal of Computing and Information Science in Engineering*, 7(2), pp. 132–140.

Alex, G., Chavez, B., and Davy, M. (2019). Methodology to design ontologies from organizational models: Application to creativity workshops. *Artificial Intelligence for Engineering Design, Analysis and Manufacturing*, 33(2): 148–159.

Ali, S., and Khusro, S. (2016). POEM: practical ontology engineering model for semantic web ontologies. *Cogent Engineering, 3*(1): 1–39.

An, J., and Park, Y. (2018). Methodology for Automatic Ontology Generation Using Database Schema Information. *Mobile Information Systems, 1*–13.

Bachimont, B., Isaac, A., and Troncy, R. (2002). Semantic Commitment for Designing Ontologies: A Proposal. In *Proceedings of the 13th International Conference, EKAW 2002*, Siguenza, Spain, pages114–121.

Bautista-Zambrana, M. (2015). Methodologies to Build Ontologies for Terminological Purposes. *Procedia - Social and Behavioral Sciences, 173*, 264–269.

Bezerra, C. and Freitas, F. (2017). Verifying Description Logic Ontologies based on Competency Questions and Unit Testing. ONTOBRAS.

Bezerra, C., Freitas, F., and Santana da Silva, F. (2013). Evaluating Ontologies with Competency Questions. *International Joint Conferences on Web Intelligence (WI) and Intelligent Agent Technologies (IAT)*, pp. 284–285.

Bowman, M. (2002). *A methodology for modeling expert knowledge that supports teaching-based development of agents*. Doctoral Dissertation, George Mason University, Fairfax, Virginia - USA.

Breitman, K. and Leite, J.C. (2003). Ontology as a requirement engineering product. In *Proceedings of the Eleventh IEEE International Requirements Engineering Conference*, Monterey Bay, California, pp. 309–319.

Brusa, G., Caliusco, M. L., and Chiotti, O. (2006). A process for building a domain ontology: an experience in developing a government budgetary ontology, *Proceedings of the second Australasian workshop on Advances in ontologies* - Volume 72. Hobart, Australia: Australian Computer Society, Inc.

---

[11] There is no doubt that the preservation and dissemination of non-traditional cultural heritage is necessary for a better understanding of cultural and social diversity.

Cardinal, R. (1972). *Outsider Art*. London, UK: Studio Vista; New York, NY: Praeger.

Chen H., McKeever S., and Delany S. (2018). A Comparison of Classical Versus Deep Learning Techniques for Abusive Content Detection on Social Media Sites. In: Staab S., Koltsova O., Ignatov D. (eds) *Social Informatics: International Conference on Social Informatics*, vol. 11185. Springer, Cham

Cunningham, H., Maynard, D., Bontcheva, K. and Tablan, V. (2002). GATE: A framework and graphical development environment for robust NLP tools and applications. *Proc. 40th annual meeting of the association for computational linguistics (ACL 2002)*.

Davies, M. (2007). On Outsider Art and the Margins of the Mainstream. [Blog Post]. Retrieved from http://www.ibiblio.org/frenchart/

Doing-Harris, K., Livnat, Y. and Meystre, S. (2015). Automated concept and relationship extraction for the semi-automated ontology management (seam) system. *Journal of Biomedical Semantics 6(1)*, 15.

Elkins, J. (2006) Naifs, Faux-naifs, Faux-faux naïfs, Would-be Faux-naifs: There is No Such Thing as Outsider Art. In: *Inner Worlds Outside, exh. Cat.,* Ed. John Thompson, Irish Museum of Modern Art, Dublin, pp. 71 - 79.

Europa Nostra. (2018). Cultural Heritage as a key resource for EU's future Cohesion Policy. The Voice of Cultural Heritage in Europe.

European Commission. (2018). *Communication from the Commission to the European Parliament, the European Council, the Council, the European Economic and Social Committee and the Committee of the Regions.* Brussels.

Fernández-López, M., Gómez-Pérez, A., and Juristo, N. (1997). METHONTOLOGY: From Ontological Art Towards Ontological Engineering. AAAI 1997.

Fujimoto, R. and Aoyama, M. (2014). A Life cycle-Based Design Methodology of the Lightweight Ontology and Its Application to Cultivating High Quality Mandarin Orange. *IEEE*, pp. 147–150.

Gangemi, A., Steve, G., and Giacomelli, F. (1996). ONIONS: An ontological methodology for taxonomic knowledge integration. *Proceeding of the Workshop on Ontological Engineering, ECAI-96*, Budapest, pp: 95.

Gavrilova, T. and Laird, D. (2005). Practical Design of Business Enterprise Ontologies. In *Proceedings of the 1st International IFIP/WG12.5 Working Conference on Industrial Applications of Semantic Web*, Jyvaskyla, Finland, pp.65–81.

Gomez-Perez, A. and Suárez-Figueroa, M.C. (2009). NeOn Methodology for Building Ontology Networks: a Scenario-based Methodology. *Proceedings of International Conference on Software, Services & Semantic technologies* (S3T 2009).

Grüninger, M. and Fox, M. (1995). Methodology for the Design and Evaluation of Ontologies. *IJCAI'95, Workshop on Basic Ontological Issues in Knowledge Sharing*, April 13, 1995.

Hiebel, G., Doerr, M., and Eide, Ø. (2016). CRMgeo: A spatiotemporal extension of CIDOC-CRM. *International Journal on Digital Libraries*.

Hitzler, P., Krötzsch, M., Parsia, B., Patel-Schneider, P., and Rudolph, S. (2012). OWL 2 Web Ontology Language Primer (Second Edition). W3C.

Hoxha, J., Jiang, G. and Weng, Ch. (2016). Automated Learning of Domain Taxonomies from Text using Background Knowledge. *Journal of biomedical informatics*. 63.

Husemann, B. and Vossen, G. (2005). Ontology engineering from a database perspective. *Proceedings 10th Asian Computing Science Conference Kunming*, China. 3818: 49–63.

Jin, L., Keqing, H., Bing, L., Hao, C., and Liang, P. (2004). A methodology for acquisition of software component attribute ontology. In *Proceedings of the Fourth International Conference on Computer and Information Technology (CIT '04)*, pp.1058–1064.

Jung, E. H., Cho, K. M., Song, K. H., Nam, S. H., and Lee, S. W. (2008). Methodology of Topic Maps creation and Semantic Web for technological information search regarding injection-mold based on Collaboration Hub. In *Proceedings of the International Conference on Smart Manufacturing Application (ICSMA 2008)*, Gyeonggi-do, South Korea, pp.78–83.

Keet, C. (2012). Transforming semi-structured life science diagrams into meaningful domain ontologies with DiDOn. *Journal of biomedical informatics*. 45. 482–94.

Koenderink, N., van Assem, M., Hulzebos, J., Broekstra, J., and Top, J. (2008). ROC: A Method for Proto-ontology Construction by Domain Experts. In *Proceedings of the 3rd Asian Semantic Web Conference (ASWC 2008) - The Semantic Web*, Bangkok, Thailand, pp.152–166.

Liu, F., Li, P. and Deng, D. (2017). Device-Oriented Automatic Semantic Annotation in IoT. *Journal of Sensors*, vol. 2017, Article ID 9589064, 14 pages, 2017.

Maynard, D., Bontcheva, K., and Augenstein. (2016). Linguistic Processing. In *Natural language processing for the semantic web.* Synthesis Lectures on the Semantic Web: Theory and Technology 6.2 (2016): 1-194.

Moraitou E., Aliprantis, J., and Caridakis, G. (2018). Semantic Preventive Conservation of Cultural Heritage Collections. In: *CEUR Workshop Proceedings, SW4CH 2018 - Proceedings of the 3rd International Workshop on Semantic Web for Cultural Heritage*.

Moraitou, E. and Kavakli, E. (2018). Knowledge Management Using Ontology on the Domain of Artworks Conservation. In: Ioannides, M. (Ed.). *Digital Cultural Heritage. Lecture Notes in Computer Science*, vol. 10605. Springer, Cham.

Nicola, A.D., issikoff, M., and Navigli, R. (2005). A proposal for a unified process for ontology building: UPON. *Proceeding of the Database and Expert Systems Applications*, pp. 655–664.

Noy, N. F. and McGuinness, D. L. (2001). Ontology Development 101: A Guide to creating your first Ontology. Stanford Knowledge Systems Laboratory Technical Report KSL-01-05 and Stanford Medical Informatics Technical Report SMI-2001-0880, March 2001.

O'Connor, M.J. and Das, A.K. (2009). SQWRL: a query language for OWL. *Proceedings of OWL: Experiences and Directions (OWLED)*, Fifth International Workshop, Chantilly, VA.

Pérez, J., Arenas, M. and Gutierrez, C. (2006). Semantics and Complexity of SPARQL. In: Cruz et al. (Eds.), *The Semantic Web - ISWC 2006. ISWC 2006. Lecture Notes in Computer Science,* vol 4273. Springer, Berlin, Heidelberg.

Philby, Ch. (2011, October 8). Can popular Outsider art still be considered 'outsider'? *INDEPENDENT.* Retrieved from https://www.independent.co.uk/arts-entertainment/art/features/can-popular-outsider-art-still-be-considered-outsider-2365948.html

Pittet, P. and Barthélémy, J. (2015). Exploiting users' feedbacks: Towards a task-based evaluation of application ontologies throughout their lifecycle. *International Conference on Knowledge Engineering and Ontology Development,* volume 2.

Poveda-Villalón, M. (2012). A reuse-based lightweight method for developing linked data ontologies and vocabularies. In *Proceedings of the 9th international conference on The Semantic Web: research and applications (ESWC'12),* pages 833–837, Berlin, Heidelberg.

Rhodes, C. (2000). *Outsider Art: Spontaneous Alternatives.* Thames & Hudson Ltd, London.

Rospocher, M., Tonelli, S., Serafini, L., & Pianta, E. (2012). Corpus-based terminological evaluation of ontologies. *Applied Ontology, 7,* 429-448.

Sarder, M. (2006). The development of a design ontology for products and processes. Doctoral Dissertation, The University of Texas at Arlington, Arlington, TX.

Schreiber, A. and Raimond, Y. (2014). RDF 1.1 Primer: W3C Working Group Note. Boston: World-Wide Web Consortium.

Silva-López, R., Silva-López, M., Bravo, M., Méndez-Gurrola, I. and Sánchez-Arias, V. (2014). GODeM: A Graphical Ontology Design Methodology. *Research in Computing Science,* 84, 17-28.

Staab, S., Schnurr, H. P., Studer, R., and Sure, Y. (2001). Knowledge Processes and Ontologies. *IEEE Intelligent Systems,* 16(1), pp.26–34.

Suarez-Figueroa, M., Gómez-Pérez, A., and Fernández-López, M. (2012). The NeOn methodology for ontology engineering. In M. Suárez-Figueroa, A. Gómez-Pérez, E. Motta & A. Gangemi (Eds.), *Ontology Engineering in a Networked World* (pp. 9–34). Springer, Berlin, Germany.

Sureephong, P., Chakpitak, N., Ouzrout, Y., and Bouras, A. (2008). An Ontology-based Knowledge Management System for Industry Clusters. In Yan, X., Ion, W., and Eynard, B. (Eds.), *Global Design to Gain a Competitive Edge: An Holistic and Collaborative Design Approach based on Computational Tools,* Springer: London.

Swartout, B., Ramesh, P., Knight, K., and Russ, T. (1997). Toward Distributed Use of Large-Scale Ontologies. In *Proceedings of the AAAI'97 Spring Symposium on Ontological Engineering,* Stanford University, CA, pp.138–148.

Tibaut, A., Kaučič, B., Dvornik, P., Tiano, P., and Martins, J. (2018) Ontologizing the Heritage Building Domain. In: Ioannides M., Martins, J., Žarnić R., and Lim, V. (Eds.). *Advances in Digital Cultural Heritage. Lecture Notes in Computer Science,* vol 10754. Springer, Cham.

Tun, N. and Tojo, S. (2006). Identity Conditions for Ontological Analysis. In Lang, J., Lin, F., and Wang, J. (Eds.), *Knowledge Science, Engineering and Management (KSEM 2006)* (Vol. LNAI 4092, pp.418-430): Springer-Verlag Berlin / Heidelberg.

Uschold, M. (1996). Building Ontologies: Towards a Unified Methodology. In *Proceedings of the 16th Annual Conference of the British Computer Society Specialist Group on Expert Systems (Expert Systems '96),* Cambridge, UK.

Uschold, M. and King, M. (1995). Towards a methodology for building ontologies. *Proceeding of the Workshop on Basic Ontological Issues in Knowledge Sharing,* pp: 74.

Vandana, K. (2007). Ontology for Information Systems (O4IS) Design Methodology: Conceptualizing, designing and representing domain ontologies. Doctoral Dissertation. The Royal Institute of Technology, Sweden.

Zalamea, O., Van Orshoven, J., and Steenberghen, T. (2018) Merging and expanding existing ontologies to cover the Built Cultural Heritage domain. *Journal of Cultural Heritage Management and Sustainable Development,* Vol. 8 Issue: 2, pp.162-178.

Zygierewicz, Anna. (2019). Cultural heritage in EU discourse and in the Horizon 2020 programme. European Parliament Research Service.

8. Language Resource References

Alexiev, V., Cobb, J., Garcia, G. and Harpring, P. (2017). *Getty Vocabularies: Linked Open Data version 3.4. Semantic Representation* (pp. 1–94). Retrieved from http://vocab.getty.edu/doc/gvp-lod.pdf

Auer, S., Bizer, Ch., Kobilarov, G., Lehmann, J., Cyganiak, R., and Ives, Z. (2007). DBpedia: a nucleus for a web of open data. In *Proceedings of the 6th international The semantic web and 2nd Asian conference on Asian semantic web conference (ISWC'07/ASWC'07).* Springer-Verlag, Berlin, Heidelberg, 722-735.

Europeana. (2017). Definition of the Europeana Data Model v5.2.8. European Union. Retrieved from https://pro.europeana.eu/files/Europeana_Professional/Share_your_data/Technical_requirements/EDM_Documentation/EDM_Definition_v5.2.8_102017.pdf

Harpring, P. (Ed.). (2019). Cultural Objects Name Authority (CONA): Introduction and Overview. Getty Vocabulary Program (pp. 1-309).

Harpring, P. (Ed.). (2019b). The Getty Iconography Authority: Introduction and Overview. Getty Vocabulary Program (pp. 1-97).

Harpring, P. (Ed.). (2019c). The Getty Thesaurus of Geographic Names: Introduction and Overview. Getty Vocabulary Program (pp. 1-133).

Harpring, P. (Ed.). (2019d). The Getty Union List of Artist Names: Introduction and Overview. Getty Vocabulary Program (pp. 1-143).

Le Boeuf, P., Doerr, M., Emil, Ch., and Stead, S. (Eds.). (2019). *Definition of the CIDOC Conceptual Reference Model version 6.2.7* (pp. 1–154). International Council of Museums.

Schriml, L., Mitraka, E., Munro, J., Tauber, B., Schor, M., Nickle, L., Félix, V., Jeng, L., Bearer, C., Lichenstein, R., Bisordi, K., Campion, N., Hyman, B., Kurland, D., Oates, C., Kibbey, S., Sreekumar, P., Le, C., Giglio, M. and Greene, C. (2019). Human Disease Ontology 2018 update: classification, content and workflow expansion. *Nucleic Acids Research.*

UNESCO. (2019). UNESCO Thesaurus. ISO 25964.
IDENTIFIER http://vocabularies.unesco.org/thesaurus

Proceedings of the 16th Joint ACL-ISO Workshop Interoperable Semantic Annotation (ISA-16), pages 102–109
Language Resources and Evaluation Conference (LREC 2020), Marseille, 11–16 May 2020
© European Language Resources Association (ELRA), licensed under CC-BY-NC

Towards Creating Interoperable Resources for Conceptual Annotation of Multilingual Domain Corpora

Svetlana Sheremetyeva
South Ural State University
76, Lenin pr. 454080, Chelyabinsk, Russia
lanaconsult@mail.dk; sheremetevaso@susu.ru

Abstract
In this paper we focus on creation of interoperable annotation resources that make up a significant proportion of an on-going project on the development of conceptually annotated multilingual corpora for the domain of terrorist attacks in three languages (English, French and Russian) that can be used for comparative linguistic research, intelligent content and trend analysis, summarization, machine translation, etc. Conceptual annotation is understood as a type of task-oriented domain-specific semantic annotation. The annotation process in our project relies on ontological analysis. The paper details on the issues of the development of both static and dynamic resources such as a universal conceptual annotation scheme, multilingual domain ontology and multipurpose annotation platform with flexible settings, which can be used for the automation of the conceptual resource acquisition and of the annotation process, as well as for the documentation of the annotated corpora specificities. The resources constructed in the course of the research are also to be used for developing concept disambiguation metrics by means of qualitative and quantitative analysis of the golden portion of the conceptually annotated multilingual corpora and of the annotation platform linguistic knowledge.

Keywords: annotation resources, conceptual domain annotation, interoperability, multilingualism, terrorism

1. Introduction

The importance of linguistic annotations and, especially, semantic annotations over raw textual data is widely acknowledged as critical in developing language technologies, such as intelligent content and trend analysis, classification, machine learning, summarization, machine translation, etc. (Mair, 2005; Pustejovsky, 2012). However, and this is also widely recognized, annotated corpora are quite sparse and their availability is often problematic due to no or restricted access, differences in volume and principles of construction, non-standardized and/or unsuitable annotations for specific language technology tasks. There are good reasons for this, - annotating a comprehensive corpus with semantic representations is a hard, costly and time-consuming task. In spite of quite a number of attempts to facilitate the problem by developing reusable annotations, including semantic annotation formats, such as, for example, XML, SGML, etc., and the introduction of increasingly convivial and hardware-independent application software, it is difficult to find a system that matches exactly end-user requirements. For quality semantic annotation, the portable annotation software packages, as the main dynamic annotation resource should contain a significant amount of linguistic knowledge, acquisition of which so far is highly problematic. If, however, genericity is considered as applied to a family of applications, i.e., applications sharing tasks and domains, one can probably suggest particular approaches to solve the problem, even cross linguistically. In this paper we attempt just that.

Our ultimate goal is to develop a methodology for developing annotation resources and resources themselves for the conceptual annotation of multilingual domain corpora, which are interoperable across languages and targeted to the automation of the annotation process primarily, but not exclusively, for such tasks as intelligent content analysis, machine learning, and classification. In our project, conceptual annotation is understood as a type of domain-specific task-oriented semantic annotation as opposed to the annotation with high level semantic properties, such as animacy, being human, person, etc.

We demonstrate our approach on the domain of e-news on terrorist attacks in three languages, English, French and Russian. Our motivation to focus on the domain on terrorist attacks is that counterterrorist activity requires, among others, operative analysis of unstructured e-information and the availability of means to speed up the creation of annotated corpora in this particular domain is of high importance. We here focus on the development of both static and dynamic annotation resources such as a universal conceptual annotation scheme, multilingual domain ontology and annotation platform with flexible settings. The platform is multipurpose; it can be used for the automation of the conceptual resource acquisition and of the annotation process itself, as well as for the documentation of the annotated corpora specificities. The resources constructed in the course of the research are also to be used for developing concept disambiguation metrics by means of qualitative and quantitative analysis of the golden portion of the conceptually annotated multilingual corpora and of the annotation platform linguistic knowledge.

The rest of the paper is organized as follows. Section 2 gives an overview of the related work. Section 3 defines the research tasks and introduces our data set. In Section 4 we suggest a methodology of building interoperable domain-specific conceptual annotation resources and describe the pool of static and dynamic resources built in the course of the current phase of the research. Section 5 describes the "first-machine-then-human" workflow of the conceptual annotation procedure. We conclude with the research overview and future work.

2. Related Work

Today the area of language annotation research witnesses the tendency towards semantization and, in particular, domain semantization (in our research, domain conceptualization), as the most realistic way to solve language technology tasks. The current trend is to use domain ontologies as conceptual annotation instruments, which, in turn, boosts the research in the field of ontology development. Ontologies are most often created for the annotation of unilingual (most often, English) domain corpora oriented to particular tasks. For example, to name just a few, the ontology described in (Roberts A. et. al., 2009) is created for the analysis of English medical records. (Tenenboim L et al., 2008) present the domain ontology for personalized filtration of English eNews. (Mannes and Golbeck, 2005; Najgebauer et al., 2008; Inyaem et al., 2009) devote their efforts to building ontologies for forecasting terror attacks and extraction of terrorist events from eNews. There is much less research on the ontology-based annotation in other languages, among which (as most closely related to our research) are (Dobrov et al., 2015) who suggest ways to semantically annotate a Russian domain corpus, and (Djemaa et al., 2016) focusing on a French corpus, correspondingly,

As ontology development is a very tough and time-consuming task, there are attempts to save effort in constructing ontological resources by making them multilingual. Multilingualism in ontologies is generally understood in two major senses: 1) as the adaptation (or understandability) of the ontology labels for the users-native speakers of different national languages and 2) as the capability of one ontology to be applied to processing texts in different languages regardless of the language used for wording concept labels. These understandings of ontology multilingualism directly depend on the interpretation of ontology either as a language-dependent or language-independent resource.

Language-dependent ontologies are thesaurus-like structures whose elements are defined by the properties of a specific language. A well-known example of such resource, often called ontological, is the famous WordNet thesaurus (Miller et al., 1990). The research on providing ontological multilingualism here goes in the direction of localization of the labels of ontology concepts, rather than modification of the ontological conceptualization. The localization procedure can go in different ways. For example, (Montiel-Ponsoda et al., 2008) propose the association of word senses in different languages to ontology concepts through a special linguistic model, while (Espinoza et al., 2008) suggest translating ontology labels into the user's language. One more localization technique is to manually annotate ontological concepts with labels in different languages (Chaves and Trojahn, 2010). (Alatrish et al., 2014) direct their efforts to the development of universal tools that could be used for semi-automatic procedure of building separate ontologies tuned to different languages. (Embley et al., 2019) suggest methodologies on how to relate unilingual ontologies by mapping both the data and the meta-data of these ontologies. The use of language-dependent ontologies for interoperable semantic (conceptual) annotation of multilingual corpora does not seem quite doable.

Language-independent ontologies, like e.g., Mikrokosmos (Nirenburg and Raskin, 2004), SUMO (Niles et al., 2003) and BFO (Arp et al., 2015), allow multilingualism in the second sense (the applicability to processing texts in multiple languages) per definition, provided that each lexical unit (one- or multi-component) in the vocabulary of a particular language is mapped (according to special rules) into such ontology concept. This is the basic feature that makes language-independent ontologies applicable to semantic (conceptual, including) annotations that can be interoperable across languages. Given the expense of manual work, unavoidable in semantic (conceptual) annotation a lot of effort in using language-independent ontologies as annotation instruments is currently devoted to the creation of different tools to increase annotators' productivity. As a rule, so far, such annotation tools are user interfaces for mapping lexical units into ontological concepts and/or postediting the results of the automated annotation (Zagorul'ko et al., 2012; Stenetorp et al., 2012).

3. Approach and Data

3.1 Task Definition

Creation of interoperable resources for annotation makes should be closely associated with the annotation procedure that in our research is defined by the intersection of the following criteria: (i) data-driven methodology directed from analysis to representation, (ii) domain orientation, (iv) interoperability across languages, (v) automation of the annotation process, (vi) reusability of resources. We argue that interoperability of content annotation across languages calls for a clear division between language-dependent lexical knowledge and language-independent conceptual knowledge that can be best represented in ontology. We consider ontological analysis as a main instrument for interoperable conceptual annotation with a tagset defined by the ontological concepts. We are fully aware that ontological analysis has a serious limitation that lies in its practical realization. The shortcomings of ontological analysis are well-known and include the difficulty of clearly specifying the boundaries of the analysis and the influence of objective human judgments. There is no universal recipe for ideal ontological analysis therefore, as a rule, in every practical project, specific approaches are developed to deal with the problems above. Our solutions are domain-constraint and data-driven. Then, to reduce manual work, a decision was made to experiment as much as possible with the "first-machine, then human" set-up of annotation work and to postpone the actual annotation process till later stages of the research and to first focus on the creation of the resources for annotation, which, following the classification given in (Witt et al., 2009) are divided into static and dynamic. In our research static resources include a conceptual annotation knowledge that consists of multilingual comparable domain corpora on terrorist acts in three languages (English, French and Russian), a universal conceptual annotation scheme, a multilingual domain ontology, domain-related unilingual lexicons and lexical-ontological mappings. The dynamic resources are tools to automate the creation of both static resources, and the annotation procedure.

The road map for this research is as follows. First, the data set for the study was acquired and conceptualized resulting into lists of conceptually classified lexical items, and then the upper-level ontology and representation formalism were decided on followed by the development of a seed multilingual ontology for the terrorist attack domain. The seed ontology was further refined and populated with the text template technique. In parallel with the research on the content (knowledge) side of the project, a toolkit to automate the work on all its stages was being developed.

3.2 Data Set

First of all, the advantage was taken of the previously built domain resources created for our earlier CAT project that include a 400 000 word Russian terrorist domain corpus of 2016-2017 e-news acquired in the Internet and a Russian-English lexicon of multicomponent lexical units built over the corpus. The lexicon includes initial corpus-based Russian vocabulary translated into English by professional translators. These data were used, first of all, to acquire knowledge for the built-in house Internet crawlers to automatically collect new portions of Russian, as well as English and French domain corpora. The crawler knowledge was decided to consist of key phrases rather than single words as the use of key phrases has the immediate effect in improving precision in keyword related tasks (Lefever et al., 2009). Then, a general opinion that content resides in noun phrases (Witschel, 2005), made us vote in favor of keywords/phrases as grammatically well-formed noun phrases. The key noun phrases were automatically extracted from the "old" 400 000 word Russian corpus by means of the tool described in (Sheremetyeva, 2012) that we trained for the Russian terrorist domain. The top 30% of the extracted Russian key noun phrases and their translations into English and French were used as the knowledge for the crawlers, by means of which the second part of the raw data, - multilingual terrorist act corpora of 100,000 words published on the Internet in 2018-2019 in the three languages were automatically acquired. For feasibility reasons, we excluded news on terrorist military activities and focused on the news on terrorist attack committed by individuals or terrorist groups in different countries.

4. Building Resources for Annotation

4.1 Static resources

In this section we describe the process of acquisition of static resources for conceptual annotation at the pre-annotation stage. The results of the acquisition were used as the knowledge base for the NLP annotation platform (see section 4.3) and were further augmented in the course of the whole research period.

4.1.1 Data set analysis

The first step in building resources for interoperable conceptual annotation consisted in classifying the multilingual corpora lexis into domain-relevant conceptual classes (or categories). It included decisions on i) the units of conceptual classification, which we took to be both single words and multi-word phrases of different POS classes, and ii) the list of categories/concepts. The set up for this work included an initial intuitively prescribed universal list of conceptual classes with definitions, unilingual (English, French and Russian) corpora-based frequency lists of multicomponent noun phrases as most closely content-related textual units (note, not only key phrases), raw corpora for context check, if needed, and conceptualization guidelines that were the same throughout the languages. The lists of noun phrases for conceptualization were constructed in two takes. First, the set of noun phrases up to four components long[1] were

automatically extracted from the English, French, and Russian corpora with the lexical extractor (Sheremetyeva, cf.) after it was trained for the terrorist domain in all the three languages. Then, every unilingual corpus was searched for longer noun phrases with the regular "find" functionality using the seed set of automatically extracted 4-component phrases. The domain-relevant units where then manually classified into conceptual classes (starting with the prescribed set) and following the guidelines. Special attention was paid to the selection of concept labels that were worded in English and made as descriptive as possible. Throughout the whole research period, weekly discussions were held by the project participants to provide for inter-conceptualization consistency and brush up. This stage resulted in the specification of the seed set of domain concepts. Other types of phrases were then extracted and classified in the same way followed by further brush up and extension of the cross-language conceptual class set. In general, the concept set was elaborated to specify a 3-level tree-like structure of concept organization with 97 fine-grained conceptual categories, assigned to 20 top-level domain categories. Table 1 shows a fragment of the top level domain concept list with definitions; Table 2 lists the second level grained concepts for the top domain concepts COUNTER-TERRORISM and CONSEQUENCES, and Table 3 presents fragments of unilingual lexica lists assigned to the conceptual class "AGENT – TERRORIST".

AGENT – TERRORIST: Executor of a terrorist act
ASSUMPTION: Assumption on who could commit a terr. act
CAUSE: What caused a terrorist attack
CLAIM RESPOSSIBILITY: terr. act responsibility claims
CONSEQUENCES: Aftermath of the terrorist attack
COUNTER-TERRORISM: People and measures against terr.
GOAL OF ATTACK: Demands of terrorists
LOCATION: Place where a terrorist act was committed
MEANS OF ATTACK: Items used for a terrorist act
NATION: person citizenship or country related to terrorism
OBJECT OF ATTACK: Who or what was hit in terr. act
TIME: Date and time when the terrorist attack happened
TYPE OF ATTACK: shooting, explosion, stubbing, arson
SOURCE : Sources of attack reports: newspapers, TV, etc.

Table 1: A fragment of the domain conceptual class list.

COUNTER-TERRORISM
COUNTER-TERRORISM AGENT : People fighting terr.
COUNTER-TERRORISM MEASURES: counter-terr. action
CONSEQUENCES
PUBLIC LOSS: killed, wounded, hostage, no damage
DESTRUCTION: objects damaged or destructed
TERRORISTS' LOSS: suicided, killed, wounded, detained
TERRORISTS' GAIN: terrorists' demands answered
PUBLIC REACTION: manifestation of support
RECONSTRUCTION: restoration of destroyed objects

Table 2: Second level concepts for the top concepts
COUNTER-TERRORISM and CONSEQUENCES.

---

[1]Constraint to four component extraction units is explained by the limitations of the extractor.

Language	Most frequent domain lexica of the class
English	terrorist, militant, fighter, gunman, suicide bomber, jihadi, female suicide bomber, female terrorist, lone-wolf terrorist, ISIS terrorist
French	terroriste, kamikaze, combattant, femme kamikaze, djihadiste. loup solitaire, terroriste de l'EI, combattant terroriste, femme terroriste
Russian	террорист, боевик, смертник, террорист-смертник, террористка-смертница, игиловец, террористка, джихадист, террорист-одиночка

Table 3: Fragments of the most frequent unilingual lexical units put into the "AGENT-TERRORIST" class.

Like any work on semantics based on human judgment, the concept specification process, in spite of all the domain constraints and guidelines, was not free from different levels of detalization, overlaps in interpretation and even contradictions. In such cases, reasonably strict decisions were taken by the project leader.

4.1.2 Ontology

In our project, we follow three basic methodological assumptions on ontology definition. The first is that ontology is a reusable language-independent resource; the second is that "domain-specific knowledge is not isolated from general world knowledge" (Moreno & Pérez, 2011, p. 233) and we, therefore, link our ontological resource to the upper-level Mikrokosmos ontology (Nirenburg & Raskin, cf.) to reuse the knowledge that is already there. We also follow the initial Mikrokosmos division of the reality into OBJECTS, EVENTS, and PROPERTIES, and use its formalism. We keep concept labels worded in English, the scopes of which, like in Mikrokosmos, are only specified by their definitions. Our third assumption is that interoperable domain ontological knowledge can be extracted from multilingual comparable domain corpora using mixed (top-down/bottom-up) acquisition techniques (Francesconi et al., 2010).

The set of domain concepts defined at the lexical analysis stage formed the seed e-news terrorist ontology, whose pool of concepts was further augmented and refined by using the text-template technique. For example, such RELATION concepts as IS-A and INSTANCE-OF can be acquired (though not exclusively) using the following English/French/Russian parallel text templates:

"A / is / are / and other/ such as/ B" (English)

"A est /somme/ comme / et autres / B" (French)

"A / это / и другие / такие как / B" (Russian),

where B is a lexeme that can signal of a more general concept; A is a lexeme of a more specific class.

The top domain concept MEANS OF ATTACK can be further split by means of such corsslingual templates as

"attack /with/ using/involving/ C" (English)

"attaque /avec/au moyen de/ C" (French)

"атака /с использованием/ с применением/ C" (Russian),

where C stands for lexemes of a weapon type concept.

The resulted ontology currently consists of 112 OBJECT and EVENT concepts and 27 PROPERTY concepts, see details in (Sheremetyeva & Zinovyeva, 2018).

4.1.3 Lexical-Ontological Mapping

Our main methodology for the interoperable conceptual annotation is ontological analysis. In practice, ontological analysis consists in mapping corpora lexical units into ontological concepts that, in our case, calls for creating unilingual lexicons, in which every domain-related unit is explicitly linked to an ontological concept. The boundaries of such mappings were specified by the domain data analysis and where allowed to be one-to-many, many-to-one or many-to-many. This had to follow human judgement, though strictly regulated by the mapping guidelines. For example, the French named entity "Charlie Hebdo" is mapped into the concepts OBJECT OF ATTACK (its office was targeted by terrorists in 2015) and SOURCE (it is a weekly newspaper that published info on terrorist attacks). Among lexical items mapped to several concepts there are, for example, the English word "police officer" and its French and Russian equivalents "policier" and "полицейский", correspondingly. Namely, following their use in the corresponding unilingual corpus, these lexical items are mapped into the 4 concepts of the multilingual ontology (the order of examples below are English, French and Russian):

COUNTER-TERRORISM: After the explosions, the authorities deployed *police officers*. / Après les explosions, les autorités ont déployé des *policiers*. / После взрывов власти выставили *полицейских*.

CONSEQUENCES: A *police officer* was killed. / Un *policier* est tué. / *Полицейский* был убит.

SOURCE: According to a *police officer*, the man shouted "Allahu akbar". / Selon des *policiers*, l'homme aurait crié « Allah akbar ». / По словам *полицейских* мужчина кричал «Аллах акбар»

AGENT-TERRORIST: Russia's ambassador is assassinated in Ankara by a *police officer*. / L'ambassadeur de Russie est assassiné à Ankara par un *policier*. / Российский посол убит в Анкаре *полицейским*.

We also introduced a convention that is not very obvious and generally accepted. It concerns the ontology mapping of multicomponent lexical units, in which individual components bear domain-related conceptual meanings that translate different aspects of content and do not contradict one another. For example, in the English phrase "airport shooting suspect", the word "shooting" conveys the information on the type of attack, the word "airport" points to the location where the attack took place, while the word "suspect" has two conceptual meanings "assumption" and "performer of the terrorist attack". All these content components are sincretically united in the phrase. Therefore, the convention is to map this multi-component lexeme into 4 concepts, - AGENT-TERRORIST, ASSUMPTION, TYPE OF ATTACK and LOCATION. Similarly, the phrase "Algerian terrorist" is mapped into the AGENT-TERRORIST and NATION concepts. Multiple ontological-lexical mappings will obviously lead to assigning multiple concept tags to textual units in the annotation procedure. However, as seen from the examples above, in our approach to annotation, it might or might not signal of lexical unit conceptual ambiguity. The situation forecast the need to make decisions on when multiple conceptual tags have to be disambiguated and when it should not be done to preserve as much domain-related content as possible. This issue is a matter of further investigation.

The domain conceptualization described in this section resulted in the acquisition of the pre-annotation static knowledge including the multilingual terrorist act domain ontology and ontology-mapped corpora-based unilingual lexicons of English, French and Russian. This knowledge was used to create the first version of the multilingual annotation platform described in Section 4.2.

4.2   Annotation Platform

A tool, which we call annotation platform, is the main part of all dynamic resources we used in our work. We approached its design with several considerations in mind. First of all, the annotation platform should automate the process of conceptual annotation and mark-up every unilingual corpus with the universal set of concept tags defined by the multilingual domain ontology. It is also desirable for the platform to contain knowledge that could help conceptual disambiguation. Further, it should be possible to configure the platform settings to different languages and language-dependent types of linguistic information. The annotation platform should allow for the knowledge administration and, therefore, be provided with the acquisition interface.

To save the development effort we reused, though sufficiently updated two software modules from our earlier (different type) project (Sheremetyeva, 2013) that meet most of the expectations on the annotation platform. The first module is the program shell of the multilingual TransDict e-lexicon and the second is the tagger to which TransDict is pipelined. TransDict is built over a powerful set of linguistic features that have a tree-like structure. It is realized as a number of cross-referenced monolingual lexicons. Every monolingual lexicon consists of a set of entries with semantic, syntactic and morphological zones of flexible settings. The TransDict entry is meant for one meaning (semantic class) of a lexeme in a given language. The morphological zone can contain the morphological information, such as part-of-speech, number, gender, etc., and word paradigms of a lexical unit up to 10 components long explicitly listed in the entry. The latter makes recognition of text wordforms straightforward. Depending on the configuration of linguistic information, every wordform in the lexicon entry is automatically assigned a supertag that codes semantic and morphological information, such as part-of speech and typed morphological features that are language-dependent. TransDict, what is important for our project, has an advanced knowledge administration user interface, built-in search module with flexible search masks and a lot of other effort-saving functionalities, like automatic generation of entry structures and entry-fillers. The TransDict shell allows increasing the number of languages as necessary and can be configured to any type of knowledge. The adaptation of TransDict for the conceptual annotation task (see Figure 1) was as follows. We configured the program to three languages, - English,

French and Russian. Semantic classes were set to the ontology concepts and some other classes like "Other" "Numerals", "Definiteness", etc., for mapping the lexemes of not specifically domain-related meaning. For feasibility reasons, so far, only upper-level ontology concepts were coded in TransDict. The morphological zones of the entries within each conceptual class were filled up with the explicitly listed morphological paradigms of the lexemes mapped to the ontology at the pre-annotation static resource acquisition stage (see Section 4.1.). If a lexical unit was mapped to several conceptual classes, several entries for this unit were created, each linked to a particular concept. Figure 1 shows a fragment of the TransDict main acquisition interface with the word list filtered by the mask "English" & "mapped into the TERRORIST-AGENT (tag A) concept" & "also to any other concept". The duplication of the lexical units shown in the left column of the interface displays multiple mappings. For example, the two-component lexeme "alleged terrorist" is listed twice as it is mapped into the TERRORIST-AGENT concept (tag A) and into the ASSUMPTION concept (tag I).

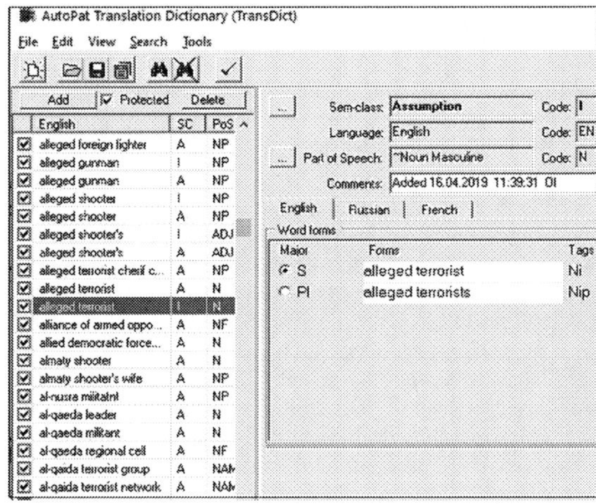

Figure 1: A fragment of the main TransDict interface.

The screenshot displays the "alleged terrorist" lexeme entry mapped into the ASSUMPTION concept. The morphological zone is filled with the lexeme wordforms that are automatically assigned supertags Ni and Nip, where N stands for "noun", "I" for the concept ASSUMPTION and "p" for plural. Supertags are positional, a concept code is the second in order; this coding format is inherited from the parent TransDict application. To allow the acquirers working independently at their own pace, TransDict is programmed in two variants, as MASTER with a full set of functionalities and as the so-called SLAVE – an empty program shell configured exactly as the corresponding version of MASTER but of a limited capability, namely, the user cannot change the dictionary settings (sets of languages, conceptual classes, entry structures and tags). SlAVEs filled by the acquirers with new portions of lexical conceptual knowledge are merged into MASTER on a regular basis. TransDict entries can be created for a single lexeme or for whole lists in batch mode. Figure 2 shows the window for ontological mapping when a lexeme is to be added to the TransDict knowledge. The window pops-up following a click on the "Add" button in the interface.

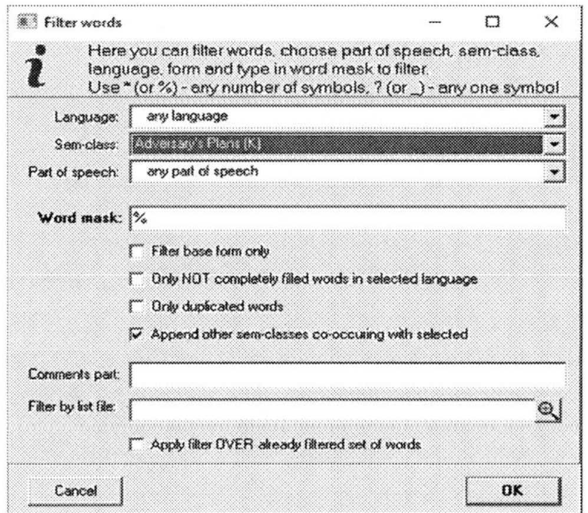

Figure 2: TransDict pop-up window for lexical-ontological mapping and assigning concept tags.

The selection of a conceptual class calls for another pop-up window for part-of-speech specification, after which an entry with typed morphological and syntactic zones appears that could be filled, if and as necessary. Fillers of the TransDict morphological zone fields supply knowledge to the tagger for conceptual annotation.

As said above, original TransDict shell was substantially updated for the annotation knowledge management and now includes quite a number of new effort-saving acquisition and analysis functionalities, substantially augmented search/filtering possibilities, export/ import functions, etc. The new TransDict search module with a lot of possible search masks is shown in Figure 3. The main update here is filtering according to the concept class parameters (combined or not with other mask parameters). One can filter lexemes of one conceptual class, lexemes of one class that are also mapped to any other concepts, and lexemes assigned to a fixed set of conceptual classes. This function shows knowledge lacuna to be filled. Filtration on the concept parameters can be done in two modes: based on lexeme main forms only or based on the whole paradigm of lexeme wordforms listed in the TransDict morphological zone. This obviously gives different results, comparing which one can find morphological hints for concept disambiguation in an automatically annotated text.

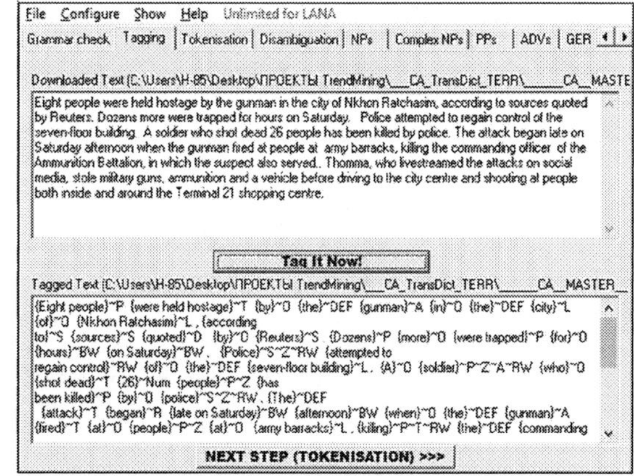

Figure 3: TransDict pop-up window for lexical-ontological analysis.

In general, all types of filtering including the concept class masks give a lot of information on the domain annotation statistics that can be used e.g., for forecasting the conceptual ambiguity rate in a particular language and for developing automatic disambiguation metrics.

The second module of the annotation platform is the tagger pipelined to TransDict. The tagger has a control interface and compilers which, if necessary, can be used for the acquisition of disambiguation rules and syntactic analysis rules. The tagger can be set to coarse-grain or fine-grain corpus mark-up. The coarse-grain mark-up outputs annotation with concept tags only, which can be enough for certain text-mining and content/knowledge extraction tasks. The fine-grain mark-up assigns a full range of linguistic features coded in the TransDict supertags that can be useful for disambiguation purposes. A screenshot of the control interface of the annotation platform tagger with the results of coarse-grain automatic conceptual tagging is shown in Figure 4 (see the concepts tags in Figure 2). Some lexemes shown in the tagger interface screenshot have multiple tags that signals of possible conceptual ambiguity. This version of the tagger does yet support concept disambiguation and, in general, the problem of automated conceptual disambiguation is out of the scope of this paper. We can only say at this stage that both statistical and, if necessary, linguistic information will be used for this purpose. This, among others, motivated the main change in the current tagging module as compared to the parent application, - two level fine-grained and coarse-grained annotation.

Figure 4: The tagger interface showing the results automatic coarse-grained conceptual annotation.

The annotation platform is currently implemented as a PC application and includes three pipelined modules, TransDict MASTER, TransDict SLAVE and Tagger that can also be used as stand-alone tools.

5. Annotation Procedure

In our approach, the process of conceptual annotation as the implementation of ontological analysis is the process of mapping text strings (in our case grammatical phrases of different types) into the domain multilingual ontology. The annotation procedure is identical for each unilingual corpus. It is "first-machine, then human" and is incremental in nature. We tested the approach, given the volume of multilingual effort and expectations about reasonable annotator tasks, on relatively small portions of unilingual corpora of 20,000 words each. However, the process and the results of such annotation, which in the long run was potedited into golden, gave us a lot of experience and leads on how to treat conceptual annotation problems.

During the beginning annotation phases covered in this paper, the types of conceptual categories included in the annotation were constrained to 21 top-level domain concepts and the concept "OTHER", to which domain-neutral lexemes are mapped. The annotators, who had already been trained in conceptualizing during the lexical analysis stage, were given a code-book with the sets of concepts associated with definitions and tags. The annotation process itself was done in several takes in an iterative manner. First, a weakly portion of the raw text meant to be gold-annotated was automatically tagged by our annotation platform described in Section 4.2 and then passed for postediting to the annotators. Conceptual ambiguity, if any, was resolved manually. In case a domain-relevant lexeme was left untagged or tagged incorrectly, it was supplied with correct linguistic information into the acquirer's personal TransDict SLAVE program to be further merged in TransDict MASTER (see Section 4.2) and the platform knowledge was thus updated, after which the annotation platform was used to automatically annotate the next portion of the corpus leading to a new knowledge update, etc. The knowledge was updated on a regular basis and the accuracy of the automatic annotation increased with very iteration. The accuracy was so far evaluated based on the annotators' reports on the amount of time spent on postediting and on the number of new lexical items to be merged into TransDict after every annotation iteration. Evidently, one cannot hope for a 100% correct automatic annotation without some risk of reducing annotation quality and, hence, human judgements cannot be avoided. However, our experiment shows that automation as used in the current research significantly augments and supports the annotation process.

The annotation procedure resulted in three golden conceptually annotated comparable English, French and Russian corpora of the e-news on terrorist acts and a substantial augmentation of the annotation platform knowledge. The TransDict lexicon currently consists of three unilingual lexicons of the English, French and Russian languages, that amount to around 43000 cross-referenced lexical entries acquired both at the pre-annotation stage, and in the course of annotation.

6. Conclusion

In this paper, we suggested a methodology of creating static and dynamic resources for interoperable conceptual annotation of domain corpora and presented actual annotation resources built along the suggested methodology for the multilingual (English, French and Russian) domain corpora of e-news on terrorist attacks. The resources include a universal conceptual annotation scheme, multilingual domain ontology, annotation platform with flexible settings and comparable golden conceptually annotated corpora in the three languages. This research is one of the major parts of an annotation project, which is significantly different from those that concentrate on morphological, syntactic or general types of semantic annotation. The emphasis of the presented work is on: i) a domain-specific level of annotation; ii) the assignment of well-defined interoperable conceptual representations based on multilingual domain ontology; and iii)"first-machine-then-human" approach to the annotation process.

Qualitative and quantitative investigation of the annotation resources we have constructed open quite a number of research opportunities for, e.g., theoretical aspects of social and comparative linguistics, as well as for research and development in Natural Language Processing technologies including multilingual Information Extraction, Generation, Question Answering, etc., and Machine Translation. The conceptual annotation knowledge can directly be used for developing machine learning techniques. In particular, the resource analysis findings can be used for developing concept disambiguation metrics, which, on top of increasing the volume of the annotation resources and annotated corpora, we see as our future work.

Bibliographical References

Alatrish E.A., Tošić D., Milenkov N. (2014). Building Ontologies for Different Natural Languages. Building Computer Science and Information Systems. – Vol. 11(2). pp. 623–644.

Arp, R., Smith, B., Spear, A.D. (2010). Building Ontologies with Basic Formal Ontology. MIT Press, Cambridge.

Chaves, M and Trojahn C. (2010). Towards a Multilingual Ontology for Ontology-driven Content Mining in Social Web Sites – URL: https://goo.gl/sZKmS2(09.11.2019).

Djemaa M., Candito M., Muller Ph., Vieu L. (2016). Corpus annotation within the French FrameNet: a domain-by-domain methodology. Proceedings of the Tenth International Conference on Language Resources and Evaluation (LREC 2016), May 2016, Portorož, Slovenia pp. 3794–3801.

Dobrov, A.V., Dobrova N.,L., Soms N., L., Chugunov A.V. (2015). Semanticheskij analiz novostnyh soobshchenij po teme «Elektronnye uslugi»: opyt primeneniya metodov ontologicheskoj semantiki Trudy XVIII ob"edinennoj konferencii «Internet i sovremennoe obshchestvo» (IMS-2015). pp. 120–125. (in Russian).

Embley D. W., Liddle S. W., Lonsdale D. W., Tijerino Y. (2019). Multilingual Ontologies for Cross-Language Information Extraction and Semantic Search. – URL: https://pdfs.semanticscholar.org/6884/41a96b6da61295 c7df39b70db2f28531370a.pdf ((09.11.2019)

Espinoza, M., Gómez-Pérez A., Mena E. (2008). Enriching an Ontology with Multilingual Information. The Semantic Web: Research and Applications. ESWC Lecture Notes in Computer Science. – Springer, Berlin, Heidelberg. – Vol. 5021. pp. 333–347.

Francesconi E., Montemagni S., Peters W., Tiscornia D. (2010). Integrating a Bottom-Up and Top-Down Methodology for Building Semantic Resources for the Multilingual Legal Domain Semantic Processing of Legal Texts . LNAE. – Vol. 6036, pp. 95–121.

Inyaem U, Haruechaiyasak Ch., Meesad Ph,,Tran D. (2009). Ontology-Based Terrorism Event Extraction

Proceedings of the 1st International Conference on Information Science and Engineering.. – P. 912–915.

Lefever E., Macken L.. Hoste V. (2009). Language-independent bilingual terminology extraction from a multilingual parallel corpus'. In Proceedings of the 12th Conference of the European Chapter of the ACL, Athens, Greece. pp. 496–504.

Mannes, A., Golbeck J. (2005). Building a Terrorism Ontology/ Proceedings of the ISWC Workshop on Ontology Patterns for the Semantic Web 36. URL: https://pdfs.semanticscholar.org/9bcb/90e48677e39da7b84939e8c8da2b2a63cde7.pdf (25.09.2019).

Mair, C. (2005). The corpus-based study of language change in progress: The extra value of tagged corpora. The AAACL/ICAME Conference, Ann Arbor, 2005.

Montiel-Ponsoda E., Aguado de Cea G., Gómez-Pérez A., Peters A. (2008). Modelling Multilinguality in Ontologies. Proceedings of COLING 2008, Companion volume – Posters and Demonstrations. pp. 67–70.

Miller, G.A., Beckwith, R., Fellbaum, C., Gross, D., Miller, K.J. (1990). Introduction to WordNet: An On-line Lexical Database. International Journal of Lexicography 3 (4), pp. 235–244.

Moreno A., Pérez Ch. (2011). From Text to Ontology Extraction and Representation of Conceptual Information. Actes de quatrièmes rencontres «Terminologie et Intelligence Artifi-cielle», pp.233-242.

Najgebauer A., Antkiewicz R., Chmielewski M., Kasprzyk R., (2008). Prediction of Terrorist Threat on the basis of Semantic Association acquisition and Complex Network Evolution. The Journal of Telecommunications and Information Technology. Vol. 2. pp. 14–20.

Niles I. & Pease A. (2003). Linking Lexicons and Ontologies: Mapping WordNet to the Suggested Upper Merged Ontology. Proceedings of the 2003 International Conference on Information and Knowledge Engineering (IKE 03), pp. 412–416.

Nirenburg S. & Raskin V. (2004). Ontological Semantics. MIT Press, Cambridge

Pustejovsky J. (2012). Natural Language Annotation for Machine Learning. O'Reilly Media; 1 edition. 342 P.

Roberts A., Gaizauskas R., Hepple M., Demetriou G., Guo Y., Roberts A., Setzer A. (2009). Building a semantically annotated corpus of clinical texts. Journal of Biomedical Informatics. – Vol. 42 (5), pp. 950–966.

Sheremetyeva S. (2012). Automatic Extraction of Linguistic Resources in Multiple Languages. Proceedings of NLPCS 2012, 9th International Workshop on Natural Language Processing and Cognitive Science in conjunction with ICEIS 2012, Wroclaw, Poland, pp. 44–52.

Sheremetyeva S. & Zinovyeva A. (2018). On Modelling Domain Ontology Knowledge for Processing Multilingual Texts of Terroristic Content. Communications in Computer and Information Science, 859. Springer, Cham, pp. 368–379.

Sheremetyeva S. (2013). On Integrating Hybrid and Rule-Based Components For Patent MT with Several Levels of Output. Proceedings of "The Fifth Workshop on Patent Translation in conjunction of the fourteenth Machine Translation Summit 2013", Nice, France, September 2-6.

Stenetorp P., Pyysalo S., Topic G., Ohta T., Ananiadou S., Jun'ichiTsujii J. (2012). BRAT: a Web-based Tool for NLP-Assisted Text Annotation. Proceedings of the 13th Conference of the European Chapter of the Association for Computational Linguistics. Avignon, France, April 23 – 27. 2012. pp. 102–107.

Tenenboim L., Shapira B, Shoval P. (2008). Ontology-Based Classification of News in an Electronic Newspaper. International Book Series "Information Science and Computing", pp. 89–97.

Witschel H. F. (2005). Terminology extraction and automatic indexing - comparison and qualitative evaluation of methods. Terminology and Knowledge Engineering (TKE) http://wortschatz.unileipzig.de/~fwitschel/papers/TKEIndexing.pdf

Witt, A., Heid, U., Sasaki, F., Gilles Sérasset (2009). Multilingual language resources and interoperability. Lang Resources & Evaluation 43, 1–14 (2009). https://doi.org/10.1007/s10579-009-9088-x

Zagorul'ko, M. YU., Kononenko I. S., Sidorova E. A. (2012). Sistema semanticheskoj razmetki korpusa tekstov v ogranichennoj predmetnoj oblasti. Proceeding of the international conference Komp'yuternaya lingvistika i intellektual'nye tekhnologii, pp. 674–683. (in Russian).